The Ride of my Life

Memoirs of a Sporting Editor

For Marilyn

The Ride of my Life

Memoirs of a Sporting Editor

MICHAEL CLAYTON

Merlin Unwin Books

First published by Merlin Unwin Books, 2016
Text © Michael Clayton 2016

Merlin Unwin Books Limited
Palmers' House, 7 Corve Street,
Ludlow, Shropshire, SY8 1DB
www.merlinunwin.co.uk

A CIP record of this book is available
from the British Library.
Printed and bound by TJ International, Padstow, England

ISBN 978-1-910723-21-0

Acknowledgement

My thanks to Jim Meads, friend and hunting companion,
for providing virtually all the hunting pictures in this book.

CONTENTS

Foreword

Mark Hedges, Editor of *Country Life*

I was advised before my interview with Michael to talk about hunting and, if he changed the subject, to bring the conversation immediately back to it. This wasn't difficult, as he spent some time recounting, in vivid detail, a run he had had with the Cottesmore the previous Tuesday. Then he offered me a job on *Horse & Hound*.

I knew nothing about editing or journalism and could barely type, but I had fluked a job with the most talented magazine editor of his generation. I owe Michael my career.

Michael was a fearsome taskmaster, but one that led by example; despite his absences on 'Foxford' duties, he approved every word and was capable of performing any role – legend has it that, during an NUJ strike, he produced *Horse & Hound* single-handedly.

He had an inspiring energy, writing more, hunting more and uncomplainingly breaking more bones than any person I have worked with; dictating the Monday-morning leader from the casualty ward was a common occurrence. Once, a reader recognised him and, as he lay awaiting anaesthetic, began to upbraid him about an incorrect result.

Horse & Hound, which he proudly referred to as a newspaper, rather than a magazine, was an exciting place to work. Michael was fair, but occasionally terrifying; a note in his spidery handwriting – 'See me, MC' – could stop the heart. He had a habit of emerging from his office, proof page held aloft, demanding: 'Who did this?' As staff ducked behind their typewriters, he'd murmur: 'Well, it's rather good, anyway'.

Yet sometimes, instead of delivering the anticipated rocket for a mistake, he would put his philosophical former war reporter's hat on and shrug: 'Life how it really is.' He kept us all on our toes.

Michael's twin passions for print journalism and foxhunting coursed through his veins. He could have done anything but, fortunately for us, he chose hunting and horses.

Mark Hedges
Editor, *Country Life*

Hacking for fun

For many people nowadays the word 'hacking' refers to raiding other people's mobile phones, allegedly used as an illegal news source.

In the England in which I was born and bred, hacking only applied to riding a horse for fun. You hacked home in the twilight after a good day's hunting. You hacked your horse across a smiling countryside on a fine morning for exercise. Your horse was simply a hack if it was an ordinary riding mount, and not a grand hunter nor racehorse.

Journalists were referred to as hacks because they put their pens out to rent, like horses in a hireling stabling. For most of my life I have been employed as a hack, and have so much enjoyed hacking about on horses.

Fatefully, I was invited to a lunch in the Reform Club in 1972 which brought me even closer to hacking horses and words. It happened like this....

'And so I wondered if you would like to take over from me as Editor...'

The words hung in the air only a couple of seconds over the lunch table before I heard a voice say firmly: 'I certainly would.'

With a familiar tremor in the stomach I realised the voice was mine. I had not guessed the purpose of the lunch invitation from Walter Case, long-serving Editor of *Horse & Hound*.

And yet, without hesitation I had committed myself to a drastic career change – from BBC international TV and radio reporter to the editorship of one of Britain's oldest and most conservative weekly magazines; a periodical whose title was used as a joke by the liberal literati. It became best known to the widest public who relished the episode in the film *Notting Hill* when Hugh Grant posed as a *Horse & Hound* reporter to interview the girl of his dreams.

When Case made his offer I reacted in the same way you should jump a fence in the hunting field: throw your heart over first. It is the traditional advice to the horseman crossing country, and it usually works well, since a horse responds instantly to boldness from the rider.

I heard myself instantly accept Case's offer with warm approval; I gave the impression I would have taken over that afternoon if necessary.

Impetuous decision-making can be equally successful off the hunting field, but when it goes wrong it proves the accuracy of Mr Jorrocks's famous remark that 'a fall is a h'awful thing'. After a working life chasing hard news in newspapers and broadcasting, would I really find a happy landing in a corner of specialist journalism which my BBC colleagues would consider quaint, or even eccentric? My fellow reporters in the TV News Room already called me 'Squire' because of my passion for foxhunting.

Horse & Hound's longevity and apparently changeless appeal caused more than a few misconceptions, even among its readers. I remembered this two years later when one of Ireland's leading hunting ladies, Bunny McCalmont, greeted me at her front door by saying: 'Good heavens! I thought the Editor of *Horse & Hound* was a little old man with a white beard. Do come in, young man. I've got a very exciting horse for you.'

I contributed little to the remainder of my lunch-time conversation in the spring of 1972 with Walter Case. Before he made his offer it was clear that he was retiring the following year with the greatest reluctance.

He told me glumly the management had an inflexible rule that all staff must retire at 65, and he would reach that birthday in 1973, 33 years after he had succeeded as Editor during the drama and bloodshed of bombing in war-time London.

Walter had immediately succeeded the magazine's first Editor and owner, Arthur Portman, when Portman and his wife were killed in an air-raid which demolished their home in Montagu Square on

August 17th, 1940. No-one knew which of them died first, greatly affecting the implementation of Arthur Portman's will.

Like the magazine's first Editor, Walter had become entirely consumed by the demands and pleasures of *Horse & Hound*. It was far more than a job; it was entirely his way of life, and he would miss it sorely, he explained. He was a slight, bespectacled figure, not given to revealing his emotions, but his reserved manner cloaked a steely will. Handing over his precious editorship was probably the most painful task in his life, and I was touched and grateful to be the recipient.

With a pang, I realised that as the elderly magazine's third Editor I could expect to find myself similarly immersed in a life-style job for the rest of my life. Would that really be enough to contain a restlessness which had already seen me move from provincial journalism to Fleet Street, and then to broadcasting at its most hectic?

I had been a hunter of news for over 20 years, most of it the bad news that makes headlines; latterly I had been reporting a series of wars, and was due to return to Vietnam and Cambodia soon after my lunch with Case.

Perhaps the pressures of such work had increased my passion for the recreations I had enjoyed most of all: riding and hunting. I had read *Horse & Hound* regularly since childhood, contributed as a freelance to the magazine on hunting matters, and had written my first foxhunting book for publication in 1967. My freelancing paid for the keep of a precious hunter, although the demands of news journalism all too frequently robbed me of hunting days I had planned and anticipated with such fervour.

Before we parted after the fateful lunch, Walter Case hesitated and then murmured: 'There is one thing I should tell you: *Horse & Hound* is a real money-maker; far more successful than most people in the horse world understand. It makes substantial profits for IPC; all you have to do is to persuade the management to let you spend it, and I am not pretending that will always be easy.'

I was not deterred: it sounded just like every other publishing management I had worked for in the postwar years of austerity. On the way back to BBC Television Centre at Shepherd's Bush I began to consider the challenge ahead. I still had to apply formally for the Editorship and pass interviews with the publishers, IPC Magazines, the huge company which I had seen somewhat disrespectfully described in a trade press article as 'the Ministry of magazines', owning over 80 titles in an extraordinarily wide range of markets – from the hip modernism of *New Musical Express* to the conservatism of *Country Life* and *Horse & Hound*. The company's most prominent group was the clutch of leading women's magazines, led by *Woman* and *Woman's Own*.

Clearly IPC was a highly professional outfit and I would fit in somehow.

Suddenly I cheered up: all doubts disappeared. I was absolutely confident I could convince the faceless magazine moguls that I was entirely the right man to take the reins of their workhorse. I had more than enough varied journalistic credentials, and above all I had something which neither Mr Portman nor Mr Case had been able to offer – I rode the Horse in pursuit of the Hound at every available opportunity, and I was determined to do so for the rest of my life.

Editing *Horse & Hound* should be fun. And if it wasn't I would make sure it was thoroughly entertaining for the readers, and for me. I wondered whether there was a cupboard for a spare pair of riding boots in the Editor's office. There soon would be, I resolved...

CHAPTER ONE

IMPOSSIBLE DREAMS

I once read a psychologist's view that a happy adult is one who feels he has made his childhood dreams come true. If that is so, my later life at the rarefied top end of the equestrian and hunting world fulfilled many of the dreams, seemingly impossible, which I fostered during my boyhood in a two-bedroomed bungalow in a suburb of Bournemouth during the second world war.

By today's average standards in bungalow land on the South Coast, we lived in straitened circumstances. My father, Aylwin Clayton, was an electrician commuting for long days by train to Southampton to work on naval shipbuilding; my mother, Norah Clayton, despite ill-health valiantly helped our meagre income by working variously as a typist and a bookmaker's telephonist.

Hitler was already gaining power, and there was an international economic crisis when I was born in 1934. Vast sorrow and strife was about to engulf the world.

During my wartime childhood, food and clothing were strictly rationed, car travel a very rare treat. Many nights were interrupted when we dashed to our homemade air-raid shelter at the bottom of the garden during German aircrafts' sporadic bombing of the area.

If this sounds grim, for me it was not. We were generally safer in Bournemouth than those living in London and Britain's major production areas, which were subject to frequent heavy bombing raids.

My normally relaxed South Coast retirement town was not entirely insulated from the war. As an infant I tasted fear when a German fighter

1

flew low over Bournemouth's Pleasure Gardens firing indiscriminately at children as we sailed our toy boats on the Bourne Stream. My father grabbed me and thrust me into some bushes, sheltering me with his body. There were a few casualties, including a schoolmate of mine.

War over-shadowed my life from the age of five to eleven, and yet overall it was a wonderfully happy childhood. This was due mainly to the sacrifices and devotion of my parents to me, their only child. My father was generally placid, and gladly made time to take me on outings. Mother, who had slim, dark good looks, had a more meteoric temperament, and a strong right hand occasionally. She assured me I could 'do anything', and frequently urged me to 'get out of doors and do something!'

My happiness was also compounded by the wonderful environment of the balmy South Coast at a time when urban development had been abruptly halted. Empty grass fields abounded around our bungalow estate, and beyond lay some of the most delectable rural landscapes in East Dorset.

My parents strived hard to ensure that, despite the shortages, life for me was as normal as possible: birthday parties, bus trips, plenty of pets, and above all freedom to roam far and wide on foot or bicycle, often with a host of neighbouring children. At the time I did not appreciate enough the sacrifices they made.

Bournemouth's wonderful sea-shore was denied to us for most of the war, the splendid pier blown in half, and the beaches off-limits behind barbed wire, as some form of protection from a German invasion. This ensured my childhood explorations were directed inland. Barred from the sea, at my mother's insistence I learned to swim in a tributary of the River Avon near Christchurch.

Without the distractions of computer screens and mobile phones, a visit to the Moderne cinema at sixpence a seat was approved by Mother as long as it involved a long healthy walk across a common.

I did not share my parents' worries that food, clothes and petrol were severely rationed. I cared only about the sweet ration, which was healthily limited. Our nutrition levels were remarkably good; there was no danger of obesity among children in the 1940s.

The war had stopped house building, and our bungalow estate

remained right on the edge of deeply rural Dorset. Perhaps it was an inheritance from my father's family who were originally Quaker farmers in East Essex, but at a very early age I developed a passion for dogs, ponies and farming. My great-grandfather, a farmer and grocer in Dunmow, was a passionate foxhunter, wearing a black coat and avoiding attending meets because hard liquor was consumed.

The possibility of launching a career as an equestrian journalist from our bungalow estate during the war seemed an impossible dream.

And yet this is how it happened....

'I want to start riding now,' I said firmly at the age of seven. To my surprise my mother did not give the response to which, in 1942, I had become all too accustomed: 'We can't afford it. Wait until after the war.'

We were enjoying a luxury: tea and scones, without cream, in the garden of a cottage café on the bank of the River Stour at Longham, in Dorset, a village of delightfully rural thatch and stone cottages north of Bournemouth.

My demand was prompted by watching an elderly lady, in impeccable riding dress and bowler hat, ride past, accompanied by an equally smart little girl on a pony.

My mother said: 'After tea we'll find the stables in Longham and see what we can do.'

By the River Stour at Longham, Dorset, where I decided to take up riding.

We walked up the village's long winding street until on our right we came to a yard of loose boxes, some with horses' heads leaning out, much to my excitement. There appeared to be no-one there, so we walked on past a grass paddock where there was a shabby notice-board proclaiming: 'Longham Riding Stables'. We did not know it, but the lady and child we had just seen riding past did not come from this yard. They were based at the far more up-market teaching and schooling establishment run on the opposite side of the road in Longham by Miss Bush.

On our right was a double-fronted, pink-walled farmhouse with a thatched roof, all in need of renovation, as were so many war-time properties. There was a narrow, dirt path by the side leading into a ramshackle farmyard, lined with wooden loose boxes roofed in blackened cast-iron.

We peered over a water butt into an open back window of the cottage where a large lady with hair in a tight bun, and wearing a capacious pinafore – her garb at all times – was busy at the sink.

'Mr Brown is milking; if you wait in the yard he'll deal with you directly,' she said severely. I do not think I ever saw Mrs Brown smile.

This was not Mr Brown's wife; it was his mother, the dominating influence on a life virtually confined to the yard, and the riding school. It was far more down-market than Miss Bush's, but it was available, and just about affordable.

The Brown yard was enjoying a busy war-time because there was an influx of servicemen and women stationed in the area who were hiring his horses.

Bernard Brown eventually emerged from a cattle shed. He was as near the human incarnation of Mr Toad of Toad Hall as I had ever seen: impressively rotund in girth, with a round, red beaming face and small bright blue eyes, under a capacious checked cap which I only once or twice saw him remove to reveal a pink bald head. The eyes were not as smiling as his mouth. He sported the drab cord breeches, brown boots and gaiters which were virtually the uniform of Longham Riding Stables. His fingers snapped a pair of bright yellow braces, and he opened his small, cupid-lipped mouth to surprise us with a light, mincing voice: 'And what can I do for this young man…?'

Mr Brown was, in the vernacular of today, undoubtedly gay. I was later to be told conspiratorially by a young male stable-hand in the jargon of the 1940s: 'He's a queer alright, but he's harmless...'

I had not the remotest idea what this meant. Sex education was an entirely unknown phenomenon in the learning syllabus of my junior school, nor later at Bournemouth Grammar School.

Bernard Brown welcomed to me to his yard, but I never had to be careful of any homosexual overtures. On rare occasions he would make a mildly salacious remark, such as: 'You really can't ride that big horse – not until your middle leg is longer.'

His tragedy, shared by many, was that he lived in a world where his sexual inclination was illegal, and if he had any sex life it had to be entirely clandestine.

Bernard Brown's yard, a 30 minutes' cycle ride from my home, was to become my first gate-way to horsemanship, and the hunting field. There were to be no formal lessons, but plenty of instruction and education in the practice of keeping horses, as well as riding them.

'Yes, you can ride at ten o'clock next Saturday morning; it's four shillings an hour,' Bernard lisped. I decided I quite liked him, although I did not understand how such a large, formidable-looking man could speak in such a little voice. I have never ceased to be utterly grateful to dear old Bernard for my first opportunity to become something of a horseman.

My cousin Nina Clayton, who lived with us, and was a year older than my seven years, accompanied me on my first ride from Brown's.

Nina, somewhat to her dismay, was mounted on an ancient, washy-chestnut gelding named Splash, hideously one eyed, with the vacant eyeball gaping beneath a large swelling.

I was put up on Kitty, an elderly Welsh Mountain pony, almost white, and proving to have impeccable manners.

We wore old trousers tucked into rubber boots, and we were hatless. It was another ten years before I managed to acquire a second-hand velvet riding hat with a peak, and that was so soft that it would have been of little aid in a heavy fall on the head.

In my early teens, in a 'war surplus' clothing shop in Bournemouth I bought for a couple of shillings a curious pair of US Army canvas gaiters that fitted down over shoes, and therefore avoided the weighty decision to spend over 30 shillings to buy new leather ankle boots to replace those I had outgrown.

The tan gaiters only needed an occasional scrub, and they served me well as a rider for a few years. It was a big day when my mother bought me English leather gaiters and matching brown boots in a Wimborne agricultural store. They protected me from many an equine foot stamping and kicking in Brown's yard.

Long before the Health and Safety Act arrived to plague riding school proprietors, Bernard Brown's establishment suffered remarkably few riding accidents. His horses and ponies never looked in poor condition; he was an experienced feeder, ensuring they were never 'above themselves'. He was shrewd in matching each novice rider to an appropriately quiet mount of which he seemed to have an abundant supply.

I only ever saw Bernard in the saddle once, in the stables paddock one evening, when he surprised me by riding in the female fashion – side-saddle. He employed two or three men and women who worked in the yard, and escorted groups of riders for one or two hour rides.

A stern, weather-beaten lady in riding breeches, boots and a felt hat, appeared on a large brown horse in the yard, and without a word to us took charge of two leading reins attached our mounts' bridles. With a pony either side, she led Nina and me out of the yard and up Longham's main street on a route I was to learn and enjoy.

Past the church we veered left into a muddy bridleway which led to the superb expanse of gorse and heather we knew as Ferndown Moor, but often referred to as 'Brown's Moor' because his animals were to be seen trudging round it seven days a week. There was a wealth of sandy tracks, and Bernard's horses and ponies knew the routes for an hour's hack with little direction.

Our instructor occasionally barked at us to 'sit up', and to keep our 'toes up' and 'heels down'. We completed a short circuit on the moor at the walk, but when we returned to the lane, we were warned to be ready for a trot.

'Keep your knees into the saddle, toes up and heels down, and rise up-down, up-down, in the stirrups,' we were sternly advised, with the added advice: '…and grab the front of the saddle if you feel yourself falling.'

Suddenly we were trotting, and I do not recall the slightest problem; within a few minutes I was mastering the rise to the trot quite comfortably, and I was not grasping the saddle pommel, although I earned a sharp rebuke for holding my hands too high. It was sheer heaven.

When I dismounted beaming in the yard I vowed to return the following week, and although four shillings was a considerable hole in our household budget, my mother nobly continued to support my riding 'lessons'. I cycled to Longham nearly every Saturday and Sunday, and as well as spending my precious four shillings on an hour's ride, I was eager to muck out stables, make-up beds and heave hay and straw into the boxes. Our enlightened society nowadays forbids children under 16 to undertake such work in a commercial yard, but for me it was a godsend, providing healthy exercise, a modicum of responsibility, and the opportunity to ride lots of different horses and ponies free, whereas children may learn far less through the luxury of owning and riding only one tractable pony kept at home. The horseman's greatest gift is to be able to mount a strange mount, sum it up immediately, and ride it accordingly. I believe it is vital to ride as many ponies and horses as possible in the early years of riding.

Although I have since read many thousands of words on riding technique, and as an adult belatedly took some lessons from experts, I am convinced that the truly effective horseman needs only to acquire two fundamental abilities: a really safe seat, whether in the saddle or bareback, and a natural aptitude to 'balance' the horse at all paces.

Leaping up on ponies and horses bareback as a child, staying aboard when the animal suddenly bucks, shies or accelerates, are vital attributes for the natural horseman.

I learned this at Brown's yard by regularly going into the paddocks to collect the horses and ponies which had spent the night out at grass. We would fit a halter and vault on to their bare-backs to ride them back to the yard. I did not realise it, but it was a huge boon in helping me acquire a natural seat on any horse.

The all-weather schooling manège was virtually non-existent in most yards in the 1940s, and everyone I knew schooled their horses while hacking out, or occasionally indulged in some jumping schooling over home-made jumps in grass paddocks, weather permitting. I first learned to jump over small gorse bushes on the moors, with uneven take-offs and landings.

I heard my mother explaining to a friend: 'It's a bit expensive this riding, but he's so restless and full of energy that it's great to get him out of the house to do something he really likes.'

She had unsuccessfully tried subsidising lessons on the piano, and even the piano accordion, to give me some out-of-school hobby, and now settled for horse-riding, fortunately without having an inkling as to the real risks – not least the possibility of her son acquiring a life-time addiction to an expensive leisure pastime.

My biggest debt to Bernard Brown was that he rewarded me with free rides for working throughout weekends and school holidays in his yard. Looking older than my years because of my increasing height, I achieved one of my goals, acting as an escort to visiting adult riders who did not know the routes around the moor. Most valuable of all, I learned something of basic horse-mastership through working in the Brown yard. You don't allow a horse to gulp down too much water until he has cooled down after a ride; you don't give a horse chopped sugar beet until it has been properly soaked first. You check a horse's feet for stones before and after every ride.

Although I was never worried about the perils of riding, I had some anxious moments in the stables. I was secretly scared of a large, dark bay horse, named Ranger, who had a reputation for savaging grooms in his box.

I think this was exaggerated to give me a fright, but Ranger swung his quarters at me ominously when I was alone in his box, and I escaped by jumping above him to swing from a rafter. He was alarmed and shied off to the back of the box, so I came down from the rafters to vault frantically over the bottom half of the box door.

Treating horses with respect in the box is well worth learning if you are to survive a life-time dealing with a powerful animal with hair-trigger reflexes.

One Sunday afternoon, at the age of nine, I led a party of about 15 US servicemen up to the moor, for an unusually spirited ride. By now I sported leather gaiters above short brown boots, and a baggy pair of war-issue cord breeches, well in line with the Brown establishment dress code.

A grinning little man, riding with very short stirrup leathers, told me he was a jockey 'back home in the States', and he and his friends repeatedly asked: 'Say, when do we get to the goddamned jumps?'

By now I prided I myself on being well in control of my mount at a canter, or even a gallop, but I had never jumped anything more formidable than a puddle or a very small bush, and I could only squeak apologetically: 'I'm afraid Mr Brown doesn't allow any jumping....'

I often rode a speedy black pony named Spider, who was very handy and taught me far more than any of the human 'instructors' in the yard.

I did my best to make up for the lack of jumping by cantering ahead of the soldiers far more vigorously than usual round the moor, even venturing at some pace off the tracks onto the heather where there were hidden holes, and two of the Yanks fell off, which pleased their friends enormously.

One of the best forms of tuition occurred every morning and evening when I was sent to nearby fields to bring in horses and ponies. Jimmy, a recent school-leaver who worked full-time in the yard, wearing the regulation dress adopted by Mr Brown, accompanied me. Jimmy became a good friend, and showed me the best way to leap onto the horses bare-back, and how to ride them with only a rope halter by neck-reining and judicious use of the leg.

It was all tremendous fun, and I simply copied Jimmy and the other grooms.

I was impressed when Jimmy confided proudly: 'I'm paid an agricultural worker's starter rate.' He did not explain how much that was, but I suspected it meant Mr Brown paid him a pittance.

I had fallen off two or three times on the moor, usually when a pony shied, but I was perilously over-confident until, as a ten-year-old, I experienced my first riding accident.

At a sedate walk on the road back to the yard, I was accompanying a lady rider mounted on her own well-bred mare, of rather better quality than Mr Brown's string, when suddenly the mare wheeled her quarters towards my pony and let fly with both hind-feet, aiming at the heart as horses naturally tend to do in such attacks. The mare was trying to kick the pony, but inevitably one of her feet caught my right leg hard, and I slid off more in shock than pain.

I was sent home in a taxi, my first time on my own in such a vehicle, and my mother examined me remarkably calmly. Our doctor assured me it was only a bad bruise, but put a plaster on the leg. I must have been a particularly pompous child, because I insisted on using a walking stick for at least two weeks, even taking it to Hillview-road Junior School where I was able to describe my remarkable escapade to all and sundry in the playground. It was a wonderful way of boasting that I could actually ride a pony, but no-one would admit to being impressed.

After the plaster was removed I resumed working and riding without a tremor, although I had received my first warning of the Arab proverb: 'The grave is ever open for the horseman.'

In my first year after failing the eleven-plus (I scraped through at a second attempt), when I was already outgrowing my classmates in height, I fell in love for the first time.

I was not conscious that it had anything do with sex, but I developed a tremendous crush on Bernard Brown's new lady instructor, in her early twenties a decade older than me.

Her name was Mimosa Robertson but she was always known as 'Mosa', and she was far smarter, more intelligent, and decidedly more shapely, than the usual riding spinster who arrived in the Brown yard.

Quite how Mr Brown came to employ a female so overtly attractive, well outside his own taste, I never knew, but I assume he was badly short-staffed at the time. Mosa let it be known she had instructed previously in rather grand yards; she was smartly turned out in the best fitting riding breeches I had ever seen, and she brought a new dimension to the Brown establishment: she wore make-up while riding.

A brunette, with a delicious twinkle in her brown eyes, Mosa was assured and well-spoken; male and female clients liked her, and asked

Mr Brown if they could go out on her conducted rides.

From the start, Mosa was kind and pleasant to me, and quietly began to give me some tips about 'improving my riding'. I thought she was wonderful, and immediately fell in with a secret plan she confided: she intended to leave Brown's yard quite soon, and set up a new riding school of her own in Bournemouth. Mosa assured me I was to be given entirely free riding in return for working part-time in her yard in the same way.

'You're very good at talking to the clients,' she told me, somewhat to my surprise.

To achieve her ambition, Mosa won financial backing from a new admirer, a wealthy gentleman in Longham. Mosa persuaded him that his niece Anne could benefit from Mosa's experience by becoming her partner in the new venture which he would finance. Anne, an 18-year-old honey-blonde with blue eyes, was a delightful personality who I liked immediately; another good reason for me to join the new venture as an eager volunteer.

It became most exciting when it was revealed to me that the new riding school was to be much closer to my home, in the former coach-house adjoining 'The Hollies' pub in Moordown, a northern suburb of Bournemouth, only just beyond Winton's busy shopping centre.

We were sure to get plenty of new clients by operating within Bournemouth's boundary, Mosa assured us. There were only half a dozen loose-boxes and stalls, but she was after quality not quantity of clients, and it was bound to be a huge success.

I was not mature enough to thank Bernard Brown and say farewell properly; I simply transferred my time and affections to the Hollies. It proved to be a financial flop which lasted little more than 18 months, and offered no threat to Bernard Brown's business, but I benefited hugely, not least because I learned a lot more about life as well as horses.

The Hollies was in an urban, built-up setting. Yellow trolley buses hummed past, amid busy traffic on the main road to Winton and central Bournemouth. We rode through back-roads to Hillview Common where I had played, and found our way on by-ways to Talbot Woods and other leafy areas abounding in outer Bournemouth.

These routes had not seen horses for years, and the hacking was never as ideal as Longham. The Hollies yard had far too few horses to make money in volume, and failed to succeed as an exclusive riding venue.

Mosa and Anne secured contracts to provide horses for visitors in Bournemouth's cliff-top hotels to ride on the beach, which was allowed in the winter months. With her usual confidence, Mosa led her small string through central Bournemouth's traffic to the seafront.

We collected a few riders, and then we hacked along the sandy beaches from Boscombe towards Bournemouth pier. It was here that I received my first jumping 'lessons', simply by following Mosa over concrete groynes jutting from the beach into the sea, and copying her style. It was a great progression from hopping over furze bushes at Longham.

'Hold on, and kick,' was the entirely correct equestrian advice she shouted, and I did just that, usually riding our only pony in the yard, a splendid strawberry roan mare who was far more attractive than her name: Stoodgie. She had the intelligence and self-preservation instinct of all good mares, and she taught me far more than any other pony I had yet ridden.

Keeping your horse on the bit, and using your legs, was the staple advice which has since taken me over a myriad of obstacles. Stoodgie would take me into fences with confidence and verve, a huge slice of luck at this stage in my self-taught equestrian career. Later we won pony races together, on the Flat or jumping over straw bales at speed which no-one in those days regarded as dangerous, although it certainly is.

I was an avid reader of riding instructional books, starting with staid but sound tomes on the 'elements of riding', but my enthusiasm was fired up most of all by a Christmas present of the 1947 edition of *The Horseman's Year*, edited by Lt.Col. W.E. Lyon. It was a marvellous survey of the current top-level of English riding.

All the contributors were male, with a heavy accent on racing and foxhunting; I was thrilled by the map of the 'Fox-Hunting Countries of Britain' printed on the fly leafs. John Hislop wrote on bloodstock and racing, Lt.Col. Jack Hance on the leading 1947 horse shows, Sir Archibald Weigall on 'The Cult of the Cob', and showjumping was surveyed by Lt.Col. Sir Harry Llewellyn, who was to partner the great

Harry Llewellyn and Foxhunter, among my boyhood heroes.

Foxhunter in winning a gold medal in the 1952 Helsinki Olympics.

Thanks to these gallant military horsemen, early postwar equestrianism was already surging ahead, and I gazed fascinated at the monochrome photographs of their activities, especially the showjumping riders, mostly men at that time, and often in military dress, soaring over obstacles which impressed me greatly, one of them no less than 5ft 3ins, nowadays a very modest leap.

An untypical picture of a junior girl rider, Pat Moss, captioned as 'very much at home on Hairpin of White Cloud' was a pointer towards the future glory of British showjumping in which women riders would play an increasing role.

Soon I was hooked on jumping anything I could find suitable, from gorse bushes on the common to piles of logs in the small paddock adjoining the Hollies yard. My voluntary work at the stables, somewhat to the detriment of my formal education, increased well beyond the scope of anything I had done at Longham.

Pat Moss "very much at home on Hairpin of White Cloud"

Mosa was increasingly preoccupied by other interests; she acquired a new boyfriend, the son and heir of a Moordown garage firm, who responded by purchasing a would-be point-to-point horse. I was still a devoted worshipper of anything and everything Mosa did, and followed her dictates unquestioningly. She was always fun, and I realised later, a sexy girl with intelligence and drive, well ahead of her time when many women were only just emerging from lives chained to dull domesticity.

Although I was well short of the necessary experience and competence, I was sent off daily into the Bournemouth traffic to exercise the hopeful point-to-pointer, which I believe never won anything. The big, powerful chestnut, well above my weight, although I had long legs and arms by now, gave me some nasty frights by jinking about on the roads, and once nearly ditched me over the edge of the bridge at Longham where I had hacked from Moordown to the farrier, old Harry Gray, who plied his trade in a small stone forge just above the river bank.

I reverted to childhood and cried afterwards on the delightful Anne's shoulder. She gave me a comforting kiss, and conveyed my fears to Mosa who relieved me of the point-to-point exercising role. Otherwise I was increasingly busy as escort to the Hollies' small but interesting groups of riders, who often liked to stop for a drink at pubs on Sunday mornings.

I was called upon sometimes to 'teach' complete novices to ride, especially the mysteries of rising to a trot. It became clear even to me, as an eleven and twelve-year-old, that the stables was soon in decline. I was increasingly left 'in charge', as the partnership was otherwise busy with boyfriends.

A few other volunteers helped out, including a riding housewife, but I was often attempting tasks well beyond my riding experience and capacity. However, I seemed to be successful in chatting to the clients, and learned something of the art of making people feel good in situations where they were in physical peril.

It was the equestrian version of sink or swim, and somehow I swam, surviving hazardous experiences of which my mother was blissfully ignorant.

She liked Mosa and Anne after they took the trouble to come to my 11th birthday party where they were even more admired by my father and an uncle.

Mosa gave me my first ever copy of *Horse & Hound*, selling then at sixpence. I thought the text was a stodgy read, although I trudged through it, but I was entranced by the 'Horses for Sale' at the back, and spent hours fantasising over the ones I would buy.

Mosa increasingly took in less suitable mounts, including an Exmoor pony mare called Molly who proved totally unreliable, and bolted with me along Winton's main road, back towards Moordown, weaving her way deftly in and out of cars stopping in alarm, and eventually charging into the dark recesses of the Moordown Trolley Bus depot where she came to a halt with her muzzle stuck over the back platform of one of the yellow trolley buses. I prayed she would not board the bus.

Somehow we were still together, she had not fallen on the bus depot's slippery cobbles – probably because she was unshod – and I slid off, to lead her back into the yard by the pub in a state of euphoria at still being alive.

The proximity of the Hollies' lounge bar was proving a negative influence on her business, since some clients were inclined to spend more money and time there than on the horses.

Inevitably, the yard folded, presumably when Anne's uncle declined to meet further mounting debts, and the rent of the coach house. Nothing daunted, Mosa quickly re-sited her venture to Bournemouth council's small yard at Northbourne, recently vacated by the council's cart-horses. This was a far more rural setting, with ample grazing to be rented nearby, and it was closer to my home.

Now I rode Mosa's half dozen horses and ponies more or less at will, since there seemed to be very little formal riding school activity, just occasional Sunday morning pub tours on horses. Sadly for me, Stoodgie was sold to a local grocer's son, but I formed a better partnership with the dreaded Molly, even though she jumped over a hedge and set off across country with me when confronted with an Army tank near Kinson.

It was too exciting, but it taught me to sit tight, and I never resorted to the foolish policy of baling-out.

Most unwisely, I taught Molly to 'shake hands' for tit-bits, and she became a dangerous nuisance, by striking out with a foreleg when not required. She lived out in a paddock near the Council yard, and was a devil to catch. My father nobly joined in the fray when eight of us used ropes to trap her in a corner one day after I had been unable to retrieve her for several weeks. She was pretty wild at being captured, and while I was grooming her she kicked me hard in the buttock, fortunately with her unshod hind feet.

I rode several very large horses off grass, including a dreadful bright bay gelding which was a confirmed shiverer, and would nap at electric pylons by repeatedly rearing nearly vertical. It was all useful experience, and somehow I survived the hazards as most young riders generally do, with resilience and luck, if not much technical skill. I frequently rode bareback for hours on end, mainly because I could not unlock the saddlery room at the Council yard.

My jumping improved because Mosa's old hunter mare, Honey,

who survived the move from the Hollies, proved an excellent coach. I erected some poles on drums in the field next to the yard, and jumped Honey regularly on summer evenings, again deriving my instruction from horse rather than from human.

Mosa's next surprise was to announce that she was about to marry Arthur Rowbotham, a navigator for BOAC – and thereafter, with his backing, she would run a riding school at Lilliput, the upmarket suburb between Poole and Sandbanks, nowadays one of the most expensive addresses on the South Coast.

Arthur was a Yorkshireman, but nothing like the stereotype of that ilk: he was cultivated, with a great sense of humour, and although he did not ride, he went to great pains to back his new wife's continuing desire to make a success of a riding school.

They were exceedingly kind to me, and invited me to their Catholic church wedding in Bournemouth, followed by a jolly reception at what seemed to me a sophisticated hotel in Old Christchurch road where I tasted sherry for the first time, and talked far too much about my illusory prowess as a rider.

Now I cycled over ten miles each way from Northbourne to Lilliput to ride Mosa's horses, and found the journey well worthwhile.

Still riding hatless, I was put up on a fiery chestnut thoroughbred, only 16 hands, who 'needed some work' before he was considered fit for the school's clients. He had an old girth gall, which was to become cancerous, and this probably accounted for his irascibility: he bucked me off three times one afternoon when I tried to test his jumping, on each occasion landing me head first in a huge forest of nettles.

Then I took off his saddle, and without a girth, he was much better behaved. For weeks I rode him bare-backed out on rides, which included the shore-line at Sandbanks, and adored his quality and style. Despite veterinary treatment his girth gall never recovered, and eventually he was put down.

At Sandbanks Mosa and I made friends with one of the first great equestrian eccentrics who would enliven my life with horses, Mrs Louie Dingwall. She was credited to be the first lady racing trainer, and she was certainly a pioneer, training her horses on the sandy beaches at Sandbanks from her yard behind the bus garage in Panorama Road where she ran her own private bus service, the Rossmore Flyer, for more than 40 years. She taught me a valuable lesson, that a true enthusiast does not look askance at the antecedents or wealth of a fellow addict who shares the same passion. She seemed to recognise that I at least had aspirations to be a horseman, and already had a passion for horses.

'Come in. Look at the horses,' she would beam. We watched several rolling happily in a sandpit, and inspected her string at close quarters.

Louie would ride them fearlessly on the old chain ferry from Sandbanks to Studland where there are miles of beach and heathland.

'Come and ride out one morning?' she invited with a smile.

I did so just one morning, and for the first time I 'rode short' in a light saddle on a thoroughbred racehorse, fortunately a remarkably benign and quiet animal which the kindly Louie selected for me. We hacked quietly along Sandbanks beach soon after dawn, with the waves gently lapping the shore on a summer's morning, and a light mist clearing over the expansive green waters of Poole Harbour, behind us on the other side of the Sandbanks spit.

'Sit quietly, and stand in the stirrups', said Louie, on a horse in front of her small string of perhaps four. I copied the other riders, and we cantered along the sand remarkably sedately. The horses behaved impeccably, although I had heard stories of Mrs Dingwall's racehorses occasionally appearing in front of a bemused holiday car driver on the Poole road.

If this was not heaven it seemed remarkably like it, I thought, secretly immensely proud to be there at all. Riding out with the Dingwall string was the greatest compliment my outsider's route to horsemanship had so far achieved, and probably totally unwarranted, but I was secretly proud of it, and grateful to the big hearted lady for the rest of my life. It was my first indication that horsemanship could open the door to acceptance in a wider and far more exciting world.

I made several other visits to the Dingwall yard, but I was also immensely busy trying to 'help out', which meant gain free riding, in Mosa's riding school in Lilliput.

During a short holiday in Sandbanks, the Labour politician Sir Hartley Shawcross and Lady Shawcross arrived one day arrived at the yard for a hack. I, a gangling and talkative youth of 13, was given the task of 'showing them the way'. They were charming, and probably to his surprise I ventured to compliment Hartley, later Lord Shawcross, on his role as chief UK prosecutor in the Nuremberg war trials. He said he was glad I had taken an interest, but replied tactfully that a ride on the beach was perhaps not the best place to discuss it.

His second wife, the delightful Joan Shawcross was a bold and highly competent rider, and 20 years later I reminded her of our first meeting when I met her again frequently in the hunting field in Sussex, and in Leicestershire. I admired her as a dashing rider with the Quorn, and with the highly exciting Mid-Surrey Farmers' Drag Hunt. In the 1967 season I would enjoy one of the most exciting short hunts in my life in company with Joan when we were among a very small group who broke away from the sedate Eridge mounted field to jump an awkward place off a road, and cut across country on a quick five-mile point behind their huntsman John Cooke.

Hartley was opposed to his attractive wife hunting because of the risks, and tragically she died not in the hunting field, but in an accident while exercising horses with another rider in 1974. The other horse fly-bucked high in the air, and with a metal-shod hind foot gave Joan a fatal injury; it was a shocking, but very rare example of the ultimate penalty of horsemanship.

Later in life I would know others who have died in disastrous falls, and all too many who would become permanently paralysed as paraplegic victims of riding accidents.

Such risks never entered my mind as I embarked blithely on my own lifetime with horses. Riding across country is far more a state of mind than it is a scientific technique.

Through ignorance, naivety, or downright foolishness, I started my horseman's life armed with supreme confidence, and an impregnable belief that no real harm could ever come to me once I was in the saddle, no matter that I wore neither a hard hat, nor such new-fangled devices as back-protectors, which are rightly now de-rigeur for many.

Such confidence, misplaced or not, communicates instantly to the horse or pony under that saddle. For the rest of my riding life that relationship, and huge slices of luck, saved me from the fate of which the Arab proverb gives all too prescient a warning.

Working as a voluntary groom in riding schools as a boy was fun, but it did not persuade me that a career 'working with horses' was a good way forward. My mother impressed on me at a very young age that it would be far better to earn a good salary in some other occupation rather than slave in a stables to be near horses all the time.

Far better to ride the horse, than muck it out, I decided. I have never regretted that decision, and I have often gently advised mothers of horse-mad children to think carefully before encouraging children to take up a 'career with horses'.

Grooms are not generally the best-paid manual workers, and you need considerable financial backing to open your own yard. In my youth there was all too much exploitation of young people's enthusiasm through rewarding them a pittance to work for long hours in stables. I am sure there are some worthwhile jobs as grooms in top competition yards nowadays, but parents should beware. Horses are wonderful animals, but their care is demanding and risk-prone. It's surely preferable to earn a good income outside the horse world so that you can afford to buy your own horses, cared for by others?

My motto has always been: 'Don't put your daughter on the stable yard Mrs Worthington.'

Chapter Two

FIVE SHILLINGS A WEEK PONIES

The tabloid press stereotype view of riding and hunting people has long been that many are upper-class twits. This persisted even after the rugged showjumping star Harvey Smith's Yorkshire vowels became widely known in TV interviews.

The reality that riding in Britain crosses all boundaries of class has more or less seeped into today's media culture, although there are still occasional attempts to use it as a badge of class and privilege.

I met some delightful people in Mosa Rowbotham's Lilliput yard, including some very pretty girls. I wore my first suit, borrowed from a cousin, to join them at a riding club dance at the Sandbanks Hotel. Lilliput, even in the 1940s, was a highly select suburb on the shores of Poole Habour: spacious 1930s houses in large gardens, slumbering in tree-lined avenues, mostly with glimpses of the great shallow harbour and its swarms of yachts and dinghies.

At my first riding club dance, wearing a flapping grey flannel suit my mother had desperately borrowed from a friend's son, I distinctly recall a waft of perfume, and a glimpse of cleavage from one dancing partner who I had never before seen in anything but grubby boots and jeans.

She clutched me close as we performed the Cuckoo Waltz played on an electric organ in half-darkness, while the waves kissed Sandbanks beach just outside. For the first time I thought time spent with girls was not entirely wasted, although I was still far more keen on the horses than the girls at Mosa's yard.

Alas, Mosa's Lilliput venture was another which did not survive long, and she devoted herself mainly to bringing up children in an exceptionally happy marriage.

I was determined to achieve the ambition of owning a pony: an optimistic project, since I had no money, and no chance of being given a pony by my parents.

By now riding offered me an incentive to do something useful, which an overgrown youth, inclined to be lazy and of short attention span, badly needed.

I saved cash avidly, and began a newspaper round for Mr Hankinson's paper shop, in Hillview Road. I nearly lost the job twice: once for being late after cycling back from witnessing my first point-to-point, held by the Portman at beautiful Badbury Rings, west of Wimborne, and secondly when I failed to turn up at all for the evening round, having been following the Courtenay Tracy Otter Hounds splashing about in the River Stour all day, my sole experience of that sport. They did not catch an otter, nor did I see one, but I fell into the river head-first at the end of the afternoon.

A friendly lady otter-hunter took me to her car and loaned me a towel which she always carried for such happenings. I cycled home still distinctly damp, and had a strip-wash in front of the fire; our bungalow's heating was coal fired and could not provide instant hot baths in those days.

I was a particularly dreadful paper-boy, often late, and far too inclined to spend many minutes reading the front pages of the newspapers, which I then failed to re-wrap properly, stuffing them in messy heaps through the letter boxes. In winter I was inclined to drop bundles into puddles.

Fortunately, Mr Hankinson never knew of the one occasion when I tried to accomplish my round on a borrowed pony. There were many still unmade roads in Northbourne at the end of the war, so I was able to canter over grass and gravel.

The main problem was tying up the pony adequately while I delivered to a batch of houses. I was alarmed by angry shouts from a man leaving his house to find a pony eating his favourite bush in the front garden while tethered to the gates.

Presumably he did not complain to Mr Hankinson, but I gave up my attempt at 'Pony Express' after that; it was fun but it took about three times longer than usual, and I was desperately late for school. It was the first direct connection in my life between journalism and horsemanship, and it was not a good omen.

The paper round remained essential if I was to be a pony owner, since I had to find five shillings a week to pay for the privilege of grazing the pony in a six-acre grass field among too many other horses and ponies.

I had become friends with a group of girl pony riders in Northbourne, who kindly allowed me to ride their ponies. Margaret Parrett, daughter of a senior partner in an estate agent's, was especially kind, since her 13.2 hands black pony, Flash, proved an ideal partner for me in gymkhana games, my new passion. My long legs gave me the essential ability to leap on and off at speed, and I was frequently able to get into the winning ribbons in such contests as Musical Sacks, or the

Riding Flash, my gymkhana partner, kindly loaned by Margaret Parrett.

Apple and Bucket class which involved galloping at speed up to a bucket, and hurtling off the pony to seize with one's teeth an apple floating in a bucket of water.

Sometimes Margaret and I would triumph in the Gretna Green class where I would leap up behind her, bareback, to race back to a winning line.

At the age of 16 when I was taking my O-Levels at Bournemouth Grammar School, I used a revision afternoon to ride Flash in the Festival of Britain Show held in Meyrick Park. The prize money was amazingly generous, going up by £1 for fifth place to £5 for the winner. I reaped a goodly harvest of placings, riding home in a daze with over £20 in banknotes in my pocket, a sum of money seldom seen in my home. I would have done better, but there was a family raiding party of gymkhana experts creaming off first prizes, led by a juvenile Terry Biddlecombe who was to become champion chase jockey, and the husband of the trainer Henrietta Knight.

I had a nasty moment when I collected my rosettes, for they were handed out by a steward who was a history master at Bournemouth Grammar.

'Aren't you supposed to be revising this afternoon, Clayton?' he asked. To my relief the woodwork master was also there, and he said soothingly: 'If he doesn't know it all now, he never will. And I expect the fresh air and riding will clear his head.'

Margaret was a sensible girl, with a lot more common sense about riding than I possessed. I had a far less responsible relationship with the flame-haired temptress, Daphne Oliver, youngest of three madcap daughters of a charming widow of a clergyman, living on the edge of Ferndown Moors.

Daphne was totally fearless and reckless in her riding and handling of their group of ponies. She believed the height of humour was reached when the sisters encouraged a friend to drive a pony in harness, but left the traces undone. How they roared when they whipped the animal to bolt forward, and the driver was ejected over the front holding the reins. I should have known that this story was a warning of future perilous japes.

At 12 and 13 I had little inkling of any relationship with girls except as tomboy companions, but I liked Margaret and Daphne enormously, and later became fond of Daphne's elder sister Poppet who was another free spirit, and a great winner in gymkhana games.

My friendship with Daphne survived her first potentially lethal practical joke aimed at me. She encouraged me to mount a friend's pony while grazing in a field near Longham. It was 'perfectly safe and quiet' she assured me, so I sprang on to its back, minus saddle or bridle.

The pony, I soon discovered, was virtually unbroken and set off round the field at a flat out gallop in huge circles. I was not too alarmed at first, but then the beast veered towards a barrier of barbed wire and posts, strung across a bridge over a large dike at one side of the field.

Without checking, the pony pounded up to this six-foot high barrier and took off, inevitably crashing through the top, and turning a spectacular somersault on to the bridge, from where it fell into the dike.

The impact catapulted me high into the air, with an extraordinary feeling of weightless flight, and I performed my own somersault far beyond the bridge, rolling head-over-heels to land without a scratch.

This was just as well since I was bareheaded as usual, and could easily have broken my back or my neck. I was supremely ignorant of the effects of head injuries, and could not have spelt paraplegic, let alone recognised it as a riding risk.

Beaulieu Road sale-yard in the New Forest where I bought my first pony.

Daphne roared with laughter, and was only chastened when we found the pony somewhat lame after the adventure.

For several weeks afterwards we shared one large, placid horse which the Oliver girls had 'on approval', although a purchase never materialised. We rode it for miles bareback, with me sitting behind Daphne, clutching her firmly round the waist, and causing much merriment by occasionally falling off backwards over the tail when Daphne gave the animal an unexpected kick.

We celebrated Guy Fawkes night by riding over Ferndown Moor bare-back on ponies, cantering round a huge bonfire, and roaring with laughter as the ponies shied every time a firework went off.

It was from Margaret Parrett that I learned the cheapest route to pony ownership could be the annual sales of ponies grazed on the New Forest.

There was a glut of these animals, owned by the Commoners, people who farmed land on the ancient forest and had grazing rights. They were selling very cheaply, many going straight into the continental horse meat trade, many suffering hugely by travelling on the hoof in terrible conditions to horse-eating France and Belgium for slaughter.

I read in *Horse & Hound* of a growing campaign to stop the trade, eventually resulting in a welfare Bill still working today.

Unbroken ponies could be bought for just a few pounds I was told.

So Margaret and I set off for the autumn sales at Beaulieu Road, near Lyndhurst, travelling free in the back of a lorry driven by a somewhat grubby local horse dealer.

The open-air sale yard, on the edge of moorland by a small railway station, was a series of post-and-rail pens, adjoining a narrow corridor leading to the sale ring. This was another pen, overlooked by a wooden platform for the auctioneer and his staff.

Unbroken ponies, fresh off the Forest, were jammed into the pens, a sea of tousled manes and troubled eyes. The air was full of whinnying and thuds as ponies crashed against the post and rails. They had been driven off the moorland in 'drifts' by mounted groups of their owners, called Commoners. The round-up was supervised by Agisters, officials who administered the grazing on behalf of the Verderers, of ancient origin, who protect the Commoners' rights by controlling stallions turned out on the New Forest, a royal hunting ground since the 11th century.

Strong men waded into the pens among the press of animals to paste numbers on the ponies' quarters. Armed with white flags on sticks they drove the ponies one by one into the auction ring where buyers packed the rails. There was a small, rough crowd who were buying strictly for the meat trade, and there were others looking out for a possible riding pony.

The New Forest pony is a tractable animal, up to 14.2 hands, with a large head, and a kind eye. During the war there had been less control of those kept on the moor; many were killed on the roads in the blackout, and overall numbers soared.

Armed with £15 in notes, a tremendous sum I had carefully amassed, I was recklessly determined to buy a pony whether I could find a suitable one or not. Margaret and I climbed the rails to peer unavailingly into the mass of matted pony coats heaving about as men drove them out to be sold. It was impossible to see their height or conformation which mattered little, since I was hardly qualified to make sensible judgements on such matters.

I was looking for a pony I liked, and with desperation I picked on a bright chestnut with a cream mane and tail, pressed hard against a rail as he strove to keep his feet.

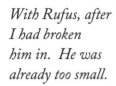

With Rufus, after I had broken him in. He was already too small.

My heart sank as other ponies were snapped up for under £10 in the auction, while others mysteriously fetched up to £30 or more. Our dealer friend told us the meat trade boys were running a ring, bidding up the prices of any ponies sought by those buying for other purposes.

I had never bid at an auction, but shrieked my bid of £10 when the pony appeared in the ring. Perhaps I was lucky, or perhaps the meat men took pity, but he was knocked down to me at £12.10 shillings.

I was thrilled, but now faced my biggest test. After I paid the auctioneers, I had to catch my unbroken pony and lead it to the lorry.

The sale yard now resembled a rodeo, as large men wrestled rope halters on to ponies who had never been handled, then drove them from the yard on the end of long ropes, often bucking and plunging.

RSPCA Inspectors were trying to prevent too much rough stuff, but some ponies were getting knocked out about on the first leg of horrific journeys to slaughter.

I located my pony, still pressed among a mass of others, and tried to make my way to him, gasping as my ribs were pressed and pounded by the mob of frightened animals. It seemed best to plunge forward as if launching into surf, and I managed to grab the cream mane of my chosen purchase, desperately grabbing his muzzle and shoving the halter over his ears.

Bruised and battered, I tugged him out of the pen with the strength of desperation, and with Margaret behind him, he allowed us to lead him to the lorry where the dealer and other men shoved him up the ramp among ponies they had bought.

In a daze of triumph I left the lorry that evening, having paid one pound ten shillings for the transport, with my unbroken pony on the end of the halter.

Suddenly he took off along suburban Northbourne Avenue, bolting down the road with a fierce eruption of energy. Dragging behind I nearly fell, but then I had a brainwave, taking a double turn with the rope around a lamp-post to bring him to a halt. Policemen travelled on bicycles in the 1940s, and a Constable suddenly appeared inconveniently to give me a telling-off, but when I gasped out my problem he propped his bicycle against a front garden fence, and kindly assisted me in releasing

*Lt. Col. Sir
Peter Farquhar,
Joint Master and
huntsman of the
Portman, with
Daphne Moore,
authoress and
Horse & Hound
correspondent on
hound breeding.*

the pony and leading it to our grazing field around the corner. It was typical of rural policing 1940s-style.

My mother made the excellent suggestion we call the pony Rufus the Red, and it suited him. He was a delightful animal, submitting easily to my inexpert breaking-in, saddling and bridling, and riding at moderate paces, and this was a highly enjoyable experience, but there was a major snag.

In my impetuosity I had bought an inappropriate animal: rising four-years-old, Rufus was a stocky pony, barely 12.3 hands, and was not going to grow big enough for me to ride much longer, for I was shooting up in height well above average for a 13-year-old.

My feet were soon dangling much too far below the pony's belly.

Next spring I advertised him in local papers, and sold him for a magnificent £25 to a family of younger children who were attracted by his flashy colour. As a four-year-old he was hardly suitable for them, but ignorance is bliss with ponies until the first drama occurs, and I had made one hundred percent profit, an entirely new experience in the Clayton household.

I soon spent £22 of my riches on Mac, a 13.3 hands registered New Forest pony, which I bought from a Christchurch dealer named Gypsy Joe.

Mac, named after my initials, was a four-year-old bay gelding with far more scope, and I rode him happily bareback for nearly three months before I bought an aged second-hand saddle at Wimborne's monthly horse market. I loved auctions, and had learned how to bid in buying and selling pet rabbits at the market.

On Mac I rode miles across the heathlands north of Bournemouth, sometimes as far as horse shows near Ringwood or Burley in the New Forest, and that winter at the age of 14 I achieved an ambition: I took my own pony hunting with the Portman foxhounds, on the eastern edge of their country.

Urged by the Oliver sisters, I had joined the Portman Pony Club, which secured my free entry to the hunting field, although I had neither suitable hunting clothes, nor any transport to take my pony to far distant meets.

It was the 1947-48 season, and Lt.Col. Sir Peter Farquhar had returned from the war to take up the Mastership of the Portman, and to hunt the hounds. He had been an eminent pre-war amateur huntsman and hound breeder, and a close friend of 'Master', the legendary 10th Duke of Beaufort who presided over his magnificent family pack at Badminton. Farquhar had returned to hunting after a tough war in Europe and the Middle East, and had been awarded the D.S.O. and Bar.

Setting off for my first hunt, wearing motley kit on an unkempt pony, as illustrated by John King.

I knew nothing of the reputation and background of the new Master of the Portman, but I liked the tall, lean man who greeted us when we made a Pony Club visit to the Hunt Kennels at Bryanston, near Blandford.

Most of the party were girls, and after Peter addressed us all on the way the Kennels were run, he took the small group of boys apart and talked to us quietly about the pleasures of hunting itself:

'Always remember, the riding is fun, but the purpose of hunting is to catch the fox. If you understand what the huntsman and the hounds are doing you will learn to love hunting for a life-time.'

I told him I lived much too far away to hunt with him on my pony, but he scoffed, and told me to hack across Ferndown Moors to any of the meets on the Bournemouth side of Wimborne.

'It's rough country where I hunt the doghounds; you will see some good hound work,' he promised.

I wrote to Uncle Hollis to tell him of my hunting enthusiasm, and without warning there arrived in the post from him a parcel containing a hunting bowler hat. It was somewhat too large, but with judicious use of newspaper inside the brim it fitted, if at a somewhat rakish angle; more suitable to a music hall comedian, my mother said.

Adorned with the comedy hat, above a school blazer, the agricultural breeches, and the US army gaiters, I hacked across Ferndown moors, and then over the A31, the Wimborne-Ringwood road, to the woodland and scrub north-east of Wimborne where the Portman were meeting at Uddens Plantation.

My pony, Mac, seemed fairly tired by the time we arrived; he was mainly grass fed, and unclipped; he was sweating after the long hack. Hounds had already moved off when we arrived; it was an unpopular meet for the riding fraternity, mainly in woodlands, and relished by the Master as a great opportunity to work his doghounds, with few people mounted.

'Stand there and holler if you see 'im!', ordered a red-coated whipper-in when I arrived at a muddy track in the woodlands, with hounds speaking somewhere in the thick belt of trees beyond. There was no sight of the Master, nor anyone else, except a dishevelled man in a grimy peaked cap, blue overalls and gumboots who arrived pushing an ancient bicycle along the track.

Mac suddenly woke up, almost alarmingly, when he heard a crash of hound music. He danced about with an amazing show of new energy. I hauled on his reins, and held him tight, making him stand, although he trembled, his nostrils flared and his eyes nearly popped out when suddenly the man with the bike screamed and raised his cap in the air.

Mac was not just responding to the noise; he was staring along the track, where I just caught sight of a streak of reddy-brown darting across. The ''im' referred to by the whipper-in was the fox, and I was supposed to give a holler, or holloa, to inform the huntsman and hounds if it crossed the ride.

I did not make a sound. Instead I concentrated on preventing Mac from suddenly converting into a bolting racehorse. Somehow I kept him on the spot, although he seemed electrified.

The hairs on the back of my neck stood on end when there was a thrilling doubling on a hunting horn somewhere in the trees, and hounds spoke again, this time far more loudly and coming my way.

Mac plunged about as a carpet of black, white and tan Foxhounds surged on to the ride, sterns waving, heads down, some baying, and then they swept into the woodland to my right, in the direction the fox had taken.

With an awesome crashing noise a large brown horse burst from the trees on to the track. Although he was now glamorous in scarlet coat, hunting cap, stiff white hunting tie, breeches, boots and spurs, it was undoubtedly the Joint Master and amateur huntsman of the Portman Hunt, Lt.Col. Sir Peter Farquhar.

Would he give a friendly greeting to the Pony Club boy he had encouraged to come hunting?

'Get out of the way boy,' he shouted loudly as he cantered past me on the ride. I was far too busy pulling Mac to the side, and then restraining him from following, to make any sensible reply even if Sir Peter had given me the time of day.

Then several other large, imposing male riders on huge horses, squelched along the track following the Master.

'Best foller 'em quick,' said the saturnine Dorset bicycle man.

So I cantered my rejuvenated pony after the others, tagging behind them up and down hilly rides, in pursuit of the sweet baying of hounds which reverberated through the taller trees like organ music.

Nothing else in life seemed to matter except keeping in touch with the hunt. Sometimes we emerged into sandy glades, then we pushed through overgrown woodland paths where my pony's size was an advantage in avoiding springy branches which hit horse-riders in the face and chest.

I could not see hounds, but I heard them all the way, until we rounded a clump of trees, and there was the whole pack, milling about in a sort of rugby scrum. Sir Peter was on his feet blowing his horn, a different note, a long drawn out one… it signified a kill. Hounds were breaking up the hunted fox they had just caught above ground, and killed instantly.

A whipper-in was also on his feet, and waded in among the hounds. He drew a large knife from his pocket, bent down and cut off the dead fox's brush.

He gave it to the Master who beckoned to me.

'This is your first hunt? Well my boy, you're in at the kill.

'It's a good time to blood you. You're happy about that?'

I could only nod my head to say yes! I was in heaven; it had been the most thrilling day I could recall.

Sir Peter dipped a finger into the bloody end of the fox's brush, and smeared a little blood down either of my cheeks. It was something like a Red Indian ritual I had seen at the Moderne cinema in Winton, I reflected later.

'You're blooded now,' he smiled. 'Don't wash it off 'til you get home. Most important, come again. And you don't need your pony every time: come on your bicycle; you'll see plenty of hunting in this country.'

Barbaric, a dreadful way of recruiting a child to a blood sport?

I was to hear all these accusations against foxhunting in years to come from the zealots of the anti-hunting lobby.

Was I brutalised, de-sensitised about the death of a small animal torn to death by a pack of hounds directed by cruel men?

As I hacked Mac slowly home I was in a reverie of bliss, recalling every foot of the way in the hunt, every check, every incident leading to the kill.

I had already seen rabbits clubbed to death with sticks at harvest time; I had seen rats chased and caught by terriers in a local farmyard, and I had sent my own pet rabbits to market to be sold for meat. I knew about life and death in the countryside long before I saw a pack of hounds instantly kill a wild fox.

Blooding is not an essential element of foxhunting; the practice was largely abandoned during the latter part of the 20th century, but in the Dorset rural communities near my suburban home in the 1940s it was still regarded by many as a mark of maturity and confidence in a country boy.

'Blooded you did 'e?' remarked the bicycle follower approvingly when he saw my smeared face as Mac and I trotted home.

My mother was aghast, and insisted on washing my face thoroughly as soon as I arrived indoors.

Yet I could see she was also impressed. She had certainly not expected me to get anywhere near hounds killing a fox.

'You may think you're very clever, but don't on any account tell anyone at school about this; not the teachers nor any of the other boys,' she ordered sternly.

'I mean it. You'll do yourself a lot of harm. They won't all understand. Keep it to yourself.'

Despite my tendency to talk incessantly, I managed to follow my mother's advice for at least half a term, until one day in the playground I confided my 'blooding' secret to a favourite friend, a clever Jewish boy named Silver whose worldly opinions on life in general I tended to value.

He listened carefully to my 'blooding' confession; then scoffed and said: 'Get real. Just think about what's been happening in the war: millions slaughtered by the Nazis. And now someone has put some fox's blood on your face? Who cares? You don't need to feel guilty – just bloody lucky!'

CHAPTER THREE

IN THE EDITOR'S SADDLE

It is comparatively rare to stumble into a working role which fits like a glove, produces a lifestyle you thoroughly enjoy, and makes you many friends. Without realising it, I had been preparing for the editorship of the weekly magazine *Horse & Hound* for a long time.

Parallel to a hectic career as a hard news journalist I had managed to find a little money and time sporadically to ride horses, and go hunting whenever I could find the time. During my impecunious three years, aged 16 to 19, as a trainee reporter on the *New Milton Advertiser and Lymington Times*, I scraped together a few pounds to hire horses occasionally in the New Forest. I achieved the reporting job through cycling to every newspaper office in and around Bournemouth.

I discovered the *Advertiser's* office purely by accident on one of these cycle rides. The Editor-proprietor Charles Curry took me on as a trainee reporter at £2 per week, which included parcelling the papers for delivery after they were printed on an ancient machine every Friday morning.

Whilst fulfilling two years National Service in Germany as a clerical RAF Corporal I was fortunate to find a farmer near our base at Laarbruch who allowed me to exercise his horses free of charge.

Via short stints on the *Bournemouth Times*, and the *Portsmouth Evening News*, based at Chichester, I reached Fleet Street at the age of 23 to report for the *London Evening News*, and later the *Evening Standard*.

It was fast-tracking into a hectic world of intense Fleet Street competition. I was sure any hopes of riding horses would be dashed for years to come, but to my surprise I found London a centre where riding and hunting were still within reach.

Foxhunting remained my recreation during nearly a decade as a BBC staff correspondent. For the BBC I reported the Aberfan Disaster in Wales, war fronts in Cambodia and Vietnam, the civil war in East Pakistan, the Palestine Liberation aircraft hi-jackings in Jordan, and other major stories ranging from the Cod War in Iceland to the Northern Ireland Troubles. I had seen quite enough bloodshed and misery at close quarters.

While at the BBC I supplemented the costs of hunting by freelance writing on hunting and equestrianism. One of the most successful projects was ghosting an annual year book recounting the exploits of the extraordinary pony Stroller and his rider Marion Coakes. By coincidence Marion was born and bred in Hampshire in the circulation area of the *New Milton Advertiser* where I had started in journalism.

I had not intended to be a ghost writer, but Bill Luscombe, head of Pelham Books, urged me to write 'just one' Marion Coakes book, after he had published my first book, *A Hunting We Will Go* in 1967.

Marion Mould (née Coakes) and Stroller – whose triumphs I ghosted in popular annuals.

Stroller's fame was based on his ability to compete with full-sized showjumping horses at the highest international levels. I interviewed Marion once a year, and garnered yet another extraordinary record of success, culminating in her Olympic silver medal won with Stroller in Mexico in 1968.

The amazing pony's continued success meant the annuals ran to four editions, all of them sold-out. Marion's marriage to the leading 'chase rider David Mould added more glamour to the annual story of showjumping triumph. Producing these books proved to be a useful method of

researching the horse world thoroughly, well before I edited *Horse &*
Hound.

One of my reporting colleagues in BBC TV news jibed: 'Clayton
writes beautifully in the manner of an 18-year-old girl.'

I could bear this with equanimity because Stroller made a helpful
contribution to my hunting costs, and I became friends with Marion and
David whose prowess as riders I admired enormously.

Between Fleet Street and the BBC, I had spent a year as News
Editor of Southern TV, based at Southampton, which provided valuable
experience before tackling broadcasting at national and international
levels.

My news reporting years, my early stint as a sub-editor, and my
spells as a News Editor, were all valuable experience in editing a weekly
magazine. An ingredient in my decision to make a career change which
many of my BBC colleagues regarded as quixotic, if not ridiculous, was
the chance to run my own show, although I was well aware that I was

Francis King, publisher of Horse & Hound (right), seated next to Dorian
Williams' wife Jennifer. I was paying tribute to Dorian for his contribution to
the magazine.

still responsible to management. I suspect I was much in need of a more ordered existence after years of rackety reporting the international scene.

I reported at *Horse & Hound* to IPC publisher Francis King, a Wykhamist, with impeccable manners, and a distinguished appearance, tall and silver-haired, but something of a chain-smoker which affected his health. I was more than sorry when he retired; he was the most congenial publisher with whom I worked, although I enjoyed good relations with virtually all the IPC management for the next 26 years.

Francis understood *Horse & Hound's* highly individual character, and he and his successors all gave me absolute editorial freedom in defending hunting hounds, no matter how vociferous the anti-hunting movement was to become in the latter 20th century.

Francis and I formed a warm understanding from the start, and I hoped I had the job in the bag after the first interview, although I was uncomfortably aware of one embarrassing snag: I had tottered into his office crippled by one of the heaviest falls I had suffered in the hunting field.

I left a supportive walking stick in the outer office, but could not hide a heavy limp and a severe black eye as I entered the publisher's office.

'Do you often have falls from horses?' Francis asked solicitously, after I confessed the reason for looking as if I had been beaten up.

I muttered that it was comparatively rare, and hoped I had not lost the job to a non-riding applicant.

The previous Saturday I rashly rode out with the Mid-Surrey Farmers' Draghounds, the equestrian equivalent of hell-on-wheels.

Our host was Douglas Bunn, owner of the famous Hickstead showjumping course. Adjoining his arena he had created a formidable cross-country challenge of strong hedges, ditches and timber obstacles. Later he used this to invent the sport of Team Chasing.

Susie Woodhouse who accompanied me on the hectic ride at Hickstead.

Accompanied by Susie Woodhouse, wife of the Portman's Joint Master John Woodhouse, we drove our horses in a trailer from Dorset to Sussex to disport ourselves over Duggie Bunn's cross-country playground. Foolish Foxford, my headstrong Irish hunter, thoroughly enjoyed the romp, pulling stronger all the time into each fence, until his exuberance made him miss his stride, hitting the fence hard, and somersaulting spectacularly on to me.

It was a heavy rotational fall which can kill a rider, but somehow I survived with some cracked ribs, numerous other bruises and the black eye. The brim of my bowler hat was hanging loose on my collar, which caused some amusement to my friends at Douglas Bunn's lavish tea afterwards.

I confided to Douglas I was to be interviewed for the *Horse & Hound* Editor's job next Monday.

'Wonderful!' he cried. 'You can do this sort of thing all the time!'

I nodded vigorously in agreement, until a terrible pain in my neck made me wonder whether I had broken it.

However, Francis King was cautious enough to appoint me as associate Editor to Walter Case for the first six months, becoming full Editor from January 1st, 1974 when Walter very reluctantly retired. My starting salary was barely higher than my BBC pay as a reporter, but I had a staff car – and I was already enjoying myself as an editor-in-waiting. I had worked for Rothermere and Beaverbrook, and knew how big London publishing houses operated within the confines of severe trade union restricted practices.

There is no such thing as a secure editorship, but I comforted myself that for the first time in my life I had a notice period of a year –and I was only the third Editor since the dear old magazine was founded in 1884.

At the beginning of 1974, when I occupied the Editor's chair for the first time in *Horse & Hound's* Edwardian offices in High Holborn I ran my hands over the leather bound desk top, checked all the drawers, and sat back to take a deep breath. I imagined the Editor's chair as a saddle on a highly experienced horse with a great many miles still to travel, but I had no illusion it was to be an easy ride.

Peter Willett, our authoritative bloodstock correspondent.

Our showjumping columnist Peter Churchill.

C.N. de Courcy-Parry who wrote as "Dalesman".

For a weekly magazine, I had a meagre staff of six: deputy editor Hugh Condry, Racing Editor Bernard Metcalfe, Shows Sub-Editor Arthur Oliver; one picture editor, and a general sub-editor, Arnold Garvey, the youngest member of the staff, plus my own secretary.

They were highly competent in producing the magazine on time, maintaining high standards of accuracy, and each had a passion for the area of the horse world with which he was concerned. Traditionally the staff talked about *Horse & Hound* as 'the paper', and indeed it had been produced since 1884 more as a weekly newspaper than as a magazine.

I had never worked on a magazine, but I was comfortably at home in a newspaper. I would strive to give the venerable publication the best of both formats. Readers wanted up-to-date news about their precious sports, but why not be entertained as well? Surely there would be room for a weekly cartoon, some by-lined opinion columns, far greater use of pictures – and perhaps, even the delights of colour reproduction?

There was ample room for updating the presentation and content of the magazine, although from the start I was cautious about introducing abrupt changes. The readership was highly conservative; many horsemen and women had grown up with *Horse & Hound*, and would strongly resent an obvious new direction in their weekly bible.

With such a small staff, I would have to be a hands-on working Editor at full throttle if we were to carry out the changes in the magazine

John Oaksey, superb racing correspondent.

I knew were needed. *Horse & Hound* still had a whiff of Victorian England, although in the early postwar years it had abandoned a Times-style front page of tomb-stone columns of advertisements, for a seasonal monochrome picture of horses, often with no heading referring to the magazine's content.

My predecessor Walter Case was a canny handler of the budget, keeping well within a very modest page rate. He had no ambition to be one of those editors who achieve success by increasing their staff and freelance contributions, even if it meant routinely over-spending the budget.

He proudly showed me a dusty file in a cupboard, containing manuscripts of what he described as 'articles', which I took to mean 'features'.

'They're useful to slip into the magazine when you have spare space. You don't have to pay for them until you use them. Very good when the weather's bad, and there's no racing and hunting,' he told me.

'Really?' I replied, thinking of the planned layouts and schedules for the feature pages of the modern newspaper and magazine. Les Carpenter, chairman of IPC, had tentatively suggested during an inaugural interview that 'the title does need a bit of dusting up; we'd expect you to bring it up-to-date, but do be careful; no need to rush it. Remember the old magazine is profitable, and plenty seem to like it as it is.'

Horse & Hound at the time was like a Victorian railway carriage rumbling entirely in the right direction, but needing the windows to be opened, and the upholstery re-stuffed. I was well aware that young women were increasingly taking up riding, and when the opportunity arrived I would add some female sub-editors and writers to the staff.

The greatest asset Walter Case handed over was a list of contributors including some of the finest equestrian writers of the day. They were a highly individual crew, headed by the BBC's famed TV equestrian commentator Dorian Williams as the weekly columnist 'Loriner', the

Dorian Williams (right) presenting me with a British Horse Society award.

superb racing correspondent John Oaksey, bloodstock correspondent Peter Willett, shows reporters Pamela Macgregor-Morris and Andy Wyndham-Brown, and the wonderful, inimitable hunting scribe 'Bay' de Courcy-Parry who used the nom-de-plume Dalesman. Peter Churchill joined us later to report showjumping most effectively, and contributing a column. They, and many other contributors, became friends, and I valued them all immensely.

The magazine had unique networks of local correspondents in Hunts and horse shows throughout the British Isles. I engaged the magazine's first regular illustrator, John King, who provided superb line drawings and colour pictures. He was a keen hunting man and accompanied me on many trips, including tours of the Irish Hunts.

Lt.Col. Frank Weldon, director and course builder at Badminton Horse Trials, was a gifted writer, and I was delighted when he agreed to report this growing sport for us, although he never reported his own event. I recruited as a staff member, Jane Pontifex, who had worked for years in the British Horse Society's Horse Trials Office. She reported the sport for *Horse & Hound*, and no contributor argued her pleas for 'more space' than Jane who combined charm with a steely core.

Anthony Crossley became our highly influential dressage correspondent, urging British dressage to raise its game at a time when the sport was wholly dominated by Germany and Holland. I was approached once by three queens of British dressage, who urged me to dispense with Anthony's services because he was 'too severe'.

I advised them they had just ensured that Anthony would not be replaced, and although dressage was not my own first love, it held a position of growing importance in the magazine deserving more space in future.

They took this rather well, although one of them, remarked with a smile: 'Yes, we know you are really just a hunting yahoo.'

Anthony would be delighted with the huge progress British dressage made, eventually gaining gold in the London Olympics in 2012.

I learned much later that it was to Dorian Williams that I owed the offer to become Editor. He had suggested the idea of my appointment to Walter Case, and hence the fateful lunch at the Reform Club. I met Dorian Williams for the first time when I was researching my first hunting book *A Hunting We Will Go* in 1967, when I was a BBC reporter.

Like millions of others, I knew his voice intimately, for Dorian was the first equestrian TV presenter – famous for his commentaries on the great horse shows at Wembley and White City, and horse trials at Badminton and Burghley, which earned TV audiences of over ten million, and made a huge contribution to catapulting horsemanship into the widest public arena.

Dorian was a complex man, extraordinarily creative and versatile: he wrote and edited dozens of horse books, created and ran a remarkable adult education centre at Pendley in Hertfordshire, and was the senior Master of the Whaddon Chase Hunt in Buckinghamshire where I was to hunt with so much pleasure. He gave me a most helpful interview on the role of Mastership, and we became firm friends immediately, a friendship which lasted until his tragically early death from cancer, aged 72, in 1985. Dorian's friendship and example was a major inspiration towards my major change of focus in journalism, encouraging me to believe there would be a fulfilling role for me in the horse world.

Dorian had a great sense of humour, was a born actor and public speaker, and I enjoyed our frequent lunch meetings when we would share confidences and information about the world of horse and hound. Dorian preferred to keep it secret that he was our columnist 'Loriner', although some equestrian journalists guessed it. We did not reveal his identity officially until the first issue after his death.

Another crucial figure in encouraging my appointment was Capt. Ronnie Wallace, Chairman of the Masters of Foxhounds Association, whose nickname in the hunting world was 'God'; of whom much more later.

Walter Case had ensured that *Horse & Hound* retained its position as the world's largest circulation weekly equestrian magazine; the circulation reached 70,000 per week for the first time shortly before he retired. It was a great achievement for which he deserved full credit. Many a weekly national title claiming distinction in politics or the arts would have revelled in such a circulation, and profitability.

We must have done something right in the way we modernised the magazine because the circulation soared to a peak of 98,000 per week during my editorship. It began to sink later because the horse world became increasingly specialist, and this was reflected in a more diverse magazine market with alternative specialist titles somewhat reducing *Horse & Hound's* circulation. Nowadays it has a keen following for its accompanying on-line editions.

The all-round horseman, engaging in a number of activities, has become rarer which seems a pity, but perhaps it was inevitable. Standards are so demanding in showjumping, dressage and eventing nowadays that the successful rider has little time for non-competitive sports such as hunting.

My good fortune when I became editor was that the tide of interest in equestrianism and hunting was still rising. Britain was painfully struggling out of austerity, and most people wanted to forget the grimness of war and its aftermath. There is no more addictive recreation than riding and owning horses and ponies.

Despite these advantages, I would have to wrestle with the nuts and bolts of magazine editorial production in dire circumstances. We struggled to get the magazine produced during the Heath government's three-day-week caused by the miners' strike. The staff coped magnificently, and we did not miss an issue.

I was sub-editing copy by the light of candles in my office when a telephone call came from a Scottish reader complaining bitterly that his *Horse & Hound* had arrived late. He had the grace to apologise when I told him of the staff's efforts to get to the office in fuel-starved London, before working in darkened offices to meet our weekly deadline.

The publishing industry in 1974 was still riven with restrictive practices in the production areas, unable to take advantage of impending new digital printing technology. The National Union of Journalists was strong in IPC editorial offices, making the dismissal of inadequate staff problematic. Union officials, called 'Fathers (or Mothers) of the Chapel' were inclined to appear on the editorial floor if there was a whiff of complaint from the staff. It was easier for management to sack an editor than one of the sub-editors or writers working under him.

There had been several major postwar NUJ strikes in the company, causing *Horse & Hound* to lose publication of a number of issues – an interruption in service to its readers. Walter Case pointed out wryly that Hitler had been unable to achieve this during World War 2 when the magazine's office was bombed, but the next issue still appeared. I learned that during the last NUJ strike Walter had locked the door between his office and the sub-editors' room, and cut off all contact with the staff until the strike was lifted.

If you wanted to appoint a new secretary you first had to interview candidates already on the company staff who wished to move from other magazines. Over the course of 25 years I usually managed to avoid this hurdle on the grounds that I must have a secretary with equestrian knowledge, but on occasions I was forced to make an internal appointment. I heard one such secretary saying on the telephone: 'Yes Mr Beaufort. I'll tell the Editor you've called, but he's very busy'.

I snatched the phone from her to assure the Duke of Beaufort, the highest eminence in the firmament of foxhunting, that I certainly had time to speak to him

A recently-joined young sub-editor on internal appointment told me she was very keen on 'gigs'. I said encouragingly: 'That's wonderful. We need someone on the staff who likes equestrian driving classes.'

The following week she left us to join *New Musical Express* where she no doubt enjoyed the sort of gigs she was talking about.

Horse & Hound editorial department, when I arrived, was housed in two high-ceilinged rooms in an Edwardian block in High Holborn. One room was my office, and adjoining it was the larger sub-editors' room and a cubicle for the picture editor. The offices were somewhat overcast, but they had large windows overlooking the busy London street. The publisher, and the advertising department occupied offices elsewhere in Covent Garden. *Country Life*, also published under Francis King, and his first love, was housed more luxuriously in Covent Garden offices designed by Lutyens, with antique furniture in the Editor's office.

Editors of various magazines housed at the High Holborn office each had a key to use a special washroom, and twice a day a homely lady in a pinafore arrived in an editor's office with tea, coffee and cakes. It was an easy stroll up the road to Soho to meet contacts in pleasant restaurants and bars, or one could walk down Kingsway to Covent Garden and the Strand. Lunch at Simpson's-in-the-Strand, where waiters in white aprons carved your beef and mutton at the table, was a treat especially relished by the top brass in the hunting and equestrian world.

I liked my new work-place, and my role in running a popular magazine in a gentlemanly setting. It was not to last: drastic changes were on the way, as usual in my life.

Chapter Four

TWO JOBS

Horse & Hound's Holborn office had a special advantage for me: it was geographically handy to BBC Broadcasting House in Portland Place, and to the BBC World Service offices in The Aldwych. I had been somewhat rash in assuming I would immediately sever all the apron-strings from Auntie BBC while I edited *Horse & Hound*.

Francis King was a little taken aback when, soon after offering me the post, I turned up again in his offices to discuss terms, accompanied by my agent, Bagenal Harvey, an Irishman who could claim to be one of the most astute sports representatives in London.

He was a key figure in arranging new contracts for Britain's professional footballers which enabled higher wages, escalating to today's huge pay-outs. Bagenal represented many high profile sportsmen, such as the cricketer Denis Compton whose income escalated when Bagenal introduced him to the advertising world where Denis became known as the 'Brylcream Boy'.

Bagenal worked on the football players' revolution with Jimmy Hill, the brilliant soccer manager, player and TV pundit. Jimmy became a friend of mine later because of an unexpected conversion to foxhunting devotee. I was recommended to join Bagenal's clients by Ian Wooldridge, a close friend since we were trainee reporters on the *New Milton Advertiser and Lymington Times*. Ian later became a legendary Fleet Street sports columnist for the *Daily Mail*.

Bagenal Harvey insisted that my *Horse & Hound* staff contract included the freedom to write books, and to broadcast, relying on my discretion to 'fit it all in'. Somewhat to my surprise this was readily agreed to, but neither Francis King nor myself expected that as soon as I resigned from my staff role as a BBC news correspondent I would, through Bagenal, be offered a plum freelance role as co-anchorman two or three days a week on 'Today', the increasingly popular BBC Radio 4 morning news and current affairs radio programme. With my usual inability to say 'no', I accepted the offer, and started my new editorship with this heavy broadcasting yoke around my neck.

I had to arrive at Broadcasting House at the unearthly hour of 4.30am, then engaging in a hectic round of writing my own links into interviews and reports which would make up the live programme, starting at 6.30am, continuing until 9am. Sometimes I would record interviews of my own, usually with overseas journalists or news contacts. It was a hectic news era, with the Watergate scandal raging in Washington, and at home an increasingly acute trade union crisis which was to bring down Edward Heath's government.

Presenting live news and current affairs radio for two and a half hours, with my own interviews and links, was not a light task at the start of a full working day in a magazine office. I must have been reasonably resilient because I managed the dual role for nearly two years, and also contributed a few pieces to BBC World Service radio.

It was some months before one of my *Horse & Hound* staff said: 'Was that really you I picked up on my car radio this morning?' I nodded and changed the subject, and no-one on the staff mentioned it again – nor did I receive a query from IPC management on the subject.

I would drive from my home near Maidenhead to Portland Place well before dawn, snatch the usual hideous BBC coffee, and work feverishly on my links, alongside the urbane and friendly John Timpson, the senior *Today* presenter. We were colleagues when I worked full-time in BBC News, and our partnership was harmonious, perhaps too much so. Some producers felt there was not contrast between the standard English accents of Timpson and myself. *Today* was growing rapidly in importance; it was the programme politicians and opinion makers listened to as soon as they woke up. Leading figures in government and opposition were keen to give us interviews, and so were many in business and the arts.

Not surprisingly, one of the producers said to me over the tasteless coffee and cardboard bacon sandwiches we wolfed down at the end of the programme: 'So when are you going to make your mind up? The Editors here won't go on much longer employing the Editor of *Horse & Hound* to talk to the nation on news and current affairs. You've got to make up your mind which slot you're really in.'

It was no surprise when the phone calls from the *Today* office suddenly dried up. I thought wryly that perhaps a few words of thanks, or even a short note, might be appropriate from the *Today* Editors. I had anchored the programme through some of the biggest news stories of the postwar years, interviewing cabinet ministers and trade union leaders, among the plethora of early morning chat.

But I knew this was not the BBC's way with freelances. Freelance presenters of other programmes have found out to their chagrin that when the BBC axe falls there is little or no warning – and certainly little or no time wasted on thanks. This is where the practices of broadcasting and showbusiness merge.

The Editors were already experimenting with different voices. I much enjoyed partnering Robert Robinson, amusing and erudite, but it was no surprise when the choice for full-time co-presenter went in 1975 to another journalist with whom I co-presented, Brian Redhead. He gave the programme a robust, Manchester flavour – and a liberal to left-of–centre political injection.

By 1975 I was deeply embedded in the world of *Horse & Hound*, thoroughly enjoying myself, and it was a relief, despite the financial loss, to be free of *Today*'s gruelling early schedule. I still listen to the programme, admiring the dedication of John Humphreys, Justin Webb, Sarah Montgomery *et al*, but I do not envy their working schedule.

Broadcasting was by no means closed to me: I appeared for many years on rural issues, and as a defender of foxhunting on news and current affairs programmes on TV and radio. For several years I was a regular on the panel of Radio 4's *Any Questions* – intended to give something of a rural offbeat contribution role as Editor of *Horse & Hound*.

Freelance broadcasting never distracted me from my principal role. No editor can escape the relentless round of deadlines if he wishes his precious publication to survive and flourish. I had a firm conviction from the start, however arrogant, that I could edit the magazine better than anyone else available. I had already decided that the Editor's office would not be a prison: I badly needed to get out of London as often as possible to explore the realm of *Horse & Hound*.

I had carefully noted the remarks of Ron Phillips, a shrewd and amiable Main Board director of IPC Magazines, when he interviewed me for the Editor's job: 'We don't care whether you never come to the office at all, so long as you turn it out on time, and it puts on circulation. You won't of course be able to do that without coming into the office most of your time. We had to dispense with a yachting magazine editor who was always out of the office when it mattered; he blamed it on the tides which always seemed to be against him when he wanted to come into land.'

Over the next two decades I was to become all-too-accustomed to 'coming into land' into *Horse & Hound's* office in a great hurry from some far-flung hunting field, or horse show. My attempts to point out how economical it would be to re-site the magazine's editorial offices in a Midlands rural setting never succeeded.

However, being sited in London enabled me to chair the British Society of Magazine Editors, and to be a founder member of the Press Complaints Commission.

Chapter Five

WEEKLY CHALLENGE

Horse & Hound's production schedule in the 1970s was by no means easy: from Monday to Wednesday the reports which made up most of the magazine, much of it hand written, sent in by post from freelances of highly varied writing skills, were sub-edited in the office; all too many needed some re-writing on a series of ancient typewriters. A messenger service transported the edited copy every day to the small, noisy printing works in far off Stratford, East London where it was set in columns of lead type.

These were 'pulled up', printed in long columns on newsprint, and sent back to the office in High Holborn. The staff then cut and pasted these paper columns into page sheets, leaving spaces for pictures and headings, and they were sent back to the print works to be 'made up'. Page proofs came back from the printers each day, but late news pages still had to be made up on Thursday nights. Pictures had to be sent earlier in the week to a separate processor to be made into photographic 'blocks' which were sent to the printer. There was little opportunity for including a 'late' picture.

Every Thursday evening, at the end of a long day in the office, the editorial staff drove their own cars through heavy traffic to the printers. Publishing conglomerates, such as IPC, appointed the printer they considered most suitable, and economical, for each of their large portfolio of magazines.

Horse & Hound survived and flourished on a basic, frugal, printing system suitable for a weekly monochrome newspaper, and thereby earned worthwhile profit.

Walter Case had ceased to go to the printers regularly for some years, but I resolved never to miss this onerous outing. It was the precious window in which the Editor could make late adjustments to the magazine, see all the pages before the issue 'went away', and make late decisions. Visiting the Stratford printing works carried me back nostalgically to my start in journalism as a teenage trainee reporter on the *New Milton Advertiser and Lymington Times* office in Hampshire. There was the same somewhat sweaty atmosphere in the print room, the never-forgotten smell of printing ink and hot lead in the pots attached to the elderly typesetting machines.

As editorial staff, under the type-setters SOGAT union rules we were strictly not allowed to touch anything, but we stood next to the chief compositors as they placed the type in the metal forms, making up the pages. An ability to read metal type in its reverse format became second nature to a 'stone sub-editor', one who worked with printers. The busy East London printing staff were cheerfully cooperative, but *Horse & Hound* was just one of their contracts, and they worked under inexorable deadlines.

The process of production was incredibly laborious. There were so many possibilities of interruptions in the lengthy chain of communication of the magazine's content, and yet the system rarely failed. Some correspondents used British Rail's quaint parcel service to send in their reports, which added to the risks of non-arrival. In dire circumstances my secretary took copy over the phone on a head-set, but in the main the dear old weekly relied on the devotion of its staff, and an antiquated, labour-intensive printing industry.

Even within the frugal editorial budget it was obvious there would be ample room for updating the magazine's presentation and content, although from the start I was cautious about introducing abrupt changes. The readership was highly conservative; most horsemen had grown up with *Horse & Hound*, and would strongly resent a sudden new direction in their weekly bible. It seemed best to endeavour to do better the things which the readers already liked.

Walter Case commissioned few pictures, except those needed to accompany horse show reports. Many useful pictures arrived non-commissioned, and would only be paid for if used to fill corners in the make-up. He was proud of never publishing a picture of any rider falling off. 'They don't like to dwell on that too much,' he said. In fact, falls are an inevitable accompaniment to riding, and most riders are not at all averse to seeing others falling off.

I vowed I would certainly be breaking this taboo, although I was well aware the riding fraternity would certainly not enjoy a fall picture in which the horse was being injured, a policy to which television sports producers still adhere.

Already there was a suggestion that a major move was pending; all IPC magazines were to be shifted from offices scattered all over central London to King's Reach Tower, a huge tower block on the South Bank of the Thames near Blackfriars Bridge. I shrugged, and took little notice, but the move when it came made a fundamental change to the rest of my life in full employment. There would be no more special washrooms for editors, and vending machines on landings would soon replace the homely ladies with my tray.

I had a firm conviction, however arrogant, that I could edit *Horse & Hound* better than anyone else available in the England of 1974. I had already decided that the Editor's office would not be a prison: I badly needed to explore the equestrian and hunting world, to become far closer to my readership. Somehow I would have to be a bridge between the old equestrian establishment, dominated by the Army, and the growing numbers of newcomers to the riding and hunting world, many of them ex-grammar school products like myself. Fortunately I was to make firm friendships in all stratas of the changing world of horse and hound.

The great sporting editors of the 19th century, Robert Smith Surtees, also a brilliant comic novelist, and Charles James Apperley, known as 'Nimrod', both travelled the British Isles as hunting correspondents, producing copy eagerly read in the journals they edited in London. Privately, I was sure I could do the same, and I shall never cease to be grateful to Francis King and his management colleagues that they did not become alarmed when the new Editor was regularly absent from the office to report from the hunting field for his new weekly column *Foxford's Hunting Diary*, named after my prized hunter, of whom much more later.

My passion for riding to hounds was the most pressing motive which made the editor's seat at *Horse & Hound* the prize I could not resist, but I looked forward with warm enthusiasm to sharing my love of horses and horse sports with the readership. A successful specialist magazine involves a close, warm dialogue with others who share your own pleasures. However, I was well aware that running *Horse & Hound* was a genuine journalistic challenge. We needed to attract more young readers, without offending the older generation of loyal subscribers, and the sheer slog of bringing the magazine out efficiently every week seemed a threat to the joys of actually riding and seeing horses and hounds far away from London.

Horse & Hound's editorial staff in our centenary year, 1984.

My previous experience in dealing with a tough team of reporters as deputy news editor on the *Evening Standard* may be the reason Arnold Garvey said at my retirement lunch that my staff nickname was 'Genghis Khan'. Perhaps like the acerbic editors I had worked for, I was inclined to express eloquent displeasure with errors, but I was quick to praise as well.

Over the next two decades I had the benefit a loyal, long-serving staff I liked very much, who treated me with respect and gave full co-operation. Our shared enthusiasms for the world of the horse were the extra bonus which specialist journalism brings.

I would advise any aspiring young journalist to get a sound training as a general news reporter before eventually specialising in the field which commands your genuine enthusiasm. It will make the latter years of your working life far more rewarding.

I am especially pleased that my former racing editor, Mark Hedges, is nowadays the successful Editor of *Country Life*; our former sub-editor Kate Green is Managing Editor of that magazine; and Pippa Cuckson, who was a key member of *Horse & Hound*'s staff, is an award-winning equestrian journalist for *The Daily Telegraph* and a leading contributor to other publications.

Our centenary was celebrated in the staff magazine IPC News.

CHAPTER SIX

FOXFORD SETS FORTH

R.S. Surtees, the satirical novelist, cruelly lampooned the famous hunting correspondent, Charles James Apperley as 'Pomponious Ego'.

When I launched myself into visiting and reporting on widely different packs of hounds I soon realised just how unfair Surtees had been to Apperley who was a skilled and brave rider across country, but suffered injury and ill health, and finally died deeply in debt.

I was soon to discover there are ample reasons for humility in the role virtually invented by Apperley who wrote under the nom-de-plume Nimrod. Surtees was a brilliant satirical novelist, creator of Jorrocks, Soapy Sponge and others, but he was a poor horseman. His barbs fired at Apperley looked too much like jealousy.

There can be few journalistic tasks as anachronistic as that of hunting correspondent. Unlike virtually any other sports writer, the hunting scribe ventures on to the field of play all day, taking the same risks as everyone else riding to hounds.

Indeed, being expected to go well when riding over a country you do not know, on a horse you have mounted for the first time, is an extra challenge. How out of date is that in a modern world where sports writers sitting comfortably in the stands are so magisterial, and even caustic, about those playing on the pitch?

I called my own weekly reports *Foxford's Hunting Diary*, named after my own sole hunter at that time. The diary format gave me an opportunity to range beyond a straight account of a day in the hunting field, and was useful when a major freeze-up stopped hunting. I rode

Riding Tex, Geoff Brooks's stallion, who gave me great hunting in Leicestershire.

with over 250 packs throughout the British Isles, and as Editor of the magazine it was much better to write under a pseudonym.

How fortunate is the hunting correspondent in tasting fully the pleasures of the sport he is reporting! Riding on privately-owned land, in other people's Hunts, is a unique privilege and pleasure. On each visit you are entering a unique rural community with its own history and customs. I shall never cease to be grateful for the ready hospitality accorded to a visiting Pomponious. Frequently I was given bed and board in country homes ranging from mansions to tiny cottages, and would be loaned horses varying from top-class quality hunters to handy cobs.

As well as 'writing up' the Hunt, I often 'sang for my supper' by speaking at Hunt Supporters' Club dinners, cheerful occasions when my limited repertoire of hunting jokes was received with amazing generosity. One Chairman summed up the situation by whispering after the meal: 'Would you like to speak now, or shall we let them enjoy themselves a bit longer?'

Apart from the rewards of the chase, the prize I received from over 40 years as hunting correspondent was a thorough exploration of our countryside on horseback which offers perspectives you can never gain from road-sides.

A hasty change of clothing for Jim Meads and myself before a day with the Galway Blazers.

Negotiating steep moorland hillsides at speed was just as much of a challenge as flitting over fly-fences amid a keen mounted field with the Quorn. There are many areas of our countryside which have disappeared under buildings and roads since I hunted with them. I grieve as much the erosion of the British rural landscape as I do the iniquitous passing of the Hunting Act in 2004.

It requires a certain amount of stamina to run the whole gamut of winter travel, speech making, then early rising to 'see a favourite farmer' on the way to the meet to mount an unknown steed. Occasionally I was even loaned a change of horses during the day. Once this encouraged me to make a foolish decision: I tried to emulate a professional huntsman by vaulting lightly from one horse to the next.

Unfortunately, the second horse bucked immediately I landed in the saddle, and I was thrown high in the air to land in a morass of mud. For the rest of the day my brown-stained back was discreetly pointed out to others in the hunting field who could share the joke about Pomponious's fall.

While I was still working at the BBC Wilson Stephens, Editor of *The Field*, invited me to take on the role of hunting correspondent which had been occupied with distinction by a foxhunter with the most resounding by-line: 'Sir Andrew Horsbrugh-Porter Bt.'

My hunting visits were sporadic due to my BBC commitments. Wilson Stephens announced, no doubt with tongue-in-cheek, that *The*

Field's hunting correspondent was unable to start reporting the start of the 1970-71 hunting season because he was trapped by heavy gunfire in the Intercontinental Hotel, Amman, where he was endeavouring to report the Jordanian war.

It is true that I was as much frustrated by missing the start of the hunting season, due to being unable to ship film from Amman airport.

War reporting alternates periods of fright with tedious waiting, and amid the booming of guns for hours I sat on floors in passages of the Intercontinental Hotel reading my slim copy of *The Foxhunter's Bedside Book* which accompanied me to Vietnam as well as the Middle East. Compiled by Lady Apsley it provides a wonderful collection of much of the best writing on the Chase, and I thoroughly recommend it to today's foxhunters.

Sir Andrew knew his subject intimately, although he was open to the charge of being far more interested in horses than hounds. He was a

Tackling a West Country thorn hedge during a Foxford's Hunting Diary assignment with the Taunton Vale hounds.

My daughter Maxine and me making a hunting visit to Exmoor.

consummate rider across country, capable of tackling any terrain, and he conveyed the thrill of the day. Ronnie Wallace let me know that while Horsbrugh Porter was 'quite interesting to read', more emphasis on hound work during a hunting report would be very welcome by the current Foxhunting Establishment (himself).

What I liked most about Sir Andrew was his willingness to write frankly. Later I appointed him chief polo correspondent of *Horse & Hound* in order to bring some refreshing candour to reports of play at the Guards Polo Club at Windsor Park and similar illustrious venues.

I confess that in reporting for *The Field* I steered myself towards the good riding countries as much as possible. Wilson Stephens was not himself immersed in the hunting world, being interested above all in working spaniels, so he left it to me to choose my hunting assignments. Clearly he was not attracting major attention from the hunting world, for the circulation of *The Field*, still a weekly magazine, was sagging badly.

Jonathan Young performed an excellent revival job as succeeding Editor, and remains in post today. When I became an IPC director in the 1990s I had the pleasure in assisting the purchase of *The Field*, now a monthly magazine, to join *Horse & Hound, Country Life* and *The Shooting Times* as an immensely strong publishing portfolio.

My best stroke of fortune as Foxford was to be accompanied from the start by the pre-eminent hunting photographer of the day, Jim Meads who became a life-long friend. He learned the skills of photographing hunting from his father Frank H. Meads who used an old plate camera to take pictures of the Enfield Chace Hunt in pre-war Hertfordshire, and then branched forth to visit packs far and wide.

In producing pictures which the hunting community treasured, Jim had an immense advantage in being a natural athlete. He ran across country, scrambling through or over obstacles on the way, so that his pictures included plenty of shots of mounted followers jumping. His knowledge of the sport ensured that his individual portraits of horses and hounds were 'correct', with the animals standing up properly.

Amateurs are inclined to produce side-on shots in which only the two nearest legs can be seen, and the animal's head is hanging or tossing. Jim sold his pictures to individuals as well as publications, and they grace many a sideboard and photo album in Britain and overseas. He refused to switch to digital photography, and continues to produce excellent results on film which are publishable, and eminently acceptable to his many patrons.

Jim's prowess as a runner produced far more plaudits in the hunting field than my efforts to cross the country on strange horses.

'Isn't he wonderful!' young ladies would gush.

'But he hasn't jumped a fence all day. I shall have to sack him,' I would reply, adding hastily in answer to their frowns: 'I'm only joking.'

Before he illustrated the Foxford column Jim Meads had already visited many packs accompanying Horsbrugh Porter, and Jim's introduction was invaluable when I arrived with a far-flung Hunt for the first time. We reported and illustrated days with packs all over the British Isles, and in North America.

Frequently Jim was greeted warmly as an old friend. He is incredibly durable, surviving a terrible injury when a horse kicked him in the face after it landed over a fence in the hunting field during one of our joint visits. In 2015, aged 85, Jim was still photographing Peterborough Royal Foxhound Show, attending it for the 69th time. He achieved great popularity in the USA, continuing to photograph American Hunts and hound shows until the present day.

Jim had already attained a remarkable status as Hunting Photographer Number One when he began accompanying me in the hunting field, although I was able to stretch the boundaries of his visits much further.

'And I believe you are the chap they've sent along to produce the words to go with Jim's pictures?' asked a Welsh Hunt secretary early in my Foxford career. Wearing full hunting kit, and mounted on a hunter at the meet, I meekly forbore to point out that I was the Editor who had commissioned Jim to photograph the day's hunting.

Later in Foxford's wanderings, I was often accompanied by Trevor Meeks, *Horse & Hound's* first staff photographer, excellent at his craft, and totally dedicated. He produced a brilliant portfolio of colour work in the hunting field, and in all the equestrian sports we covered. Although officially retired, he continues to work frequently as a freelance.

Whatever I lacked as a stylist I tried hard to bring to Hunt reporting the same standards of accuracy I would expect in the news pages of a respectable newspaper. As a visitor riding a strange country, the only way to discover exactly what happened, and where you have been, is afterwards to cross-examine the huntsman. He and his whippers-in are the only members of the chase who can answer these questions reliably. Members of the mounted field in pursuit have widely varying levels of knowledge on such matters.

I insisted on interviewing the huntsman at the end of every visit, then using an ordnance survey map to check the routes thoroughly. Ronnie Wallace asserted that anything under a five-mile-point achieved in a run was hardly worth reporting because hounds had 'hardly left the parish'. I did not agree entirely, but I certainly reserved detailed reports to the longer runs, and just occasionally I would encounter an epic run which demanded more.

Such a day occurred when I visited the Fernie in February 1977. I tried to convey my joy at the start of my Foxford report by quoting from *Mr Sponge's Sporting Tour* by R.S. Surtees.

"Ooray, Jack! Hoo—ray!' exclaimed Lord Scamperdale. His Lordship was the picture of delight. He had had a tremendous run. The hounds had behaved to perfection; his horse had carried him well, and he stood with his crownless flat hat in his hand and one coat lap in the pocket of the other – a grinning, exulting, self-satisfied specimen of a happy Englishman.'

My report continued: 'I had more than an inkling of how Lord Scamperdale felt when his hounds had achieved a first-class 14-mile hunt. For when I visited the Fernie hounds the other day, they treated me to as good a day's hunting as I have had in a long time.

'From the first draw until home was blown at 4.40pm, life was a matter of seemingly endless galloping and jumping, in following a superb pack of hounds working brilliantly throughout. From the first draw we had a good 60 minutes hunt. Then after changing horses there followed a wonderful 2hrs 30 minute run, with a six-mile point and some 16 miles as they ran. Only about half a dozen of the field finished the day which had started with some 150 riders at the meet.

'Thanks to being extremely well mounted I was able to finish the run, plastered in mud and with a great rent in the knee of my breeches. I can only echo Lord Scamperdale again when his friend Jack Spraggon pointed out that he was 'mud from head to foot':

'Never mind the mud you old badger,' roared his Lordship. 'The mud will come off or may stay on; but such a run as we have had does not come off every day.'

'It was certainly one of the best scenting days I have experienced for a long time, in a season which has generally been noted for poor scenting conditions everywhere. But you need a first-class pack of hounds, a good huntsman, and a well-managed country to take best advantage of good scent – and I had every opportunity to observe that the Fernie has these in abundance.'

I paid warm tribute in my report to my hosts, headed by Lt. Col. G.A. (Tony) Murray Smith, ex-cavalry officer, who had been Joint Master of the Fernie since 1960, and was previously a famed Master of the Quorn from 1954.

Unfortunately Tony Murray Smith was suffering from a bad back, and unable to hunt on the Great Day I reported. He provided me with an excellent chestnut hunter at the meet at Foxton Grange. Bruce Durno had been hunting the Fernie for a decade, and continued altogether for 31 years; a quiet, unflappable huntsman with a great rapport with his hounds. He said afterwards modestly that on such a day

Col. Tony Murray Smith, Joint Master of the Fernie 1960–83, and huntsman 1962–66.

of sport, it was best 'to let 'em go; they just kept on hunting.'

It was a damp, raw morning, with spells of heavy rain developing. From the first draw at the Bunker's Hill covert it was clear we were in for something special. I tightened my girth another notch as a crash of hound music told us they had found a fox straight away. Hounds surged away to hunt their fox at a good pace in a circle to Lubenham Lodge and back to Bunker's Hill where they marked to ground.

It was a good 60 minutes run, but only the entrée. I reported:

'We changed horses, and I mounted one of the cleverest little hunters it has been my good fortune to ride in the hunting field. It was barely 16 hands and is normally ridden by the whipper-in, Michael King. It was a smallish mount for a 6ft 2ins hunting correspondent, but I was never conscious of this, and the little horse gave me a grand ride throughout, no matter how big the fences nor how demanding the pace.'

First draw after second horses was the Fernie's famous covert, John Ball, planted early in the 19th century for the illustrious Master and huntsman, Squire Osbaldeston. I wrote:

'It was a wonderful moment when Bruce Durno put his hounds in at one end, and they were soon speaking. There was one of those splendid holloas which make the hairs stand up on the back of your neck, and suddenly we were galloping along the top side of the covert to come round the far end, and be confronted by a wonderful sight – a classic 'gone away'.

'The Fernie hounds were running beautifully together over the grass with a wonderful head, and the pace was fast enough to make you sit down and ride, but not too fast to spoil the pleasure of jumping the delectable variety of timber and fly-fences criss-crossing the downhill grassy slopes ahead.'

The great run, mostly in pouring rain, took us in a loop over the superb upland grasslands west of Market Harborough, passing Saddington, nearly to Fleckney and back through the John Ball covert, before this strong travelling dog fox crossed the Mowsley road, over the Laughton Brook to Bunker's Hill, past Laughton village and Gumley covert to Lubenham Lodge, this time crossing the canal. They ran on hard, with Gartree Prison on the right.

Wet through, daubed with mud, I suddenly became conscious I had become detached from the small group of remaining mounted followers behind our Field Master, Joe Cowen. I was following Bruce Durno and Michael King, and one other follower, Robin Smith-Ryland who has claim to being one of the most devoted foxhunters in the land.

We were clattering along a disused roadway when a locked gate barring our way confronted us. Bruce jinked his horse to the left and neatly popped over a slightly lower rail adjoining the gate. Michael King followed, and so did Robin. Viewed from my small horse it seemed a stiff test, but suddenly I found myself safely on the other side. Top marks to the horse, if not the horseman.

It was a formidable obstacle, and a fall onto the gravel landing side would have been be disastrous, preventing me from being 'in at the finish' which was nigh. From a lane on our right Joe Cowen and a small handful of riders joined us, and we rode for only a few minutes behind hounds before they marked their fox to ground in old earths at Gallow Hill, below the A6 main road between Leicester and Market Harborough.

In my experience, and according to accounts of Great Runs of the past, the fox more often escapes at the end of a long hunt. Some claim that hounds change lines on to a fresh fox in the longest of runs. Perhaps they do, but I never saw any sign of it on this great day, which I was touched to see recorded as 'The Foxford Day' in the Fernie's official Hunt history.

Bruce Durno, huntsman of the Fernie (1966-97) with his father, Percy Durno, former Heythrop huntsman, and his mother.

I have had many other highly enjoyable days with the Fernie since, and like everyone who has followed this Shires pack, the only one geographically entirely within Leicestershire, I owe much to Joe Cowen and his family for their immense contribution in maintaining the grasslands of the Laughton Hills so ideally for foxhunting. Joe Cowen, one of the great foxhunters of the Shires, has achieved a remarkable record as senior Joint Master, 44 years in office by the year 2016, with his son Philip Cowen among his Joint Masters.

As Jim Meads often says to me during a session of reminiscences: 'Whatever happens, they can't take all that away from us now.'

FOXHUNTER NUMBER ONE

The most daunting experience of my Foxford assignments was reporting a day with 'Master', the 10th Duke of Beaufort, Master of the Horse in the Royal Household, and the leading figure in foxhunting, throughout most of his life. He was Master of his own pack of hounds for 60 years until his death aged 83 in 1984, and hunted them brilliantly as amateur huntsman for 47 seasons. His creation of that annual miracle, Badminton Horse Trials, and his long support of the British Horse Society, established him as the number one in British equestrianism, below the sovereign. Tall, slim, with a slightly booming voice he was the epitome of what a sporting Duke could be.

I loaded Foxford into a trailer from Wendover in Buckinghamshire, and chugged through thick fog on the M4 to Gloucestershire, panicking slightly because I was clearly not going to reach the meet at Badminton House on time. I knew that Henry Hugh Arthur FitzRoy Somerset was a stickler for time.

To my consternation the Master and the whole mounted field, formidable in their blue and buff Hunt coats, were standing in the yard at Badminton as I drove up.

Looking down through his steel framed spectacles, the Duke said: 'We've been waiting for you.' I was aghast to believe a field of over 150 had waited for me. At Badminton the fog was less dense.

I apologised profusely and clambered into the saddle. Master had reluctantly given up hunting his own illustrious pack after 47 years (1920-

*"Master", the 10th
Duke of Beaufort,
in his element
hunting his hounds.*

67). Now he was an almighty Field Master controlling his followers and all too closely observing his professional huntsman Brian Gupwell.

It was a difficult day in receding fog and Master's temper was not improving. I happened to be in the front throng landing over a stone wall when hounds checked just in front of us.

'One more step forward and you all go home!' Master advised us in threatening tones.

Later hounds pursued a fox through part of the village of Badminton, through the front gates and up the drive. Rather a good story, I thought, but then Master turned and faced his followers.

'Get off my bloody gravel,' he roared. The field scattered like starlings. I reported the day as a hunting 'occasion' rather than as a moderate day's sport. The day with the Duke was a memorable experience, and so was my night at Badminton House.

No matter if the Duke had his tetchy moments, the very extensive Beaufort community adored him, especially a coterie of admiring ladies. The Duke could exhibit great charm, and was a very considerate host. Very soon after every storm there was radiant sunshine He was a remarkable example of a benevolent, generous aristocrat of the old school who freely made available his estates to generations of followers to enjoy foxhunting at its best. He bred superb hounds, and was deeply engrossed in all aspects of the sport.

"Master" at home at Badminton with Mary, Duchess of Beaufort.

The Duke's chief henchman, Gerald Gundry, a remarkably droll character who was Joint Master and hunted the doghounds, told me a story that said much about the reign of the 10th Duke. One day out hunting Gerald said: 'Master, there's a farmer standing over there who's very annoyed with us for going on his wheat. Could you talk to him.'

The Duke cantered over to the farmer and engaged in deep conversation. When he returned to Gerald he said: 'There doesn't seem to be any problem. He didn't complain at all, just pleased to have a chat.'

The 10th Duke followed Jorrocks's dictum: 'Tell me a man's a foxhunter and I loves him.' Perhaps for that reason he was extremely supportive of my editorship, and in a foreword to my *Foxhunting Companion* book, he wrote glowing praise of *Horse & Hound* for its 'many excellent and interesting articles which appear regularly – long may it continue.'

Master was a nickname he had acquired as a child when he hunted a small pack of beagles. He said he was blooded by his father when he killed a fox with his doghounds on the doorstep of the South Door of Badminton House.

Master was likeable, and held in much affection because he was sincere and direct, and blessed with a remarkable simplicity of purpose. I loved it after supper when he took me out of doors, and said with a beaming smile: 'Just listen to that; they're singing'. It was the hound music of his beloved pack, baying to the moon in their kennels nearby.

My visit to Badminton House on that frosty night would have been better recounted by Evelyn Waugh.

'We've had a bit of a leak in the roof,' said the Duke pointing to stalactites of ice hanging from the ceiling in the hall. He showed me to my small bedroom, which was his dressing room, bitterly cold and heated by a small two bar electric fire of ancient vintage, and doubtful safety.

After supper we repaired to a drawing room, threading our way past large leather screens, meant to keep the intense cold at bay. We sat round a small open fire where the best position had been given to Daphne Moore's parrot, sulking in its cage because it did not like the winter weather. Master explained that the leather armchair had been made from the skin of a favourite horse ridden by his father, the ninth Duke.

'He still wanted to continue sitting on the horse,' Master explained.

I enjoyed the simple supper, cottage pie followed by apple pie and cream, in a small dining room. Also at the table were Mary, the Duchess of Beaufort, and Daphne Moore, *Horse & Hound's* veteran hound shows reporter, and one of the great eccentrics of the hunting world.

Tall, willowy, and with a fluting voice, she followed hounds on a large, iron framed bicycle, and lived in Pond House, a cottage next to Badminton House where she had been housed by Master to keep his hound pedigrees up-to-date, and enter his hounds in the major shows.

Daphne once made a mistake in not entering some of the Beaufort

So pleased to be the winner: "Master" receiving championship cups from Queen Elizabeth the Queen Mother at Peterborough Royal Foxhound Show.

bitches in a class at Peterborough Royal Foxhound Show, the holy of holies of hound breeding, and scene of Master's many triumphs. The Duke was famous for his exuberant pleasure in winning at Peterborough, and his intense disappointment if he lost.

When I once remarked to him that we had all enjoyed a 'good morning' at Peterborough, he exploded: 'You think so, do you? I've never seen such judging in my life!'

Master exploded in vain after his bitch hounds were barred from the ring due to Daphne's error. She retreated to the car park in tears, later making her way home by train instead of in Master's car. They were quickly reconciled, and Daphne remained at Badminton well into the Mastership of David Beaufort, the 11th Duke who was very kind to her. She died in her nineties in a Tetbury nursing home.

Ian Farquhar, son of Sir Peter, joined the Beaufort Mastership the year after Master's death, in 1985, and is still in office. Ian, thoroughly supported by the 11th Duke, has made a tremendous success of this major Mastership before and since the Hunting Act hit the sport from 2005. I have enjoyed some remarkable days' hunting with Ian, marvelling at his ability to keep the traditions of the Beaufort Hunt alive in good times and bad.

My wanderings throughout the British Isles as a hunting correspondent revealed to me the beauty and diversity of our countryside, and the staunch individuality of the characters associated with foxhunting.

When I gave up foreign news reporting, including the war zones, I thought my most exciting adventures were over. Riding strange horses in new hunting countries afforded me more thrills than I could have imagined, and in a setting I grew to love deeply.

Far too many of Britain's hunting countries from which I reported have been eroded by building developments and new roads since I first visited them. Of course a vastly expanding 21st century population needs infra-structure, and much more is on the way, but I fervently hope that society takes a deep breath and pauses before going on to destroy the very core of our countryside, uniquely beautiful and the greatest gift inherited by the British people.

Chapter Seven

HUNT SUBSCRIBER

Fun though it is to be a travelling Soapy Sponge, visiting Hunts far and wide, I paid a subscription to one pack that I hunted with throughout the season, in addition to the Foxford hunting correspondent role.

There are huge rewards from being part of a rural community, and there is continuity in your days in the hunting field.

I should add, there may be a downside in becoming part of a Hunt: the Great Hunt Row is a negative part of hunting life. Fortunately acrimonious disputes are rare, but when they occur they are similar to the disputes you will find in most clubs, although it must be admitted that hunting issues can raise hackles to an alarming degree. Although they are unpleasant and damaging, in my experience Great Hunt Rows eventually have a cleansing effect, resulting in a long period of peace thereafter. Some of the worst malcontents depart for other Hunts, or even give up hunting. Often the cause of a Great Hunt Row is local factions jockeying for control in the belief that each one can do the job better.

Strong Hunt Chairmen and Masterships working together are the best answer. It is significant that, although there may be low key grumbles, Great Hunt Rows have not erupted in the few remaining Hunts where the hounds, the kennels and much of the land have long been in the ownership of a titled family.

Nowadays many Masterships operate through each Master making a fixed cash contribution, or perhaps providing Hunt horses. The Committee pays all other costs. In the 'good old days' many Masters received a fixed annual guaranteed sum from a Committee, but the Masters still had to find considerable cash to fund the Hunt. Since they were paying the piper they had no problem in calling the tune on all Hunt matters.

However, considering the huge amount of work required of modern Masters in organising sport, hours spent in liaising with farmers and local shoots, the present day system works well. It puts extra pressure on the Committee, and the Hunt Supporters' Club to raise money, and it emphasises the need for everyone who hunts to pay an appropriate subscription. Fund raising is hard work but it ensures many local Hunt functions are held throughout the year, providing the cement to bind together the hunting community.

Somehow I managed to be a Hunt subscriber, as well as a roaming correspondent, for well over 40 years. I was fortunate to subscribe to eight of the finest packs in the land. In the last of these, the Cottesmore, I succumbed to an invitation to become Hunt Chairman for a five years term, giving me an insight into the backroom stresses as well as the joys of hunting, and increasing my admiration for everyone who works behind the scenes to keep a Hunt in existence.

OLD SURREY AND BURSTOW

Working for the *Evening Standard* in central London in the 1960s I had feared I would have to renounce foxhunting, but soon I discovered that London was a remarkably good launch pad to reach packs far and wide, with plenty close at hand in the Home Counties. I became firm friends with our South Coast correspondent, the late Sydney Curtis, who lived in rural bliss near Haywards Heath in the Old Surrey and Burstow country. A lean, tense individual who seemed to live on his nerves, Sid was at home spinning out crime stories in Brighton, but he liked rural life too.

Thanks to Sid's generosity in lending me a horse, a somewhat flighty filly who gave me a couple of falls, I tasted several days with the OS&B in their Sussex country, and in their splendid grass country around Lingfield. It was tremendous fun – and I discovered it was quite easy to drive from my home at Blackheath down to the Elysian Fields of hunting in Surrey and Kent. In view of the fun I experienced, I strongly refuted the old hunting man's advice to his son: 'Get your hair cut once a week, and never hunt south of the Thames.'

I should have remembered that Mr Jorrocks managed to hunt in Surrey by travelling down from the City of London in horse-drawn transport. Indeed I seemed to be taking a similar route through Croydon to Jorrocks's trips to ''unt in the Surrey 'ills'. The Old Surrey in those days hunted as close to London as Biggin Hill, site of the war-time RAF fighter station.

My great-uncle Hollis Clayton, who had provided me with my first bowler hat, had just died, and generously remembered me in his will. With this unexpected windfall I decide to buy a headstrong blue roan gelding I had been hiring for £4 a day from the Stangrave Hall riding stables at Godstone, near East Grinstead. Margaret Reeves, the kindly lady in charge, confessed that the 16.1 hh blue roan, named Ballyn Garry after his Irish origins, had jumped a fence into a garden while being hired for a day's hunting by a lady who was so terrified that she dismounted and led him all the way back to the horse-box.

Fortunately I had already discovered that Garry was happiest if given his head in the hunting field, and when aimed towards the biggest timber or hedge he would soar over superbly. He clearly enjoyed hunting as much as I did, and he was ideal for the Old Surrey country in being able to jump boldly off his hocks from a short take-off. He was indeed a handy hunter.

Now I had discovered the best of all escapes from the pressures of working in London could be found in a hunting field which was accessible. Best of all I met a splendid sporting community who made me feel welcome from the start. Some of them worked in London too,

Riding Ballyn Garry, my blue roan who "ran away" with his previous owner.

and shared my joy in our Saturday jaunts and jollities.

The mild and reserved demeanour of the senior Joint Master, Sir Ralph Clarke, of Borde Hill, cloaked a great passion for foxhunting. I never met a more courteous Master of Foxhounds. At my first meet in Sussex I noted that he dismounted from his horse and approached each visitor to give a welcome. He chatted with me, learned that I worked for the *Evening Standard*, and said no more. Whether he really welcomed a Fleet Street reporter in the hunting field I do not know, but he made it plain that if I was a foxhunter that was good enough.

Legend had it that he had returned from a parliamentary trip to Russia, remarking that 'Russia could be marvellous for hunting. I never saw any barbed wire between Moscow and the Urals.'

His Joint Master, Uvedale Lambert, was a staunch practising Christian, and seemed somewhat austere, but he warmed to anyone who was a keen foxhunter. His estate at South Park, near Godstone, was one of the key areas of grass and fences in the country. A signed copy of his history of the Hunt, 'Jorrocks' Country', published in 1961, is a treasured item in my hunting library. His son, Stephen Lambert, became a successful amateur huntsman at the Taunton Vale, and with the Warwickshire and Heythrop. His excellent Masterships were followed by his chairmanship of the MFHA.

I made friends in the Old Surrey country with many others, especially the Joint Masters John Robson and Diana Barnato-Walker. Diana, one of the intrepid wartime lady pilots delivering new aircraft to RAF stations, was a vivacious personality who 'did her own thing'. When we hunted on the day of the Grand National she attached a mobile radio to her saddle and switched it on to receive a commentary of the race while hounds drew for their fox in a dense covert.

I was particularly hard-up at the time, and was relieved when Philippa Andrea and Brigadier Munn, the Joint Hon. Secretaries, gave me practical encouragement by allowing me to pay the £30 subscription in two £15 instalments, the second just after Christmas. Fortunately Ballyn Garry was never sick nor sorry, and did not need replacing.

Whenever possible I scrounged a Wednesday off from the *Standard* news desk, and rushed down to Surrey to enjoy a mid-week day.

Riding after hounds was especially beguiling over the grass and fences in the Arden Run country near East Grinstead. Another choice hunting area was over Joint Master Sir Derek Greenaway's grass and fences at Four Elms on the Kent side. Sir Derek, I was told, once distinguished himself by jumping a railway-crossing barrier during a hunt, apparently when riding a hard-pulling horse.

The man who ensured that we all had such fun was Jack Champion, huntsman of the OS&B for 38 seasons, from 1947 to 1985. When I first followed his hounds, my experience of hunting had been confined mainly to the Portman and the New Forest Hounds. I was soon impressed by Jack's ability to provide sport in even the most unlikely area of the country. His ebullience ensured no day was ever dull.

I can still vividly recall Jack shouting 'Tally Ho! Tally Ho!' as he cantered over a roadside verge to jump a hedge or timber to take his hounds to the line of a fox seen going away across a field. His verve,

Jack Champion gave us so much fun as huntsman of the Old Surrey and Burstow.

75

his enthusiasm, and his skilled horsemanship and hound control were the major key to the remarkably good sport we enjoyed. The Old Surrey country was constantly being eroded by new roads and buildings, but Jack made the very best of rural areas all too close to suburbia.

Jack was especially good at the 'quick thing' which he must have learned in his pre-war days whipping-in in Leicestershire.

The M25 had not scythed through the country; many other forms of urbanisation had not arrived; there was still a remarkable amount of grass.

Jack, coming from a long line of huntsmen, was an old-fashioned foxhunting character who could have come from the pages of Surtees. When I returned much later to report an Old Surrey Day for *Horse & Hound*, he kindly provided me with a horse of his own to ride. It was beautifully schooled over timber and other fences, and gave me a great ride. Jack was a fine horseman, and I only recall him having one notable fall when he disappeared in a deep ditch.

'Are you alright Jack?' enquired an anxious Diana Barnato Walker.

'It's alright Madam. I just got me bum wet,' came his foghorn voice from the ditch, much to the mounted field's joy.

My memories of the Old Surrey and Burstow in the 1960s and early 1970s are a bright and shining light in my hunting life. Hunting behind Jack Champion at that time fired my enthusiasm for the sport even more, and helped me to make the crucial decision to change from 'hard news' reporting to accept the Editor's chair at *Horse & Hound*.

Diana Barnato Walker, Joint Master of the Old Surrey and Burstow Hunt, a vivacious personality, whose wartime role was as an intrepid Air Transport Auxiliary pilot.

At that time the ring road had not been created, nor had the urban sprawl of Gatwick Airport extended far. The Surrey side below Croydon had a vale of grass and fences around Lingfield, although hounds also hunted in the Surrey Hills on the edge of Greater London. There was an attractive country over the Kent border, and the Sussex country to the south offered woodland and grassy dingles ideal for hound hunting. I am glad that despite amalgamations of South East Hunts, the onward march of urbanisation and major roads, foxhunters are still enjoying some of the Old Surrey country where I rode my blue roan, but there are large areas lost forever in the march of 'progress' in the South East.

THE DRAG

Although I never subscribed to them, occasionally I fitted in an afternoon with the Mid-Surrey Draghounds, one of the most hard-riding outfits I ever encountered. The field included a contingent of City businessmen and lawyers, riding with tremendous dash behind the senior Joint Master, the Hon. Philip Kindersley, who lived in Sussex. He had a formidable war record, escaping from a German PoW camp to return to duty with the Coldstream Guards.

With a booming voice and genial manner, Philip gave a fearless lead across the most daunting country the Mid-Surrey could find for their drag lines. The scent dragged across country was the urine of jackals and wolves, provided in tins by the London Zoo; it must have been very powerful because hounds zoomed away the minute they hit the line, running more or less mute.

One Saturday afternoon I saw the drag pack, all drafted from Foxhound packs – and perhaps not the most reliable at that job – dodging through a gate-way on their way to the first line. They proceeded to hunt a couple of ponies who galloped and jumped ahead with great abandon over a few fields, followed by the drag pack and some of the mounted field. We ascertained at the usual après-drag pub party that no harm had been done.

The first time I took my blue roan out with the Mid-Surrey, Philip Kindersley's old horse Ranger somersaulted through a huge bullfinch hedge, and lay on the ground with one foreleg trapped in its tangled running

The Hon. Philip Kindersley, who gave a fearless lead as Master of the Mid-Surrey Draghounds, accompanied by his assistant Archie Kay.

martingale. Philip lay alongside, but was soon staggering to his feet.

'Are you alright, Master?' shouted members of the field as they landed alongside.

'Don't bloody wait for me! Go on!' Philip thundered to his followers.

We rode on to complete the first line, and after a few minutes Philip and Ranger appeared over a hill, plastered with mud, and with a broken bridle and martingale tied up with string.

Without a word Philip led the charge over the remaining lines. I finished in a cloud of rapture, and gratitude to my splendid little horse: Garry had soared over hedge and timber alike. I reported days with the Mid-Surrey for *The Field* and *Horse & Hound*, quoting Philip Kindersely diplomatically making the point that he never intended the Drag Hunt to supplant foxhunting.

'I would hunt in Leicestershire if I had my way, but I'm one of those chaps working in London who simply doesn't have the time for a full day's hunting anywhere. So an afternoon's draghunting fills the bill.'

His enthusiastic City following over choice lines in Surrey and Sussex later included as Joint Masters Edward Cazalet QC, Douglas Bunn, owner of the Hickstead showjumping arena, and George Goring, owner of the illustrious Goring Hotel behind Buckingham Palace.

I introduced George to the Drag which suited perfectly his devil-may-care attitude to hunting and its perils. George appeared to have no nerves, taking some crashing falls with equanimity as he alternated draghunting with point-to-point riding and team 'chasing, riding with his own team, the Boring Gorings. He tells the story that when he went to try a new horse, it gave him a tremendous fall over an artificial fence provided. The vendor was furious, shouting: 'You jumped the fence the wrong way round – from the landing side!'

George responded: 'The horse is no good to me if he can't jump the fence from both sides!'

The Mid-Surrey were a very jolly gang, and I thoroughly enjoyed their company in the hunting field and at their annual dinners where I saw Uvedale Lambert, as guest of honour, wincing a little at the latest stockbrokers' ribald stories from Philip Kindersley.

I rode later with the Cambridge Drag, and the Coakham and the Readyfield Bloodhounds, and they were all fun, but I was never tempted to forswear foxhunting for drag-hunting. I adored a good ride across country until I ceased to hunt in my seventies, but the joy of hunting has to be compounded by the art of venery, and the uncertainties of the Chase.

My experience draghunting proved useful later, in the thick of the anti-hunting debate, when I could speak about the sport from personal experience and make the case that it contributed nothing to the conservation of wildlife and the growth of animal sanctuaries in the form of coverts, as Foxhunts have done for hundreds of years.

RETURN TO THE PORTMAN

When I left the *Evening Standard* in 1963 to become News Editor of Southern Television, it enabled me to return to the country where I had hunted as a boy. A rented house at Cadnam in the New Forest enabled me to reach the TV studios in Southampton. Equally important to me, it was an easy drive westwards to the Portman country where I had started hunting as a boy.

The return to hunting in Dorset was happier than I had possibly imagined. The Portman was largely in the hands of the Woodhouse family, owners of Hall and Woodhouse, of Blandford Forum, one of the few privately-owned brewers at that time in the country.

Edward Woodhouse, the eldest, was Hunt Chairman, and his brother John served as Field Master and Hon. Secretary. The youngest brother, Dick Woodhouse, was soon to become Joint Master with John. This could not have been better for a young man looking for some fun in the Portman's lovely grass vale country, stretching from Shaftesbury southwards past Sturminster Newton to the Okeford Fitzpaine area.

John, who was the brewer at Blandford, gave a tremendous lead as Field Master over the vale's huge thorn hedges, growing on banks, and guarded by daunting ditches. Dick, who farmed, and was a leading amateur chase rider, liaised successfully with vale farmers to keep the country open to the Hunt.

Dick and John were married to hard-riding foxhunting ladies, both called Susan, and generally known as Susie-Dick and Susie-John. The Woodhouse children all hunted from an early age, ensuring that following the Portman was similar to joining a happy family party on a horse. I was lucky to join in some of John and Susie's uproarious after-hunting dinners at their Blandford home, or at the Crown Hotel in the town, which the family owned.

So loud was the laughter and banter in the mounted field that one neighbouring foxhunter with the South and West Wilts remarked sourly: 'When the Portman holloas a fox in their country another one goes away immediately in the next door country.'

No-one was bolder, nor more devoted to foxhunting, than monocle-wearing Capt. Sandy Maxwell-Hyslop who rode almost stride-for-stride with the Field Master, no matter what lay ahead. Sandy made annual visits to Leicestershire to hunt, and to take part in the Melton Hunt Club Ride, of which more later.

Here, I am riding a horse of Douglas Bunn's over his own formidable fences at Hickstead, during a Mid-Surrey Draghounds run.

As in all families there were just occasional fall-outs in the Woodhouse team, which added to the amusement of the subscribers. On one occasion Dick and John differed strongly on a route to be taken across the Saturday country. Eventually they went in different directions with the field split between the two.

'Is this just a family row, or can anyone join in?' asked one follower as the row reverberated above the hedgerows. Mostly good humour prevailed, especially when one of the family 'had a jerk', as they described falling heavily. This was sometimes caused by another local expression, 'hitting a mock', which meant your horse had struck an old tree-trunk in a hedge, causing him to fall.

The true perils of foxhunting in a stiff country were underlined ·for me when a visiting lady foxhunter died after a fall in the Portman country, but the local hard-riding contingent survived remarkably well, partly because the ground was usually soft to land on, and I believe

John Woodhouse, Joint-Master and Field Master of the Portman, to whom I owed so much for the best of my fun.

because John Woodhouse gave a galloping lead which ensured our horses had enough pace to get over or through the great hedges and the yawning ditches beyond.

I suffered a tragedy much later when a horse I had owned briefly was lamed by one of the vale's vicious blackthorns which penetrated a tendon, and could not be located nor extracted by the vets, all too quickly leading to a cancerous condition, causing the horse to be put down.

A less dangerous, but spectacular 'happening' was a fall by one of the field when jumping the Manston book meandering through the Vale. I recall Dick Woodhouse lying on his back after one such swim, kicking his legs in the air to get the water out.

We were aghast, and then amused, when John Woodhouse disappeared once into an enormous bullfinch, reappearing eventually with a double-bridle in his hand, while his horse cantered off into the distance.

The 'Woodhouse way' was not always popular with Stewart Tory, a leading Dorset stock farmer, and the Portman's senior Master who hunted the hounds. He was the tall, imposing, silver-haired figure

I recognised from childhood days. He was inclined to glower over his shoulder when joy in the mounted field became unrestrained.

After a particularly heavy fall in the Wednesday vale, John Woodhouse lay winded on the ground next to his horse, similarly knocked out. Stewart Tory leaned over a hedge to look down on them, and said sternly: 'If I was to treat my horses like that I wouldn't have any at all. Now, what's he going to do?'

The answer came when, to muted cheers from the mounted field, John staggered to his feet, took out his stock pin and stuck it into the quarters of his huge, recumbent horse. The noble beast sprang to its feet immediately. Our portly mud-stained Field Master regained the saddle and continued to give us a marvellous lead over a very stiff line of country.

Now in his sixties, Stewart had succeeded Sir Peter Farquhar in hunting the hounds, and he proved a canny fox catcher, hunting patiently for hours to secure a proper end to a run.

Stewart was not a bold rider in the vale, frequently using gateways while the mounted field romped over the obstacles after John Woodhouse.

Percy Tory, son of Stewart, showing the way across the Portman country.

Yet the huntsman had a detailed knowledge of his country, and kept in touch with his hounds remarkably well, aided by his veteran professional kennel-huntsman Barry Boyle, with Stewart's son Percy Tory giving a tremendous support as second whipper-in. Percy was an excellent rider, and sometimes unselfishly missed a good hunt through being sent on some errand to fetch a few hounds who had got left behind.

So wet was the Portman's vale country after Christmas, that foxhunting was abandoned there at the end of January in the interests of the dairy farmers who so valued their spring grass. Hounds were hunted until the end of the season in the beautiful upland country stretching eastwards past Blandford to the downland country around Crichel where the Tory family farm.

I recall one spring evening being the only follower still out with Stewart Tory as he patiently hunted his fox in the hills above the Okeford Vale. I had the greatest respect for him as a foxhunter, and was grateful when, after our 'goodnights', Stewart said: 'I'm glad it's not just the riding, with you. You'll enjoy this game a lot longer that way...'

The Woodhouse brothers became Joint Masters after Stewart retired in 1969, and appointed an excellent professional huntsman, Geoff Harrison. He had Leicestershire experience whipping-in at the Belvoir, and Geoff had hunted the North Staffs pack.

To the joy of the Woodhouse family, and all who hunted with them, Geoff Harrison rode in front over the Vale country boldly, ensuring the Portman pack hunted with drive. We had some terrific hunts from which I would emerge elated with pleasure, and just occasionally dazed from a heavy fall. By then I was living near Maidenhead, and in winter darkness I made the long drive back up the A30 re-living every inch of the day's sport. Geoff was a shy man with a warm smile, who we all liked, and he made the most of the sporting possibilities of the Portman country. Riding regularly in front over the vale country for a decade was a considerable feat, for which he paid with a damaging fall. I am one of the Portman followers considerably in his debt.

I owed most to Sue Mitchell who nursed Garry and several of his successors with great skill and care in her hunting yard at Sturminster Newton. When I returned on foot leading Garry after an especially heavy fall in which we were both battered, Sue said sternly: 'I'm not worried about you; it's the horse I care about. You won't be taking him out next Saturday, even if he's sound.'

In the 19th century some villages in rural Dorset would ring the church bells to celebrate the Hunt catching a fox. The need to control the thriving fox population in the Portman vales, who flourished in hedgerows as well as coverts, was underlined when Sue and Jeff Mitchell held a meet at their yard. Just after the Hunt departed, a fox broke into the Mitchell's chicken run, and killed all their hens, plus a few ducks.

Sue's husband, Jeff Mitchell, ran a horse transport business, and was most obliging in delivering me to nearby meets with the South Dorset, the Blackmore Vale, the Cattistock, and the Taunton Vale. They are lovely grass countries, all strongly fenced in their vales, which I was so privileged to explore long before the Hunting Act arrived – preceded by visits from some of the most aggressive gangs of hunt saboteurs on the South Coast.

The Dorset hunting communities are strong and closely knit, and it says much that all these Hunts survive today, even though there is still some ludicrously inappropriate harassment from the saboteurs.

Dick Woodhouse, Joint Master of the Portman with his brother John. Dick was a superb amateur 'chase rider.

If I had never hunted again after my years with the Old Surrey and the Portman, those seasons would still be a golden patch in my memory to be cherished forever. I made friendships which I have valued all my life, and acquired hunting memories I savour.

Very sadly the Woodhouse brothers all died far too young, but most of their children remained part of the hunting community in Dorset.

I had wonderful hunting with the Portman's neighbours, the Blackmore and Sparkford Vale and the South Dorset. I had much admired Simon Clarke's prowess as Master and huntsman of the South Dorset, and he was a hard act to follow for his successor, Alastair Jackson, in 1969. Alastair, fresh cheeked and youthful, seemed young to take on the challenge, but he made a great success of the Mastership, and hunting the hounds, well supported by his wife Tessa. They became great friends, and I hunted later with Alastair in his Masterships with the Cattistock and the Grafton, his career culminating as Director of the MFHA. A talented artist, he contributed illustrations and was my co-author in producing *A Short History of Foxhunting* (Merlin Unwin 2013).

The difficulties of commuting regularly to Dorset to hunt became insoluble, and near the end of the 1970s I was grateful to be invited by Dorian Williams to subscribe to the Whaddon Chase, little more than 30 minutes' drive away from my home near Maidenhead.

It was the start of my foxhunting life in the Midlands where the sport was still flourishing in the last decades of a more expansive mode. It was all too soon to be squeezed by urbanisation, increasing arable farming, and the counter-demands of organised shooting, the number-one sport in many areas of our countryside today.

From the Whaddon Chase country it was an easy drive up the M1 to the Shires, and I was determined to explore those Elysian fields as soon as possible.

Chapter Eight

MIDDLE ENGLAND

The Whaddon Chase thoroughly deserved its nickname, 'The Londoners' Leicestershire', because its two-day-a-week country in north Buckinghamshire, though small in area, contained some splendid riding country, and in parts was as formidable to cross as any hunting country in the illustrious Shires. In Dorian Williams it had the great good fortune to be led by a senior Master who linked foxhunting tradition with an ability to adapt to modern conditions.

Dorian was a remarkably versatile professional as a broadcaster, author, and educationist, and his skills as an equestrian commentator were underpinned by his background in foxhunting. His father, Col. V.D.S. Williams, had been a Master of that formidable jumping country, the Grafton, between the wars, and Dorian was a Joint Master there for three seasons until he began his great Mastership of the neighbouring Whaddon Chase for 26 years (1954-80).

Dorian's early life was dominated by foxhunting; he said his first childhood ambition was to become a Master of Foxhounds. Adding this background to a natural ability as a communicator fitted him for Mastership in a fast-changing world where hunting was facing increasing threats. Dorian's excellent horsemanship enabled him to ride at the front of a hard-riding field in a big country, again aided by his upbringing; both parents were immersed in all aspects of the horse world, his father being one of the founders of the British Showjumping Association, and a keen racing man.

Dorian applied his talents and experience to making the Whaddon Chase one of the most effective Hunts in the land. He and his professional huntsman, Albert Buckle, ensured good sport in a hunting field which was to become increasingly cramped by the growth of Milton Keynes new town. Albert, a trim figure on quality horses, was a canny personality with a dry sense of humour, and won a keen following among the Whaddon Chasers.

'You're antis are you?' he greeted a group of Hunt Saboteurs at a meet.

'Well you just stand over there quietly and we'll deal with you later,' he said with a disarming smile.

Albert was adept at 'keeping the tambourine rolling': he had the Shires huntsman's knack of knitting together the hunting of a fox, and lifting hounds to hunt the next one, producing an exciting ride for the mounted field.

Under Dorian Williams the Whaddon Chase formed the first Hunt Supporters' Club, soon copied by most other packs. The mounted field was mainly well mounted, and comprised a mix of sophisticated metropolitans with Buckinghamshire landowners, farmers, horse-dealers and leading showjumpers and eventers.

Albert Buckle, remarkable huntsman of the Whaddon Chase throughout Dorian Williams' Mastership (1954-80).

There were visiting and subscribing celebrities, such as the bearded Turkish-Armenian Nubar Gulbenkian, the cowboy star Wyatt Earp, and the co-owner of the Bunny Club, Victor Lownes, who set-up a ritzy country club in the Whaddon Chase country. I accepted an invitation to a rural supper from Victor, and found myself among a cheerful crowd entertained by a jazz band, with Bunny Girls providing friendly escorts for those who needed them.

Dorian Williams, far more than a TV commentator – an excellent horseman who gave the Whaddon Chase a great lead.

Instead of the old Master-and-man relationship, Dorian formed a virtual partnership with Albert Buckle, who continued to hunt hounds throughout Dorian's Mastership. Albert not only ran the Hunt Kennels, but also bred the hounds and helped liaise with farmers.

Foxford, the 17 hh, rangy hunter I had bought in the Whaddon Chase country, enabled me to keep near the leaders of the field, although he did once dump me in front of everyone else, leaving me clutching his double-bridle while he galloped off, to be caught later with great difficulty.

'Puggy' Wyatt, Hunt Secretary and one of Dorian's Joint Masters, was an excellent horseman who once led me over a fearsome place into a narrow lane, to exclaim triumphantly: 'Michael! We've pounded them all – including Dorian!'

A less tolerant Field Master would have given me a verbal pounding, but Dorian mainly relied on natural authority and charm to ensure discipline. His wrath was so rare that it was immediately effective when deployed.

With the Whaddon Chase I had time at the end of the day to accept invitations to that great institution, the Hunt Tea, exactly what was needed after a cold winter's day on a horse: delicious feasts of eggs, scones piled with jam and cream, fruit cake, and steaming mugs of tea, with generous helpings of whisky. Jim Cunningham, who ran a specialist veterinary unit, and his wife were especially hospitable, becoming firm friends.

The Whaddon Chase's postwar Indian summer proved all too short. Dorian died five years after his Mastership ended, and by 1986 so much of the hunting country had been lost to urbanisation that the only solution was amalgamation with its neighbour, the Bicester, hunted with great dash by its Joint Master, Capt. Ian Farquhar, son of Sir Peter Farquhar with whom I started hunting in the Portman country. Ian has since become legendary as the 11th Duke of Beaufort's Joint Master and huntsman.

The Bicester with Whaddon Chase Hunt, which survives and flourishes today, is yet another example of the huge contribution which foxhunting makes to many people's lives, and their refusal to let their sport die, no matter what modern urban society flings at our unique countryside in the way of ignorance, prejudice, and urban sprawl.

HEYTHROPIA

Before I finally made my home, and my foxhunting future in Leicestershire and Rutland, I experienced a unique style of hunting with Capt Ronnie Wallace, nicknamed 'God' in the foxhunting world, much to his considerable annoyance.

I was a subscriber to the Heythrop during the final five seasons of his extraordinary Mastership of 25 years up to 1977.

'Ronnie Wallace is the one name in hunting that will be most remembered, certainly in the 20th century, beyond any other man – Master or professional huntsman – as being head and shoulders above anyone else involved in foxhunting.'

This glowing tribute was paid by Alastair Jackson, then Director of the Master of Foxhounds Association, to Ronnie Wallace's hunting career in which he had been a Master of successive packs for 58 years. Alastair was one of a number of young Masters of Foxhounds who were heavily influenced by Ronnie Wallace in all aspects of venery. They tended to breed hounds, and hunted them in the manner Wallace deemed correct – and he was usually right.

Wallace thoroughly recognised the importance of foxhunting as a riding sport, attracting those who would pay for it, but he put his emphasis heavily on hound rather than horse. His own ability to communicate with hounds was astounding; he exhibited similar powers of mesmerism on people, and especially on the ladies.

Like all truly formidable leaders, Wallace inspired respect, but occasionally some resentment from those he sought to rule. This expressed itself sometimes in mockery behind his back. One apocryphal story was that one night in bed, his wife Rosie said: 'God, your feet are cold.'

To which Ronnie was alleged to have replied: 'It's alright Rosie. You don't have to call me God in bed.'

There were many other much-prized anecdotes about 'God'. For example, he inspired such awe in the Heythrop mounted field that a group of them hid in a tin shed on one occasion when they had transgressed by getting in front of him during a hunt.

Capt. Ronnie Wallace, formidable leader of the foxhunting world, renowned as a Master and huntsman of the Heythrop and finally the Exmoor.

During a hunting day he seldom spoke to the mounted field at large, but I was there when he was trying to listen to his hounds in a wood. He turned to the field, which included at least one Duke, and said: 'Shut up, you bunch of idiots.' There was immediate silence.

On another occasion Wallace halted the large mounted field, and called for the devoted foxhunter Robin Smith-Ryland to dismount from his horse. Wallace peered down, and declared: 'I am told you went to a meet of the North Cotswolds this morning but they couldn't hunt because of fog, so you boxed-up your horses and came here. Is that right?'

'Yes Ronnie,' said Smith-Ryland, a keen foxhunter to the point of eccentricity.

Wallace drew breath, and we waited for the imperial command to 'Go Home!'. Instead Wallace said: 'What you did is totally contrary to etiquette. Don't do it again.

'Now, get mounted.'

Robin did so in silence, but had his revenge later in the day when Ronnie's hounds were giving tongue in a hedgerow. He shouted to the Master: 'I think they're hunting a badger, Ronnie!'

Wallace thundered in reply, aka Capt Mannering of Dad's Army: 'You stupid boy! I suppose you read that in a book!'

Wallace undertook an intense life-style to partake in his life-long ruling passion for the Chase. Added to his hunting prowess was a formidable intellect, and an Etonian charm cloaking the will of a dictator. This was exhibited in the way he dominated all the Hunts of which he was Master, and in his 22 years as Chairman of the MFHA. He established a remarkable hold on the appointment of Masters and professional huntsmen throughout the land, working for his vision of the best interests of foxhunting. Most professional huntsmen held him in the highest regard, although he could be caustic to his whippers-in in the hunting field.

On Dartmoor one day Wallace's hounds had checked, and a visiting huntsman in the field could not resist blurting: 'Oh sir, if I was you I would....'

Wallace responded immediately: 'Hold your tongue!'

It is worth repeating the true story told by Bill Lander, Wallace's kennel-huntsman at the Heythrop. A visitor asked Lander if he enjoyed hunting hounds on occasions, such as when Ronnie was ill.

'Ill?' replied Lander. 'I've been here ten years and the bugger hasn't coughed once yet!'

Although he hunted five days a week at the Heythrop, Wallace found time to make firm friends in Westminster and the City to find allies in defending, and paying for, foxhunting at the high standards he sought to achieve. Some said he was so formidable that he would have been Prime Minister if he had entered politics. I doubt, however, that he would have cared to share power with a cabinet.

I first met Wallace in 1966 when I gained an interview with him at a small house at Glympton, Oxfordshire, where he was living with Rosie Lycett-Green who was about to become his fourth wife. I was researching my first foxhunting book *A Hunting We Will Go*. I was immediately impressed by his clarity in discussing foxhunting, and recorded an interview with him which I used verbatim in the book, and also ensured it was published in *Horse & Hound*.

I freely admit I fell under Ronnie's spell, and bought into his vision of foxhunting, although journalistic cynicism intervened occasionally. In return I received a life-long friendship and considerable, warm hospitality from both Ronnie and Rosie, especially when life had dealt some of its harder blows.

I did my best to use my journalistic experience as fully as possible to assist him in the defence of hunting against the growing attempts at abolition by the animal rights lobby. We disagreed later on the need for modern foxhunters to wear modern safety caps instead of top hats if they wished, but on the fundamentals of the sport his judgement was impeccable. He was the key figure in maintaining the highest possible standards in the practice of foxhunting.

Wallace spent his summers attending all the major hound shows, competing every year at the holy of holies, Peterborough Royal Foxhound Show where he won 33 championships. He judged at scores of Hunt puppy shows each year, travelling hundreds of miles, later extending his travels to leading packs in the USA. He was one of the finest judges of a hound ever seen, and was notably helpful and instructive to his junior judges. Summer was the key period of the year when he stamped his authority and influence on the breeding of the modern foxhound.

To reinforce his views he organised regular educational seminars for Masters of Foxhounds, many of which I was privileged to attend. There was no question of magisterial rule here: Ronnie was prepared to debate with those who did not hold his views, and gave plenty of opportunity for other Masters to lecture.

Rosie was to remain Ronnie's wife for the rest of their lives. She had been a society girl, daughter of a Yorkshire steel magnate, but she was thoroughly adjusted to country life, having been partly brought up at the family's second home on Exmoor. Although much later her life was blighted by ill-health, she retained many friendships because of her great sense of humour, and her loyalty. I was grateful to be among her closest friends, and much enjoyed her company.

Ronnie's much-married status came up during a Gloucestershire forum on foxhunting, which he chaired. A questioner asked the forum: 'Is the fox monogamous or polygamous?'

Wallace, somewhat patronisingly, turned to Sir Newton Rycroft, said: 'I think we'd better ask our naturalist.'

Sir Newton, without a hint of a smile, replied in his distinctive high-pitched voice: 'I think we can take it for granted the fox is considerably more monogamous than some Masters of Foxhounds. '

Wallace hastened to the next question, ignoring the chortling from the audience. The cognoscenti knew that Sir Newton, when Master of the Dummer Beagles, hunting part of the Heythrop country, once confessed to have killed a fox with his splendid hare hunting pack, and received stern admonishment from Wallace.

Foxhunting with Wallace in Heythropia was a reminder of just how different is the character of each hunting country. The well-drained grass and arable fields of the Cotswold, bordered by small limestone walls or trim jumping places, was like another planet compared to the deep riding vales and massive obstacles on banks of my native Dorset.

My horses from Dorset skipped over the well-drained going as if on holiday, and found the jumping little or no problem. It was refreshing to go home with a comparatively clean coat. Wallace had stamped his personality on the landscape as well as the operation of the Hunt. Some perfectly jumpable hedges had small tiger-trap timber obstacles set in them to facilitate the portly huntsman's progress across country, and there were convenient small hunting gates everywhere. The front rank of the mounted field was usually led past these escape routes, but they enabled plenty of less intrepid followers to cross the Heythrop.

Wallace maintained superb preservation and care of the hunting coverts, and ensured that the Hunt was virtually the only controller of the fox population. Vulpicide by any other method than the use of hounds was practically a hanging offence in the Heythrop country. This resulted in the largest fox population I had ever seen; a classic example of culling for sport being by far the most effective means of conserving the quarry species.

I hardly recall a Heythrop covert not holding foxes when Wallace's hounds were sent inside to draw. For a mediocre huntsman this would have posed considerable problems. Foxes would often explode in all directions, and it needed all the Master's extraordinary skill to ensure that his pack went away on one fox, instead of splitting in different directions to chase a number of foxes going to all points of the compass.

He achieved this repeatedly, and the Heythrop mounted field seemed to take it for granted. His hounds adored him so much they would bay at him at the meet as his large figure, swathed in the Heythrop's green livery, walked from his car.

Ronnie's two whippers-in used whistles instead of holloaing when a fox went away. This ensured that hounds did not leave the covert until Wallace's voice and horn told them to do so.

After the pack went away with a tremendous cry, the Field Master would lead the large, well-mounted field thundering in pursuit, and the hunt would progress in a well-ordered fashion. If hounds checked, Wallace would suddenly appear as if by magic, often through a nearby gate, to cast them impeccably to regain the line. No hunt was considered satisfactory unless hounds eventually caught their fox above ground. As Gerald Gundry, the sagacious Joint Master of 'Master', the 10th Duke of Beaufort, used to say: 'There should be no mystery tours in the hunting field; a hunt should have a beginning, a middle and an end.'

As Foxford I reported the following example in *Horse & Hound*:

'It was towards the end of day and there were not many of us left. Ronnie stood at the side of the wood and said: 'Shut up all of you. Stand absolutely still, and I want to hear no holloaing. Not a sound.'
'With that he disappeared into the covert with his hounds. Foxes came out in all directions, but not a single hound. I was astonished; this was quite incredible. Eventually a fox emerged, presumably heading in the direction that Ronnie wished to go, and then came the pack; hunting as one, they swept off like a carpet. I don't remember seeing Wallace while we had a fast and brilliant 25 minutes round the Evenlode Vale, hounds catching and killing their fox just in front of us. I looked up, and the Master of the Heythrop trotted through a small gateway, dismounted and told the bitch pack they had been 'rather good girls'. It was an astounding performance, and one I have never seen matched. I asked him how he did it; how it was that all the other foxes had been ignored; nobody else could do that. He said: 'You just wait your chance.'

The consistently high standard of venery, achieved in an environment specifically organised for it, meant that Wallace had a devoted band of hound watchers on the roads, and from the backs of a various mounts who scarcely jumped a twig. From this throng there emerged admiring lieutenants to do his bidding. I noted that they carried out his wishes with amazing alacrity. None was more effective than Lavinia Jenkinson, a rather superior school teacher, naturalist and artist, who led the damage repair teams with incredible efficiency, while another formidable lady, Diana Hastings, worked on the kennel accounts and many other tasks.

Wallace's hounds were adept at hunting foxes well across hunt boundaries into their neighbouring countries, but if neighbours such as the North Cotswold, Warwickshire or VWH crossed into the Heythrop country there were likely to be eruptions of protest from God.

Stephen Lambert, then the keen young Master and huntsman of the Warwickshire was summoned to the phone one evening to speak to Wallace while dining with Geoffrey Cragghill. 'Craggers', a genial lecturer at the Royal Agricultural College, Cirencester, was perhaps more importantly Master of the Dummer Beagles. He was popularly known to encourage young hunting enthusiasts to embark on careers as Masters of Hounds, rather than the estate management careers their parents had fondly expected. I thoroughly enjoyed Cragghill's company at all times; we were once partners in a Dorset hunter-trials, completing our round amid a fit of the giggles on the part of the beagler.

The group of hunting friends around the table was convulsed with laughter as they heard Stephen Lambert on the phone in the hall, trying to explain to Ronnie Wallace how his hounds had trespassed on Heythrop territory: 'No Ronnie, we were definitely on a fox found in our country I assure you... It was just one of those things....No Ronnie, I don't think we did any damage or left any gates open....No Ronnie, I'm sure it won't happen again soon....'

The laughter reached crescendo when Stephen re-entered the dining room to be told he had actually been speaking to Cragghill who was on an extension line in the house, employing his remarkable impersonation of Ronnie Wallace's voice, with which he was wont to entertain select groups.

I observed Wallace himself in action as a martinet, admonishing a group of young Masters of Foxhounds for not wearing bowler hats at Peterborough Royal Foxhound Show.

'How can you expect anyone else to keep high standards when you don't give a lead?' he barked.

They nodded dumbly and went their way, as if suddenly transported back to their schooldays. If Wallace was occasionally mocked he was far more often highly respected for giving a firm lead to the foxhunting world at a time of increasing pressures: shorter masterships, modern farming methods, and a growing threat from the animal rights lobby.

One morning in 1976, Wallace telephoned me uncomfortably early while I was still in bed, as he often did, to advise me briefly and unemotionally that he was resigning from the Heythrop to take the Mastership of the Exmoor from the 1977-8 season.

'Good Lord,' was all I could think of in reply. From my point of view Ronnie's decision was to open a marvellous opportunity to sample

Ronnie Wallace with his hounds on Exmoor where he relished moorland hunting.

moorland hunting at its best. Many others were to trek to Exmoor in autumn and spring to see Wallace's magic at work with a pack of hounds hunting superbly on beautiful heather-clad hills above deep valleys.

It was an earth-shaking move in the foxhunting firmament. Heythropia gave Ronnie and Rosie a protracted farewell, culminating in a final, tremendous hunt in the best of the country, followed by a large-scale dinner party addressed by 'Master', the 10th Duke of Beaufort.

Although Ronnie was irreverently known as God, the Duke was the true deity in the hunting world. Wallace was always quick to give due deference to the Duke, and much valued the privilege of judging the Beaufort puppy show every year at Badminton, one of the holiest of the holy foxhunting occasions. The Heythrop is historically an offshoot of the Beaufort, which is why the hunt staff of both packs wear the green livery coats of the Beaufort family, although only Beaufort subscribers wear their distinctive blue and buff coats.

Hunting with the Heythrop I was once summoned into a dense covert where Wallace rode alongside, and said in a stage whisper: 'Because it's such an unusually wet spring Master has actually stopped hunting next door in deference to the farmers. I think he's got it wrong because once you stop for rain you'll always have to do so. I am definitely not stopping – but we shall be extra careful, and only ride round the edges of grassland.

'So don't publish in *Horse & Hound* any statement by the Beaufort that they've stopped hunting because of heavy rain. We don't want every farmer here knowing it.'

It was the sort of cunning you will read of Flurry Knox, Master of Hounds in the immortal Somerville and Ross novels. I could only nod, and hope for the best. Fortunately, the Beaufort Hon. Secretary ceased sending in fixtures, but wisely did not state why, so editorial integrity was saved – just.

The farewells in the Heythrop country were only to be exceeded by the hugely-attended memorial service for Wallace, held on March 19th, 2002 after his death aged 82 when a car he was driving collided with a lorry near Taunton, Somerset, on 7th February. St Edward's church at Stow-on-the-Wold was packed, and many more friends and admirers from all over Britain overflowed into a tent and a hall. We heard Stephen Lambert, who became a distinguished successor as Master and huntsman of the Heythrop, give an address full of affection and humour.

David Wallace, Ronnie and Rosie's son, showed he had inherited his father's gift for organisation in arranging impeccably a remarkably well-attended funeral on Exmoor, and then the tremendous memorial service, attended by Rosie in a wheelchair. David and his family are nowadays held in high regard by the hunting communities of which they are part in Yorkshire and on Exmoor.

Even before Ronnie Wallace had retired from the Heythrop I had been exploring other foxhunting countries, partly to provide articles for Foxford's Hunting Diary, but also through sheer curiosity.

Billy Oliver, owner of the livery yard at Wendover where I kept my horse Foxford to hunt with the Whaddon Chase, took a short-term rent on a small hunting yard at Great Dalby in the heart of the Quorn's delectable Monday country.

He transported Foxford to Great Dalby for my first day's hunting in the Shire of Shires. It was magic – I was lost to the charms of Leicestershire.

Chapter Nine

DISCOVERING THE SHIRES

I arrived in the Quorn country when it was at one of the high points in its illustrious history since it was founded in 1753 by the 'Father of Foxhunting', Hugo Meynell. The Quorn country, north and south of Melton Mowbray, had been the Mecca of generations of visiting foxhunters ever since – and was still regarded as a 'must' in every ardent hunting person's career, if only for a one-day visit.

The Quorn in the early 1970s was still hunting in a manner reminiscent of foxhunting's golden years: a sharp bitch pack hunted on Mondays and Fridays on the light going of High Leicestershire, and a doghound pack hunted westwards in the woodlands of Charnwood Forest and beyond on Tuesdays and Saturdays. The Quorn hounds were of the most modern stamp, at that time bred under the direction of none other than Capt Ronnie Wallace. It was somewhat like having Harrods in to do the furniture, except that Wallace provided free after-service – by judging the annual puppy show to check on the new entry.

The Quorn's best country north and south of Melton Mowbray was still mainly grassland, but the march of arable farming was quickening. I was to enjoy Leicestershire in a condition ideal for foxhunting we shall never see again. Today's four-lane A46 main road scything through the Monday country was a lesser main road which the Quorn field often crossed by leaping rails or hedges from adjoining fields. I was there when lorry drivers halted on the A46 by the Hunt were astonished to note the rider holding up the traffic was Prince Charles.

Most of the mounted field on the fashionable Mondays and Fridays in the best country each had two horses out, and changed mounts during the day. The Quorn was unusual in that most subscribers lived outside

Michael Farrin, huntsman of the Quorn (1968-98), a great friend who I especially admired as a superb horseman across country.

the hunting country, and this included two of its three Masters.

This was a long-standing tradition in the Quorn country accepted by most of the farmers who afforded the mounted field the privilege of riding over their wonderful old turf and cut-and-laid fences. In return the Quorn went to exceptional lengths to entertain and reward farmers as much as possible, with annual dinners, free tickets to point-to-points and free hunting for themselves and their families if their land was crossed by the Hunt. The Chase had long added extra value to property and land in Leicestershire, and in the past provided farmers with a ready market for locally grown horse-fodder, plus many jobs in livery and dealing yards.

I noted the Quorn field was an entertaining mix of personalities, all out to enjoy themselves and warmly welcoming to a newcomer, which was fitting since most were themselves 'carpet-baggers' (visitors seeking a good country to ride). They ranged widely across English society from

High Court judges to bookmakers. There were some notably pretty girls in the field, wearing beautifully tailored breeches and coats and riding quality horses.

In a Shires mounted field there was always someone interesting to talk to, and ripples of laughter were not infrequent. One young lady, I was told, was mortified to find she had arrived with two left riding boots, but put up with the excruciating pain of wearing both in order not to miss her day's hunting in the Shire of Shires.

Aside from the gaiety were the underlying risks attending a sport involving steering more than half a ton of horse over fences, surrounded by many others likely to barge into you, or bring you down. Amid the crush in a Quorn gateway there were some wry smiles when someone remarked: 'So nice to get away from the crowds in London.'

The arrival and departure of scores of lorries bringing horses to

One of the Quorn's most successful Masterships: Fred Barker, Ulrica Murray Smith, and James Teacher.

the second horses meets half-way through the day, and the throngs of car followers all day, needed a miracle of rural traffic management to avoid jams in country lanes, but in the 1960s they were still tolerated by most of the local community. Avoiding holding up local traffic became an increasing headache later.

The dress code in the mounted field was still traditional: male subscribers in top hats, red or black coats, white breeches and top boots with spurs. A few men still sported white buckskin breeches on wet days, and had white 'champagne' tops to their boots. Quorn farmers wore black coats and caps with fawn breeches. Most lady subscribers breached tradition by wearing dark blue hunt coats with matching caps, instead of traditional bowlers and black coats; some had shiny black tops on their plain boots.

A few ladies persisted in riding side-saddle, wearing top hats and habits, none more elegant than Venetia Barker, blonde wife of Joint Master, Capt Fred Barker. No one went better side-saddle than the more mature Lady Margaret Fortescue, a hereditary West Country landowner who came up from her home near Barnstable to take a hunting box each season in the Quorn country. She was noted for affecting a certain parsimony by remarking well after the opening meet: 'I haven't paid my subscription yet; I shall wait to see if I am still enjoying myself.'

She invariably did so, and her hunting career was only halted by a disastrous fall with the Belvoir in the mid-1980s. From personal experience of seeing horrible accidents when horses fall with side-saddle riders I would never recommend ladies to ride side-saddle in the modern hunting field.

I was one of several men striving to rescue Margaret Fortescue when her horse fell from a bridge into a stream, trapping her underneath, and I saw her last fall, downhill with the Belvoir, when she was similarly rolled on by the horse, and terribly injured. When a horse falls you need to be thrown clear, which is far more likely riding astride. Side-saddle riders are too often trapped by the saddle's leg pommel.

The vital collection of Quorn caps and subscriptions was handled with tactful efficiency at that time by their full-time Hunt Secretary Jonathan Inglesant. I noted that he also carried out many duties which in other Hunts were solely the task of the Masters, such as visiting farmers and arranging dismantling barbed wire.

Michael Farrin had just started his remarkable 30 years' career as the Quorn's huntsman, having been promoted from whipper-in at the early age of 25 after whipping-in to Jack Littleworth who had to retire early with a brain tumour.

It was a happy decision to retain Michael rather than import an older huntsman from elsewhere. From his first season, 1967-8, he exhibited all the qualities needed to hunt hounds effectively in front of huge mounted fields; sometimes more than 200 strong on Mondays and Fridays, on the Quorn's old turf and fly fences.

He was a natural horseman, beautifully balanced on quality horses, some of them ex-chasers loaned by Queen Elizabeth the Queen Mother. He presented his mounts correctly at every obstacle, flitting across country with deceptive ease. Rather shy, with a slight stutter, during a day's hunting Farrin was a virtually silent idol we never tired of watching as well as following.

He was a worthy successor to generations of spry Quorn huntsmen, including the great Tom Firr of late Victorian times, who could seize opportunities to provide the famous Shires 'quick thing', a thrilling dash across country of perhaps 25 minutes at top speed, ending with a kill in the open. There were plenty of longer hunts too, spread-eagling the Quorn field across miles of country.

I only had my one horse, Foxford, to ride on my first day with the Quorn, but he had the stamina to perform brilliantly for three-quarters of a day, still full of going when I took him home in mid-afternoon. He adored Leicestershire's grass and fences, and was not deterred by the press of the mounted field. I was to ride many more horses in the Shires, but none more exciting and bold than Foxford who never fell with me in Leicestershire.

Despite the crowd, I was surprised when hounds ran that there was far more room to take on the fences than in the more cramped hunting countries of the south. In many areas of the Quorn country you could ride reasonably straight across each pasture, taking on whichever portion of the fence faced you when you reached the boundary.

Riding my impetuous chestnut Becher in pursuit of the Quorn hounds hunted by Michael Farrin.

For the first time I heard a Field Master, David Keith, shout the famous Shires injunction as we approached an obstacle: 'Spread Out!' The wider the front on which the field tackled its fences, the less chance there was of those in front being over-ridden and jumped on if they fell, the cause of some of the worst accidents in the Shires hunting field.

Due to Foxford's headstrong ways, and my inexperience of Leicestershire, my first day nearly ended much earlier than I had intended. The field was massed in a pasture on Muxlow Hill, near Old Dalby, an area of impeccable turf and fences beautifully maintained for hunting by its owner, Doctor Tom Connors, renowned for combining the roles of GP and horse-dealer. He imported horses from relatives in Ireland and sold them far and wide.

While the mounted field remained stationary I thought I saw a movement to my right, and assumed it was the Field Master. I must have communicated this to Foxford who bounded forward with a fly-

Jim Webster, veteran huntsman of the Belvoir (1956–83) where I relished thrilling Saturdays following their Old English hounds.

buck which nearly unseated me. He surged ahead to leap a hedge which proved to have an appreciable drop on landing. Then I pulled up, with the horrible realisation that I was on my own. The mounted field was still waiting on the take-off side.

'Now you can jump back,' I heard David Keith commanding from afar.

Jumping a drop-fence upwards from the wrong side is a tall order when you are performing under the gaze of the entire Quorn mounted field. Fortunately I spotted a small dip in the fence, kicked on and aimed Foxford at it. He had to clear a ditch on the take-off side, and the hedge-top which was above his ears. To my intense relief he just cleared it, landing impeccably. I had the sense to ride up to David Keith to apologise. He waved me on with a smile.

Ulrica Murray Smith, David's Joint Master, was most amused and said later: 'Don't worry. David's not a great sender-home. And after all, you had to keep near the front as a hunting correspondent.'

I wrote up my first visits to the Quorn and the Belvoir for *The Field* in dispatches full of my enthusiasm for the Shires. This did not entirely please those elements in the hunting world who chose to regard Leicestershire foxhunting as frivolous; a provincial assessment far from the truth if you had seen a Shires pack adhering to a line of scent efficiently and catching their foxes above ground. There is plenty of opportunity for slow, painstaking hound work in the arable areas of the Shires.

The Leicestershire terrain is great for seeing a hunt as well as riding it, especially compared with the more wooded countries of the South. Later I wrote regular reports from Leicestershire for *Horse & Hound*, and there was plenty of evidence they assisted circulation.

It was no surprise to my friends that soon after Ronnie Wallace retired from the Heythrop in 1977 I moved my newly-bought Irish mare, Josephine, to the livery yard run by George and Barbara Rich at Thorpe Satchville in the Quorn's Friday country.

I had been warmly encouraged to do so by James Teacher, third member of a notably successful Quorn Mastership. James joined Fred Barker and Ulrica Murray Smith in 1975, David Keith having retired three years earlier. Fred remained in charge on Mondays, James on Fridays and Ulrica on Tuesdays and Saturdays. Barbara and George were high-class dealers who ran a small livery yard, generously providing a Hunt tea at the end of the day, enlivened by illustrious clients such as Douglas Bunn, the Master of Hickstead, and Dick Hern the leading Flat trainer whose riding was to end tragically when he became a paraplegic after breaking his back in the Quorn Friday country.

Fred Barker inherited family traditions of high foxhunting standards in the VWH country which he communicated firmly to the mounted fields of the Quorn, insisting on proper behaviour in the hunting field, and giving them an excellent lead as a Field Master mounted on quality horses.

James was a countryman and naturalist with a gift for eloquent writing and public speaking. He could be somewhat eccentric as the Friday Field Master, sometimes seen leading the field between the huntsman and his hounds, but Michael Farrin never twitched a face muscle in protest.

I forgave James for remarking in an after-dinner speech that Foxford's Hunting Diary reminded him of Napoleon Bonaparte's memoirs: always saying what a good time he had just had on Josephine (a reference to my favourite hunter).

Ulrica had hunted with the Quorn since the fashionable 1930s. All three Masters shared a vision of the Quorn as the premier pack in England with standards they were determined to maintain.

Teacher, whose sunny personality and happy marriage to Chloe endeared him to many, died far too young at 65 in 2003.

Ulrica achieved a Mastership of the Quorn for 26 seasons (1960-85), second only in length to that of the 48 seasons of the Hunt's founding Master, Hugo Meynell.

My friendship with Ulrica was strengthened by my discovery that, although she claimed to be unable to spell, she could convey her memories of the Shires to paper with the same wit she habitually employed in her drawling 1930s accent.

I encouraged her to write amusing articles frequently for *Horse & Hound*, finally preserving her special brand of dry humour in her memoirs 'Magic of the Quorn', published in 1980 by Joe Allen who ran the Horseman's Bookshop in central London. I thoroughly recommend Ulrica's book to anyone who would like to know what Shires foxhunting was like at its pre-war grandest.

Ulrica's father, Col. Ulric Thynne, brought her from their home in Sussex to hunt for a month in Leicestershire shortly before she came out as a debutante. He thought she would enjoy the Crawley and Horsham all the more after experiencing hunting in the Shires, but after tasting Leicestershire Ulrica hardly ever returned to hunt in Sussex.

Her marriage to Army officer and landowner Tony Murray Smith having foundered in the late 1950s, Ulrica thereafter lived alone in their former hunting box in the Quorn Friday country, while Tony resided in the Fernie country where he hunted hounds and was a Joint Master for 23 years. Although Tony swiftly re-married he was all too soon widowed, and he retained a friendship with Ulrica. During supper at her house near Gaddesby he would pocket silver table ornaments, and Ulrica would ritually take them from him as he left by the front door.

Elegant and slim, Ulrica was a superb horsewoman across country, hunting four days a week with the Quorn throughout her Mastership. As Field Master on Saturdays and Tuesdays when the 'locals' formed most of the field, she would occasionally dart off a lane to pop neatly over a formidable timber fence or gate, leaving her followers the testing choice of following or finding a longer route. She was utterly devoted to the welfare of Michael Farrin, and suffered badly later when he was the object of a cruel scam by a leading Hunt Saboteur.

Ulrica did not employ the same care to her house as she did to her horse or her person: she allowed her home to moulder away, an eccentricity not a financial necessity. When I visited her frequently in her latter years she would lie on a chaise-lounge talking of the Quorn past and present, oblivious of her decaying surroundings, with damp glistening on the inside walls, and a small tree growing out of the exterior brickwork. Lying on a mat by her side was her large Rhodesian Ridgeback dog whose fierce exterior cloaked a duck-heart. When I clapped hands to make a point the dog jumped up in terror, knocking over a table and a wrought-iron standard lamp.

Ulrica developed a late passion for ocean liner cruising, once defying a broken hip to be carried on board; she hated infirmity and the ageing process. She claimed to be an atheist, and believed in voluntary euthanasia. Following her death aged 80 in 1999 she had left instructions for only a brief funeral service at Loughborough crematorium, with no eulogy. I dreaded a drab farewell, but it was a moving occasion which brought me to tears. We entered the chapel to hear on the loudspeakers Noel Coward singing wryly *Somewhere I'll Find You*, fitting Ulrica's 1930s persona.

She had ordained that I should read the text *Death is Nothing* which did not give much comfort, but finally when her coffin trundled on the rails through the screen towards cremation, I could not resist smiling at Ulrica's last jest: the chapel resounded to the thunderous rendering of *Land and Hope and Glory*.

In the late 1980s the Quorn enjoyed a particularly happy Indian summer, before the eventual arrival of the Hunting Act in 2005. The Mastership was led by Jim Bealby who farmed near Grantham, and who had benefited from serving as a Joint Master for the South Notts. His tact, and cheerful demeanour, won him many friends among the Quorn farmers and subscribers, and he gave a great lead as Field Master in the Monday country, supported by his wife Sue and his sons Chris and Ashley, the latter eventually becoming a Field Master of the Quorn and a Joint Master of the Cottesmore, while their sister Emma served as Joint Master of the Belvoir.

In the 1991-2 season the Quorn, the first season after Jim Bealby had resigned, the entire foxhunting scene was rocked when the Hunt was targeted by an anti posing as a Hunt supporter who took video pictures of a botched digging operation. The fox after being dug out unharmed was set free, but was killed almost immediately by the pack which was waiting nearby. Traditional practice was for a fox bolted from an earth to be given 'law' to get well away across country before the pack was put on the line again.

The video was widely broadcast on national TV, causing much consternation to the Masters of Foxhounds Association and the Countryside Alliance.

Two senior Joint Masters, Joss Hanbury and Barry Hercock, were suspended from the MFHA for four years, and two new Masters for the remainder of that season. There was much criticism in Leicestershire of the MFHA for 'over-reacting' in seeking to make an example of the Quorn, and there were grounds for this because the rules regarding digging procedure were not specific.

Soon afterwards the MFHA's disciplinary process was changed radically, and its rule made much more precise on the question of foxes run to ground: '....when a hunted fox is run to ground in a natural earth, there shall be no digging other than for the purpose of humanely destroying the fox,' and it added the caveat '... a fox which has been handled must be humanely destroyed immediately and under no circumstances hunted.'

Even the League Against Cruel Sports, which published the video, said in a press conference that the incident was not against the original rules of the MFHA.

After the digging incident Fred Barker nobly stepped in immediately as Master of the Quorn, returning suddenly to this arduous role after six years. He achieved much in restoring calm and firm control immediately, but when another Mastership was set up later, not including Fred, there followed an unfortunate period of turbulence in the Hunt, again all too widely reported in the national press. The loyalty of the landowning and farming community in Leicestershire throughout all this was a shining example of foxhunting's role as a much-valued part of country life.

Joss Hanbury never relinquished his support for the Quorn, nor his involvement in it, returning as a Field Master even before his re-appointment for a second term as Joint Master from 1977, a role he has continued until today, testifying to his popularity in the Hunt.

I was one of many in foxhunting much grieved by foxhunting's inability to deal quickly with the public relations crisis which erupted when the video was published. It was a case of too little response to the media storm, too late.

I was asked to assist in framing statements on behalf of the Quorn, but by then much of the PR damage had been done. The matter was not helped by the Quorn Hunt not having a written constitution and rules, a gap remedied by Sir David Samworth who stepped in as Hunt Chairman at short notice, and achieved a great deal in bringing the management up-to-date.

After the Quorn incident the public relations structure of the MFHA and the Countryside Alliance relating to hunting throughout the UK was considerably improved.

Some questioned whether these improvements were outweighed by the significant damage done at the time, but I think the Hunting Act 2004 was due entirely to the arrival of Labour governments with huge majorities led by Tony Blair. (*see* Chapter 18 – The Battle)

THE BELVOIR

My reception in 1976 when I visited the Quorn's neighbour on its eastern boundary, the Belvoir, might have sent home a more sensitive soul. When I said 'Good Morning' at the meet to Lord (Ronnie) Belper, who was in a second brief Mastership, he demanded: 'Where d'ye come from?'
Dorset sounded better than London, so that's what I told him.

Belper retorted: 'Well, I should go back there! Hunting up here is just a racket! A racket I tell you!'

I murmured thanks and edged Foxford back into the press of horses at the meet at Holwell on the hilltop above the northwards stretch of the Vale of Belvoir. Within an hour of hounds moving off I was a firm admirer of the Belvoir's Old English hounds – and of Ronnie Belper as their Field Master.

Somewhat portly by then, and with only one functioning eye, Belper still held his place at the front of the Belvoir's Saturday throng. As a pre-war amateur race-rider he finished fourth in the 1936 Grand National, and in later life could still get a remarkable tune out of a quality horse across country.

'Rugby on a horse' was the somewhat derisive description of a competitive Belvoir Saturday by another Meltonian, Lord (Marcus) Kimball who preferred the Cottesmore and Quorn. From my first Saturday following the Belvoir over grass and fences I disagreed with Kimball: a day with the Belvoir was more than just a shoving match; you had to be a goodish horseman to stay anywhere near the front of the Belvoir field, cheerful, thrusting, and manifestly out hunting to have some fun. Our Field Master on my first visit, John Parry, was not then a Master, and hunted in a top-hat, but he was easy to espy because of his forceful lead. He still went remarkably well when he became a Joint Master later in his seventies.

Because it was a Saturday many men from the City of London came up from London to hunt horses they kept at livery in the Belvoir country. This boosted the competitive, masculine element in the field, although there was also a band of hard-riding ladies…

The most notable were two of Leicestershire's best known resident characters: the Hon. 'Urky' Newton, daughter of Lord Rank, and the Hon. 'Migs' Greenall, daughter-in-law of Lord (Toby) Daresbury, hereditary owner of Greenall breweries, and a famed former Master of the Belvoir who decamped to Ireland as Master and huntsman of the Limerick. An invitation to their hunting teas was indeed to be cherished, the meal enlivened by a frank analysis of the achievements and shortcomings of those engaged in the day's sport.

Urky and Migs were unalike in appearance, since the bespectacled Urky became notably more weighty in the saddle in later years, but they shared an equal passion for the Chase, hunting at least four days a week with the Shires packs for most of their lives, stoically taking heavy falls and painful injuries as inevitable.

Urky was a compulsive organiser, running Pony Clubs and point-to-points with immense zeal, and most notably the Melton Hunt

The Hon. Ursula (Urky) Newton, one of the great characters of Shires foxhunting.

Club, founded in 1959 by her late husband Lance Newton. The Club enables outsiders to hunt with the Leicestershire Shires packs on visits at reduced cost. In return the Club makes annual donations to the Hunts for improvements to their hunting countries in fencing and coverts.

The Club runs its own point-to-point at Garthorpe, near Melton Mowbray, and its annual competitive 'Ride' held in each of the Shires countries in turn, attracting visiting riders from far and wide. Urky Newton continued to run the Club with huge efficiency following Lance's death in 1969.

I rode my headstrong risk-taking hunter Foxford in the 1975 Melton Hunt Club Ride from Scalford in the Belvoir country, amid a huge field of over 70. I was in a team with the Woodhouse family from Dorset and including Douglas Bunn. He remonstrated with me for not walking the course beforehand, but I pointed out that I simply had to be in the *Horse & Hound* office putting the paper to bed the previous day.

In fact it was Douglas who had a fall, and then had a terrible time endeavouring to re-mount standing a log pile while his horse whirled round and round.

Finishing the ride in a glow of satisfaction at Foxford's unusually consistent performance over the fences to bring me home safely somewhere in the middle of the field, I was surprised to find that the best was yet to come.

On a second horse, hired for the day, I followed the Belvoir hounds in one of their best postwar hunts on record. They ran almost non-stop all day over the superb grass and fences then surrounding the hilltop village of Holwell, north of Melton Mowbray. In the middle of the afternoon my horse and I were fairly worn, and I stopped to take liquid refreshment from the Scalford pub, a most unusual practice for me.

I was wending my way home outside the village when I heard hounds speaking beautifully. Riding towards them I saw a brown shape along the hedgerows as a fox went away. The Belvoir hounds spoke joyously and went away yet again. I joined a very diminished mounted field, led by John Hine, a colourful sporting character. With the evening sun a big red ball in a hazy evening sky, the Hunt was a stirring sight as it surged across the grass, and right glad I was to join them again until their huntsman Jim Webster blew for home.

The Melton Ride and the hunting afterwards were filmed that day by professional film unit directed by Alan Mouncer, former BBC TV sports director. I wrote the script and voiced the commentary, for a mere £30, and somewhat to my surprise the film, called 'Wednesday Country', gained a showing on the Odeon national film circuit. My former agent Bagenal Harvey would have been horrified at my fee.

Urky Newton was a stickler for correctness in hunting dress, once summoning me to the back of a Quorn meet to exclaim in a stage whisper: 'Michael! Your sock is showing above your boot!' I tried to explain that

Tom Connors, GP and horse-dealer.

I had changed into hunting kit in a lay-by on my way from Heathrow Airport that morning, but it was not accepted as sufficient excuse.

She phoned me once at *Horse & Hound* to announce dramatically: 'Richard Henson (brother of Robert, later a Belvoir Joint Master) has just had his house burn down!'

When I said I sympathised, but it wasn't really a *Horse & Hound* news story, she retorted impatiently: 'Of course you must publish it. All the point-to-point entries were in the house. Tell everyone to phone me to sort it out!' I duly complied.

The Belvoir field was highly appreciative of the sport achieved by the pack, still owned by the current Duke of Rutland, and at his command bred on strictly Old English bloodlines, unlike nearly all other 'Modern' Foxhounds who contained Welsh outcross blood. Old English breeding was derided by those who added Welsh blood to create the 'modern' lithe Foxhound early in the 20th century.

The Duke of Rutland's hounds, kennelled in historic kennels in the parkland of Belvoir Castle, are living proof that the pendulum had swung too far away from Old English breeding.

From my first visit I was impressed by the Belvoir hounds: in the traditional black, tan and white colouring of the Foxhound, they were tremendous hunters even if they did not fit the more rangy conformation demanded by the modernists whose hounds, mostly lemon and white coloured, were those favoured by judges in the hound show rings in the postwar era. Lately Old English breeding has become valued as a source of refreshing the breeding of the modern hound, and there are now separate Old English show classes at leading shows, including Peterborough Royal Foxhound Show.

I wrote fondly of the Belvoir in the form of a detailed Hunt history published in 2011, inspired mainly by one of the most enjoyable periods in my hunting memory when the Hunt was under the Masterships of Robert Henson (1978-87) and John Blakeway (1983-92). As Field Masters on the Leicestershire side of the country they gave a terrific lead, following the old precept of 'over, under or through I will go'. They remained cheerful no matter what disasters occurred, and inspired a devoted following from such passionate enthusiasts as the brothers Roger and Mike Chatterton.

I have abiding memories of such thrills as hurtling downhill over fence after fence in pursuit of the Belvoir hounds, after finding their fox in the hillside covert Clawson Thorns, then soaring down into the Belvoir Vale where an excursion over the big enclosures and inviting cut and laid fences awaited.

Somewhat ruthlessly raiding the Quorn country to the west was a favourite pastime after the Belvoir pack had found on their side of the River Smite in the Vale. I recall a sense of panic as the Belvoir hounds

Robert Henson, always cheerful Joint Master and Field Master of the Belvoir (1978-87).

and field careered on over a certain forbidden patch of country, a cricket field no less, on the Quorn side. Robert Henson, one of a family of hunting farmers and businessmen, remained cheerful despite the fall-out of such 'happenings' in the Belvoir hunting field. Acrimonious telephone calls from a Quorn Joint Master Fred Barker on a Sunday evening were part of the price.

Jim Webster, imperturbable and canny, was nearing the end of his 27-year career as Belvoir huntsman (1956-83) when I began subscribing. Sensibly, he avoided jumping unless he had to, and was quite happy to wave on the thrusters of the Belvoir field if they overtook him: 'Go on, sir! Go on! I don't mind.'

Despite this Jim understood the temperament of the Old English hound – persistent to the point of cussedness – and produced plenty of memorable days in his latter years.

He had a splendidly Victorian style of public speaking, and a dry sense of humour. I heard him tell a Quorn puppy show gathering he liked their country and so did his hounds: 'When the wind is in the right direction the Belvoir hounds is very keen on running into the Quorn country, and very apt to do so...'

When I unwisely rode an ex-showjumping horse on its first day with the Belvoir its mind was blown by the thrills of the Chase, and it subsided into a deep ditch. Jim Webster paused on the brink of the ditch to look down at me as I struggled in the mud, remarking: 'When they does that, sir, they needs a younger man on them...'

However eccentric and forceful were the cast of characters in the Belvoir Hunt, the dominant figure through most of the postwar years was Lord King, who was a Master for 15 seasons until 1972, and thereafter Hunt Chairman for 25 seasons (1976-2000). A self-made industrial magnate in Yorkshire, John bought the Friars Well estate above Broughton Hill in the

Lord King, former Master and Hunt Chairman of the Belvoir; a tough industrialist and a generous friend.

Quorn country, but soon found his sporting niche with the neighbouring Belvoir where he ruled with a very firm hand.

Later he became a nationally-known figure as Chairman of British Airways, which earned him his peerage. Known locally as 'King John', he could be excessively dictatorial, but it was leavened with wit, if at times caustic.

He was wont to say that being chairman of the Belvoir was more rigorous than his British Airways post, and he liked to recount halting a BA board meeting to take a telephone call from the Belvoir country about the need for more split rails to be stored at the kennels. He was accustomed to controversy, and stirred up some in Leicestershire by ploughing up much of his Friars Well estate. There were always foxes in residence, and the Belvoir and Quorn hounds were always welcome, but

'King John' seemed unable to avoid achieving maximum profit in all his ventures.

During my short stint on the Belvoir Hunt Committee I recall John telling us with an emperor's smile: 'Just remember you are not like other Hunt Committees. The hounds belong to the Duke of Rutland and you are here only to advise the Duke and I how to run the Hunt – not to make decisions yourself.'

King was a generous host and friend to many, and I enjoyed his company, and that of his wife Lady Isabel, in Leicestershire and in London. He loved his foxhunting, and like myself he did not take it for granted. As we galloped up the Belvoir Vale one afternoon in a sharp hunt, he called out to me: 'Just remember this! Always remember it!'

He was loyal and supportive to Jim Webster when he was unfairly criticised as 'slow' in his latter years, although I recall John King saying to Jim on a quiet afternoon: 'Come on, Jim. Do something to astonish us all!'

Jim just smiled and hacked on with his hounds. He had cheerfully survived a demanding life as a hunt servant, trained in pre-war harsh conditions in kennels, and on giving up hunting at 60, he well deserved his 25 years' peaceful retirement with his wife, Sheila. They were among the nicest couples in hunting I ever met, and after he died aged 85 I tried to convey this in obituaries for Jim I wrote in 2009 for *The Daily Telegraph* and *Horse & Hound*.

Michael Farrin also died in 2009, at the early age of 65. Unlike Jim Webster, Michael had not retired unscathed by the demands of a huntsman's life. A leg injury he received in his last season developed into a cancerous tumour which spread fatally and all too quickly. In his retirement Michael and his wife Di remained good friends, and we met frequently. His stoicism during the terrible last phase of his affliction was an inspiration.

I was touched that Michael had requested that I should speak about him at his funeral, although it was a heavy responsibility as well as an honour, addressing the packed Roman Catholic church in Melton Mowbray, everyone mourning a great huntsman who had brought them so much pleasure for 30 years.

Chapter Ten

RUSTICATING IN RUTLAND

'Leicestershire is somewhere you hunt, but you don't live there,' Douglas Bunn warned me when I told him I was buying a cottage in the Cottesmore country. Douglas used to make a return trip by helicopter to Leicestershire from Hickstead in Sussex to hunt for a day with the Quorn.

Thank heavens I did not follow Douglas's advice to settle permanently in the South East. It is true there is still plenty of horse-riding in that most populous of English regions, but so much of the country I enjoyed when I hunted south of the Thames has been swamped by bricks and mortar, new motorways, airports, golf clubs, sewage stations and all the other paraphernalia of modern 'progress'.

Douglas's warning was wrong geographically too: the Cottesmore country is largely in Rutland and Lincolnshire, and only a little in Leicestershire. I am fond of all three, but they have distinctly different personalities. Rutland, England's smallest county, still retains farming as the main producer, and has only two towns, Oakham and Uppingham, charming and under-stated. The latter in 2015 was voted in the *Sunday Times* as one of the 15 'happiest towns in which to live' in England. There is far less gentrification of Rutland's stone villages, and traffic levels are far lower than you will find in the fashionable Cotswolds.

People who view the East Midlands only through car and train windows miss the subtle beauties of the landscape: miniature uplands, charming valleys, uncluttered hinterlands, unspoilt woodlands and copses, and silvery streams winding shyly through pastures.

Those pastures, clothed in miles in undulating old turf when I arrived over 40 years ago, have been increasingly invaded by the pale green of winter wheat and the garish yellow of oilseed rape. Yet there are still areas of grassland that gladden the eye, and traditional tall church spires still point to the skies from villages which sprawl far less than those in the South East.

As for social life, Rutland, Leicestershire and neighbouring Lincolnshire, offer all that one could wish for informally, and in a host of local clubs and societies. It is possible here to enjoy life in a rural setting, with only a short drive to shopping centres, concert halls and other cultural opportunities in Leicester, Nottingham and Peterborough.

No clubs are supported more staunchly than the Hunts, enabling me to make lasting friendships in the rural community. For many years my hunting was made possible by the friendship and generosity of Geoff Brooks and his family, who farm near Widmerpool at the northern end of the Quorn country.

The showjumper Chris Farnsworth kept my horses impeccably in Geoff Brooks's livery yard on his farm. I was even more fortunate that Geoff made available his own excellent homebred hunters when my horses were lame. Through availability of the stallions on his stud, Geoff enabled me to start breeding my own hunters from my mare Josephine. *(see Chapter 19)*

After a cold mid-winter day's hunting it was wonderful to return to the warmth and fellowship in Geoff's farmyard kitchen where there was always a helping of ham and eggs. Among the guests it was not unusual to find Prince Charles enjoying these hunting teas, chatting informally about the day's sport and clearly enjoying the company and the setting.

Geoff often provided a friendly base for the Prince's hunting visits to the Quorn, and loaned him horses when he was short of a mount. (See Chapter 17). Since giving up hunting themselves, Geoff, and his son Richard retain strong links with the horse world, having developed their farm and stud into one of the most successful haylage horse feed businesses in England, supplying leading racehorse yards among many clients. In doing so they have put back to grass many acres of Quorn country which had succumbed to the plough.

My wife Marilyn and I bought a weekend cottage in Rutland when we married in 1988, enabling us to commute from our London flat. I was relieved of publishing deadlines for the last four years before my retirement in 1997.

Marilyn, from the Cattistock country in Dorset, thoroughly enjoyed Shires hunting. It was wonderful for the first time in my life to have hunting on my doorstep for we were living at Braunston, in the heart of the Cottesmore's best Tuesday country, near Oakham.

Thanks to supportive landowners, such as former Cottesmore Master Sir David Samworth, this area is still mainly down to old turf divided by fly-fences and timber, with superb spacious coverts devotedly maintained by generations of Cottesmore stalwarts. More than any other Shires pack, the Cottesmore has a tradition of a strong following of resident foxhunters, led by Masters who were leading amateur huntsmen and hound breeders.

Such Masters varied in their commitment to venery, from the purist hunting achieved by the pre-war leading amateur 'Chetty' Hilton-

My wife Marilyn at a meet of the Cottesmore.

Green to the more relaxed style of the popular postwar enthusiast Bob Hoare who exhibited a cheerful smile and a quip in the hunting field.

Ronnie Wallace, supremo of modern venery, visited the Cottesmore during Major Hoare's reign, and was horrified by what he considered the 'larking around' of the mounted field during a hunt.

After the run concluded, Wallace said to Hoare: 'Now's your chance, Bob. Get them all together and tear them off a strip.'

With one of his disarming smiles, Bob Hoare replied: 'My dear Ronnie, we only hunt up here for fun you know.'

Bob Hoare was, in fact, anything but a frivolous MFH : he performed a great service for the defence of hunting by organising a national fighting fund, and he left the Cottesmore in good heart. He was succeeded by Simon Clarke, who had won plaudits hunting the South Dorset, and with whom I first tasted the Cottesmore's delightful country in my hunting correspondent role. I was much assisted in enjoying the Hunt by Di Hellyer, who was to be an effective Joint Master, and her husband Tim. They were very hospitable and encouraging, and Di later did me a great service by selling me a cottage in Braunston.

Major Bob Hoare, Master and Huntsman of the Cottesmore, who said "we only hunt up here for fun."

When Marilyn and I became Rutland residents, the Cottesmore was being hunted brilliantly by one of the greatest amateur huntsmen of the postwar period, Brian Fanshawe, bred to foxhunting, and totally dedicated to ensuring that it was carried out to his highly exacting standards. He was of the school that believes in making it very clear to the mounted followers exactly what is required.

'Get involved!' was Brian's fierce warning to the mounted field if they showed signs of inattention

122

at crucial moments of the chase. Woe betide anyone in the wrong place at the wrong time as the Master thundered away from a covert in pursuit of his hounds going away on a fox. His pack absorbed his own burning dedication to hunting their fox with a view to catching it above ground at the end of an exciting run, 'no matter how fools nor fate divine' as the hunting poet Will Ogilvie said.

Although Brian did not tolerate fools in the hunting field, out of the saddle he was, and is, one of the most charming and polite of individuals. Marilyn and I have been privileged to remain ever since warm friends of Brian, his wife Libby, a remarkable foxhunter herself, and their sporting family which includes a leading trainer and a top-class polo player.

Most of Brian's Cottesmore human followers quickly developed the same levels of devotion as his hounds, even those who had been

Brian Fanshawe, Joint Master and Huntsman of the Cottesmore (1981-92).

chastised. Nothing succeeds better in hunting than consistently good sport, and this Fanshawe was able to ensure, organising the country, and overseeing the kennels and the hunt stables with the benefit of experience in successful former Masterships with the Warwickshire, North Cotswold, and over the Galway Blazers' turf and walls in Ireland.

Lord (Marcus) Kimball was clearly not fully informed about Brian Fanshawe when he asked me, just before his first season: 'Do you think he will be able to ride our country?'

I replied: 'There will only be one problem – keeping anywhere near him.'

Unlike some amateurs, Brian was a superb horseman as well as a hound man, and crossed the Cottesmore country with skill and elan, giving his field plenty to do in keeping anywhere near him when his hounds were benefitting from a good scent. He was a bold experimenter in hound breeding, introducing Welsh and American outcross lines, and welding them into a great working pack.

The keen Cottesmore hounds were increasingly apt to hunt into the Quorn country to the west. We relished some tremendous Cottesmore runs far into the neighbouring Quorn Friday country of grass and fences, a delectable piece of Leicestershire I knew well with the Quorn hounds.

Brian had a supportive team of Joint Masters throughout his term (1981-92) but inevitably the departure of a Master carrying out so many roles leaves notable gaps in the organisation. Brian's kennel huntsman and whipper-in, Neil Coleman, succeeded remarkably well as huntsman for the next two decades (1992-2012), a severely testing period for the sport, including the imposition of the Hunting Act from 2005.

I became closely aware of the stresses and strains which make modern foxhunting possible through accepting an invitation to become Cottesmore Hunt Chairman from 1997. It was a somewhat rash decision because I was at the time Chairman of the British Horse Society which was demanding enough.

Overall I enjoyed being truly at the heart of the Hunt, but there were stresses as well which detracted at times from my own pleasure in hunting. These were sometimes due to mistakes of mine in attempting to deal swiftly and firmly with problems which arose. Unlike a business, a

Hunt needs an ability to coax as well as manage.

We were entering a period of all too frequent Mastership changes in which there was increasing pressure on a Hunt Chairman to be a reliable anchorman, making most of the major financial decisions and becoming far more involved in the running of the country than Chairmen were required to do in the past.

I was occasionally made very aware that I was a comparative newcomer as a resident in the country, but even when there were inevitable differences of opinion in the Committee and among Hunt members, one could rely upon a bedrock of firm support from within such a long-established Hunt. The farming community remained wonderfully staunch as hosts to our hounds, and proved this beyond measure when, as in all other Hunts throughout England and Wales, they continued to allow hounds to cross their land despite the strictures of the Hunting Act.

Neil Coleman, Cottesmore huntsman (1992–2012) with his wife Philippa.

I filled the maximum five year term of a Cottesmore chairmanship, and if anything was achieved it was gaining a highly problematic planning permission for the conversion of our decaying Hunt kennels into a housing estate. I could not have achieved this without the property expertise and hard work of Marilyn, who had become a local partner in a leading estate agency. After a tense public enquiry we were successful, enabling the later sale of the Kennels for a handsome sum which was to make it possible for the Hunt to move into new purpose-built kennels and stables at Ashwell.

A sign of fast changing times in the Shires was a proposal from Joe Cowen, long serving Master of the Fernie, our adjacent Hunt to the south, that we should consider a merger. This did not happen, but it reflected the increasing pressures on land suitable for hunting in Leicestershire, not the least being the competing claims of the major growth of private shoots.

Today, ten years after the Hunting Act was passed, all the Leicestershire Hunts survive, not without difficulty. They cannot now rely on 'outside' subscribers to the same extent they did in their heyday, but the local sporting community has rallied as strongly as possible to keep its historic Hunts in being.

HUNTING MUSEUM IN DANGER

Since 2006 I took over from Lord (Marcus) Kimball the chairmanship of the Museum of Hunting within the Melton Carnegie Museum at Melton Mowbray. I was one of the original trustees, but Marcus did all the groundwork in arranging for Leicestershire County Council to include a hunting gallery within the museum at Melton, simply because the town's history is linked so strongly with foxhunting. It was, of course, the Mecca of hunting people from far and wide from the late 18th century when the Quorn was attracting so many visitors under the Mastership of Hugo Meynell who virtually invented the modern sport of hunting the fox from covert to pursue it in the open. Previously the fox's overnight scent was hunted slowly back to its earth where the fox was dug up and killed.

Through *Horse & Hound* I did my best to assist the establishment of the Hunting Museum, raising money at our annual ball and elsewhere. Altogether Marcus achieved some £120,000 to enable the launch of the Museum with the hunting gallery in 2002. This matching sum enabled the Heritage Lottery Fund to contribute £370,000. Since then, during my chairmanship, a further HLF grant of nearly £1 million was achieved by Leicestershire County Council to virtually double the size of the Museum building, including a new rural affairs gallery, and an upstairs lecture room and offices.

Since I took over as chairman we began a series of Hunting History Evenings at the Museum. We arranged illustrated lectures on historic aspects of the Chase, mainly with a Leicestershire and Rutland angle.

They were so popular we could not accommodate the response within the 40-seater lecture room. We had to hold some of them in the ballroom at the Melton Tavern in Melton Mowbray where we attracted audiences of over 200.

The enthusiastic response reassured me that no matter what anti-hunting politicians may do, the hunting community in rural Britain has remained remarkably strong. With our modest profits on History Evening tickets we have donated funds to assist development of the hunting gallery. I have visited local Hunts to give illustrated lectures based on our Melton programme, receiving an especially warm welcome in the Fernie country.

Sadly in 2015 we were facing something of a crisis: the huge financial cuts forced on local authorities made Leicestershire County Council start pruning its costs on museums and libraries. My fellow Trustees and I are faced with attempting to save the hunting gallery at some other venue, if Melton Carnegie has to close down. It's yet one more battle in support of hunting – and we are determined to win it.

France and the United States have excellent national foxhunting museums. It has long been a disappointment that Britain, the home of foxhunting, has none. The cost of maintenance is a major deterrent, but I would urge the Masters of Foxhounds and the other hunting bodies to work together to produce a top-class on-line history of their sport, using sporting art and other memorabilia before it disappears. Using the internet millions of people all over the world could appreciate the history of our great sport, and its contribution to British rural life.

Chapter Eleven

COME TO THE SHOW

If I ever had doubts about giving up the rough and tumble of news reporting, they were more than assuaged by sitting in mid-summer sunshine, after a splendid lunch, watching the elaborate ritual of a hunter showing class.

Horse & Hound's long list of horse show sponsorships required the presence of the Editor to present the cups, a summer treat which I never ceased to enjoy. We accompanied these trophies with fairly modest prize-money, but the riders and owners of the horse show world were ecstatic to receive a *Horse & Hound* Cup, and better still it would be followed by a photograph of their precious horse in the next edition of the weekly bible of the horse world.

As in our racing sponsorships, the presenting of trophies at horse shows enabled me to explore in depth this important specialist branch of the horse world. There is an underlying professionalism in these apparently amateur endeavours. Winning rosettes adds value to show horses, increasing their value to the shrewd dealers who used the show-ring as a shop window.

Professional riders who brought showing a horse's best qualities to a fine art dominated the top end of the hunter-showing world. Jack Gittins, Robert Oliver, Vin Toulson, and David Tatlow were leaders in the showing galaxy. No matter how well I had lunched at, say, the Royal Show at Stoneleigh, I grew to admire the subtleties of riding which enabled these great specialists to achieve championship trophies

Above: Walter Case, my predecessor as Editor, presenting a Horse & Hound Cup to showjumper David Broome.

Left: I inherited Walter Case's presentation role– here bestowing championship honours to show hunter rider David Tatlow at the Royal Show.

on behalf of grateful owners. Pamela Macgregor-Morris, who reported horse shows for us with great authority, was nevertheless inclined to give Jack Gittins an admiring write-up even when he did not win the championship. When I asked her to report a class rather than re-judge it in print, she was most put out.

'You must remember that I also write for *The Times*, and if it's good enough for them, it's good enough for *Horse & Hound*,' she said.

When I offered her the opportunity to write solely for *The Times* she calmed down, and I was glad that we continued to benefit from her considerable knowledge of showing and showjumping. Pamela regarded herself as a doyenne of the equestrian correspondents, and without question on a higher plane than a mere newspaper reporter. She certainly exhibited some of the eccentricities of the highly specialist writer.

Pamela and her husband Rudi, a former circus animal trainer, lived on the edge of Dartmoor. This made it necessary for her to drive thousands of miles to shows all over Britain, usually accompanied by a large Irish Wolfhound. Where possible, shows were expected to find her exclusive ringside parking space so that the dog was not left in a car park.

Pamela somehow acquired a huge bundle of unpaid parking fines in South Devon, and was risking a short jail sentence, when I sent the outstanding sum to the parking authority, deducting it from Pamela's forthcoming freelance payments.

Far from being grateful, Pamela complained: 'I had every intention of going to jail –and then writing an exclusive article for *The Times* on what it was like inside.' She was only a little mollified when, with tongue in cheek, I apologised for causing her to miss a scoop.

In later life, confined to a wheelchair, Pamela gamely decamped to Ireland where she lived for a while in the household of Lord (Toby) Daresbury, Master of the Co. Limerick Hunt of whom she had become extremely fond. At Dublin Horse Show His Lordship, by then a venerable figure, could be seen pushing Pamela's wheelchair around the ringsides. During an Irish downpour Toby Daresbury joined me under cover in a stand, and then exclaimed: 'Goodness, I've left Pamela somewhere.'

We searched several outer rings before finding her, drenched in her wheelchair. 'It's quite alright Toby,' she said. 'It was a very good class, and well worth getting a wetting.'

Pamela treated with hauteur our veteran shows correspondent Andy Wyndham-Brown, a lifelong horseman, especially experienced in the harness classes. I decided to ignore Pamela's assertion that Andy would leave a showground with his car boot clanking from bottles given by leading Hackney drivers. Andy told me that as a boy he used to 'ride a cockhorse': he would wait by a hill, and earn money by riding a spare horse, 'the cock horse', which would be attached to a team of horses to give them extra power up the hill.

On one occasion Walter Case arrived at a show to find that he had double-booked two correspondents to cover it. He asked Andy's devoted wife at the ringside to ask him not to send a report on this occasion. She had her revenge by ensuring that the ring announcer loudly broadcast a bulletin saying: 'Mr Wyndham Brown is NOT to report this show for *Horse & Hound!*'

During my editorship Peter Churchill, broadcaster and writer, most capably succeeded Pamela as showjumping correspondent, and for a while I published a showjumping column by Harvey Smith, undoubtedly the greatest character the game has ever produced, and for whom I have immense respect, if sometimes we did not agree.

Harvey's Yorkshire bluntness soon produced numerous letters disagreeing with the trenchant points of view he propounded in the column. For example, he was fiercely opposed at that time to the use of modern headgear with chinstraps. One day Harvey telephoned me to complain: 'Why put in those letters saying I was wrong? I know I'm right, and I don't need it to be corrected by people who don't know what they're talking about.'

I patiently explained that this was how journalism worked: we gave the readers the right to reply. Vainly, I tried to argue that many young riders regarded him as a hero, and it would be a good idea to encourage them to wear safer headgear because they were riding in an increasingly unsafe environment on modern roads.

'Well, that's it, then, 'said Harvey. 'The light's going out for you.' I replied tartly that the light would be going out for him as far as being a columnist was concerned.

Harvey, to his credit, never bore a grudge and remained friendly when we met at the shows. He has made a great success as partner and supporter of his second wife Sue in their chasing yard where his knowledge is a huge asset. The Yorkshire showjumper Graham Fletcher took over the showjumping column which remains a valued part of *Horse & Hound* today.

The British male rider I much admired for his style was Graham's brother-in-law, David Broome, who liked his hunting as well as competing. His partnership with Douglas Bunn's horse Beethoven was a classic example of David's ability to produce great performances from widely different horses. Beethoven could be difficult, and this contributed to David's World Championship win at La Baule in 1970. In a world championship riders have to perform on each other's horses, and they did not find Beethoven an easy ride. David meanwhile performed magnificently on the Italian horse Fidux, another problem ride.

Marion Mould (nee Coakes) and her amazing pony Stroller, stars of top-class international showjumping.

I especially liked the world championship for its emphasis on horsemanship in testing circumstances. The men's world championship in 1974 when Hartwig Steenken won gold for Germany on the mare Simona was the finest contest I ever saw.

My own favourite showjumping rider above all was Marion Coakes who continued to make a great success of her career after marrying the leading steeplechase jockey David Mould in 1969. As I have explained (Chapter three), Marion and her amazing pony Stroller made a contribution to my own riding costs through the success of the annual books I wrote about their exploits, running in to four annual volumes.

WEMBLEY GLAMOUR

Hacks, hunters and ladies' side-saddle classes, all added glamour and prestige to the programme of provincial shows, earning qualification to appear in the spotlight of the autumn Horse of the Year Show at Wembley's indoor stadium.

Walter Case had established an annual booking of an Editor's table for four in the ringside dining area at the Horse of the Year Show each October, entertaining different guests from Tuesday to Saturday. On Monday nights he and his wife sat in the royal box before presenting the trophy to the opening major showjumping class for the *Horse & Hound Cup*.

I was more than happy to maintain this enjoyable ritual, but it was a demanding schedule, requiring wearing a dinner jacket and black tie every night, and rushing from our South Bank office through heavy London traffic to Wembley's indoor arena.

Sitting in the royal box was anything but restful: Col. Sir Mike Ansell, Chairman of the Horse of the Year Show, was a stickler for time-keeping. At the interval the bevy of guests, mainly sponsors of various classes, rushed into a small cramped room behind the royal box.

We consumed supper and wine with haste, before anxious stewards bundled us back into the box so that the show should not resume while it was empty, a crime worthy of heavy censure by Sir Mike. Members of the royal family were allowed more time to avoid indigestion over supper, but I was among those discreetly whisked out of the back-room before the royals had finished supper, so that we could fill the front row of royal box seats.

SHOWS SUPREMO

Sir Mike, silver haired, and using a walking stick, was a tall, distinguished figure, seemingly benign, but this cloaked an iron will imposing military-style discipline on the timing and conduct of the show. His blindness made him even more careful to ensure that he knew precisely what was happening. On the arm of an assistant, he often entered the ring while trophies were being awarded in showjumping classes.

Mike Ansell would chat to the winners and pat their horses just behind the saddle. 'While he's congratulating the rider he's also checking to see if the horse is wearing the British team saddlecloth. If Mike can't feel the saddle-cloth on the horse's back the rider will get a terrific rocket next day,' Dorian Williams told me.

I never suffered the illusion that Mike Ansell was just a charming old Army officer. If it had not been for his blindness, suffered during the retreat to Dunkirk when he was accidently shot by a British soldier, I am certain he would have ended the war as a general. He spent his years as a blinded PoW in a German camp working out a plan to re-launch British equestrianism after the war – and he succeeded.

Col. Sir Mike Ansell, hero of the equestrian world, in uniform as Colonel of the 5th Royal Inniskilling Dragoon Guards.

At the original BHS and BSJA headquarters in Bedford Square, London, Mike used a windowless office under the stairs. It was not uncommon for him to receive guests in total darkness, which put him at a considerable advantage.

I first met him when I was a BBC TV and radio reporter. I had interviewed, for the *World at One* programme, the author of a showjumping book who dared to suggest that some few riders had used improper means of training their horses to jump clear. Allegations of showjumpers using caustic substances under a horse's leg bandages, or using electric shocks, were made in the press on the continent.

Sir Mike at first ordered the book taken off the stands at the Royal International Horse Show taking place at the time. Then he thought better of it, and came to BBC radio headquarters at Portland Place to give me an excellent interview firmly defending his sport.

After I became Editor he invited me often to suppers with him at the Cavalry Club where he would keep me up-to-date with equestrian politics, and would ask me to regale him with stories of my latest hunting trip. Not being able to resume after the war his outstanding career as an international showjumper, and keen hunting man, was one of the heaviest burdens he bore stoically.

After his first wife Victoria died, Mike found happiness in re-marrying in 1970 his second wife Eileen, a delightful personality. Within a year she was run down by a lorry and killed. The depth of his distress at this latest blow of what he called 'a malign fortune' was indescribable, making his courage in re-shaping his life again all the more remarkable.

Of all the characters I met in the horse world none was more impressive than Mike Ansell. The eloquent tribute at his military funeral was given by another great soldier and horseman, General Sir Cecil Blacker, better known in the horse world as 'Monkey' Blacker. Another consummate horseman, steeplechase rider and showjumper, Monkey put a great deal back into the horse world, serving as President of the BSJA and the British Equestrian Federation.

I liked his modesty, his acute sense of humour, and much admired him as a true horseman. Ansell and Blacker were among a significant group of military men who led and re-formed the horse world after the war, and gave it the impetus to attract many new riders in the 1950s and 1960s. They included one of the great war leaders, Field Marshal Sir Gerald Templer, who served as a President of the British Horse Society. I was thrilled to meet him one morning as a fellow judge of turnout in

Sir Mike with his second wife Eileen whose tragic loss was another cross he bore stoically.

the annual Heavy Horse Parade in the City of London.

The military horsemen made a great contribution to the horse world I knew: they were incorruptible, adept at planning and administration, and above all they gave excellent leadership to sports trying to recover from the war and the postwar austerity years. As I later discovered, running sporting organisations is demanding voluntary work. I was by no means an unquestioning worshipper of the military caste, but in the horse world I experienced the true value of that generation of professional soldiers who had served nobly in war, and conducted themselves admirably thereafter.

COMMENTATOR NUMBER ONE

Dorian Williams was born into a military family, but through his work in adult education he brought a creative contribution to the horse world. His fought his own private battles against recurring ill-heath: his courage and stoicism during his struggles to beat cancer were inspiring.

Dorian's input to the Royal International and Horse of the Year shows was crucial, using his talents as a communicator to make equestrianism popular for the first time to millions of TV viewers. The BBC would put back the start of the nine o'clock news on its major channel so that Dorian could complete his commentary of a tense jump-off at Wembley or White City. That could never happen today on any major TV channel.

Dorian often acted simultaneously as ring-announcer as well as TV commentator, although sometimes he felt his value as a mass communicator was not fully appreciated by Mike Ansell, the supremo of the horse shows world. Perhaps their family connections were too close: Dorian's father became the guardian of Mike Ansell after his father died in 1914. Ansell's father had been Dorian's godfather.

Through his strict control, Mike Ansell achieved a far more slick format than any other horse show I had seen. Time-keeping in the ring was much more of a priority than at many county shows, which were inclined to saunter through the day.

Ansell's shows were ideally suited to the demands of BBC TV which achieved audiences of over ten million a night with its transmissions from Wembley.

Dorian also wrote and produced annual, colourful pageants in the ring, such as enacting the 'Cat and Custard Pot Day' from Surtees' Handley Cross. His abilities as a writer and actor enabled him to impart considerable drama to a showjumping class jump-off, using carefully timed silences far more effectively than any of today's commentators who simply cannot stop babbling when it is not necessary. He would hiss, or tap his teeth to add atmosphere to a tense moment in the competition. As one of the early postwar sporting commentators to build an audience of millions, Dorian built a bridge between his specialist sport and the wider public. The Royal International and the Horse of the Year Show have been bereft of national terrestrial TV coverage by the BBC for many years since Dorian handed over.

The ringside dining restaurant on the other five nights of the show was a treat, and it was useful in ensuring that the Editor of *Horse & Hound* was thoroughly acquainted with current leading horses, riders and owners. Entertaining senior IPC management figures at least one night a week helped to remind them just how important their magazine was in the firmament of the horse world.

By Saturday night I was still enjoying the ring competitions, but was all too well acquainted with the much-loved set pieces: the parades of the heavy horses, and of leading horse personalities of the year, and the Pony Club Games. One Saturday I engaged my guest, Lord King, head of British Airways, in a £1 a time betting contest based on whether each showjumping horse would get a clear round. His Lordship left Wembley nearly £100 poorer, and not entirely cheerful, so I resolved not to try that pastime again.

I thoroughly enjoyed the Horse of the Year Show, but after six nights happy memories were inclined to be mixed with gastric and allergy symptoms due to eating regularly indoors amid dust kicked up by horses from the sand ring.

Dorian's successor, Raymond Brooks-Ward, managed the feat of succeeding in horse shows management as well as commentating.

His greatest success was the creation in the 1970s of the great Christmas show at Olympia which survives and flourishes. Our relationship was edgy at times in the early years of my editorship, heightened by tensions which arose when Raymond achieved a key position in the horse shows world as head of British Equestrian Promotions, in partnership with Bob Dean, the canny publicist of the agency Pearl and Dean.

They created a situation where they ran the major shows, organised sponsorships for individuals as well as shows, and had a great influence on the horse shows calendar. In 1983 Douglas Bunn accused Raymond and BEP of 'not doing anything' for Hickstead, and a row ensued. It was said that Douglas banned Raymond from Hickstead, an ironic move since Raymond had been Hickstead's first TV commentator when it was first covered by Southern TV.

Raymond sensibly ignored the ban, if it existed, but although he continued to commentate on Hickstead, now for the BBC, he was not seen in Douglas's private box as a guest for some years.

Keeping an enormous number of projects going, whilst working as a broadcaster, was a huge toll on Raymond's health. We had become good friends, and I was somewhat concerned that he looked unwell at the Barcelona Olympic Games in July 1992 where he had to commentate in intense heat, and in a rainstorm. Yet we were all shocked when Raymond collapsed and died on August 22nd, aged 62.

I believe his passing contributed to some loss of impetus in the horse show world, the decline beginning in the 1990s. Raymond's role in horse shows management has been continued by his sons Simon and Nick.

In the late 1970s Dorian was assailed with a cancer recurrence, and could not broadcast for several months. Having previously been a professional broadcaster, I was asked to deputise for him as one of the commentary team at Hickstead, and at Badminton Horse Trials. I was surprised just how tightly the commentary team was controlled by the outside broadcasts director Alan Mouncer. Raymond Brooks-Ward, immensely ambitious, was not too keen on my joining the team, but he need not have worried; I was not yearning to become a full time showjumping commentator.

Raymond Brooks-Ward, TV commentator and leading shows organiser.

I tried to fill in the somewhat tedious gaps in the action by trying to explain what type of bridles the horses were wearing, and why a horse jumped less well away from the collecting ring entrance, but this was not what was wanted, I was told.

Also deputising for Dorian was Mike Tucker who pursued the task of saying something meaningful over yet another showjumping round with perhaps more enthusiasm than I did and has made a life-long career in the commentary box. I found long afternoons of somewhat synthetic enthusiasm over yet another clear round fairly boring, and it probably showed.

Perhaps that was why, when Dorian thankfully returned to commentating, I was not asked to remain in the team, and I was not at all sorry. I much preferred one-off interviews on radio and TV as an occasional freelance. Making films was more fun, and I enjoyed working as script writer and voice commentator, in making a film of the Melton Hunt Club Ride in the Belvoir country.

I had a brief, and bizarre, return to TV shows commentating when I was asked by HTV (Harlech Television) to perform this function at the Royal Bath and West Show in Somerset. The producer decided to add novelty by pairing me with the West Country comedy mimic and impersonator Johnny Morris who became famous for the *Animal Magic* zoology programme for children. I had enjoyed Morris's radio broadcasts for BBC West of England when I was at school, so I was pleased to meet him.

He added a first-ever comedy dimension to showjumping commentating that had me in stitches, making it difficult to treat the task before me with due gravitas. It became a double act, with me as the straight-man.

This was not at all appreciated by the judges and stewards in the box, accompanied by Raymond Brooks Ward as ring announcer. They were most unhelpful when I asked them for further information, and afterwards Brooks Ward told me he had written a letter of protest about the broadcast to the Independent Broadcasting Authority. Since he was at the time commentating for the rival BBC I doubt this was treated very seriously, and I never heard the outcome.

Our broadcast reached its height when suddenly the Bath and West was assailed by a mid-summer storm of almost tropical intensity. The ring became blocked out by the storm; we could see nothing, and the class was abandoned. This meant a great deal of filling-in until the show resumed: Johnny Morris convulsed me by imitating agitated chicken noises in response to a report that floods were sweeping through the poultry section of the show, causing chickens to float down the aisles.

Personally I thought the injection of a spot of Johnny Morris humour was an excellent innovation, and it might have helped to stem the tide away from TV coverage of the major shows late in the 20th century.

There was nothing amusing about my assignment to commentate for ITV on the controversial 'Alternative Olympics' Three Day Event, held in Fontainebleau in 1980 for the nations who had boycotted the Moscow Olympics that year.

I found the live commentary far more testing than expected, when a South American rider whipped a manifestly tired horse over a fence, following a refusal; the horse staggered over, and broke its leg. I decided to broadcast a forthright condemnation of the rider, and ITV later switched to a race commentary in England where the respected horseman Brough Scott backed my broadcast view that the rider's action was 'totally unacceptable'.

After an inquiry the FEI gave the offender a lengthy ban. That incident was the worst offence I had seen in eventing, and I went way beyond the normally bland commentaries you would normally hear during a three-day event.

THE HICKSTEAD EXPERIENCE

While at BBC Television News I reported the major showjumping row which broke out at Douglas Bunn's All-England Jumping Course at Hickstead in Sussex. After winning the 1971 British Jumping Derby on Mattie Brown, Harvey Smith, ever a blunt Yorkshireman, raised his right hand in a clearly executed V sign, apparently aimed at the directors' box.

Harvey Smith after winning the 1971 British Jumping Derby at Hickstead, on Mattie Brown.

This was interpreted by some of the directors as an insult, and that evening Bunn sent a message to Harvey advising him he was disqualified, forfeiting the £2,000 first prize. Harvey stoutly denied he intended to be insulting, and amid huge publicity Douglas Bunn set aside the disqualification, but asked the British Showjumping Association to hold a disciplinary inquiry. At the end of a lengthy process the BSJA exonerated Harvey from breaking their rules.

Douglas and Harvey patched up their differences amicably; Hickstead and Harvey Smith achieved huge publicity, and the V sign incident became part of showjumping legend.

It indicated to me, well before I edited *Horse & Hound*, that Hickstead was like no other showjumping venue in the land, run by one of the largest sporting personalities in Britain.

The famous Sussex course had a refreshingly relaxed atmosphere compared with the London shows. Douglas Bunn adopted an informal style in the royal box at the course he created next to his back garden at Hickstead, which had been open 12 years when I arrived at *Horse & Hound*. One afternoon we were still enjoying an excellent lunch in the spacious dining room at the back when a military band came to attention in the ring in front of the royal box.

'My God, we need to reply to the salute,' exclaimed Douglas.

He need not have worried. My infant son Marcus was standing at the front of the box alone, giving a cheerful wave in reply to the band's salute.

During the showjumping later in the afternoon, Marcus told us: 'Oh look, that baby bulldog has fallen on that man's head.'

He was right: a small pug dog had fallen through the front of the box, landing on the head of a BBC TV cameraman below. It caused the live picture suddenly to slew out of focus on millions of TV viewers' screens.

Despite such incidents, there was nothing amateurish in the way Douglas ran his unique project by the London-Brighton road. Even before I took over *Horse & Hound* I wrote admiringly of his great contribution to showjumping in producing courses which gave our riders valuable experience of the sort of modern fences they would encounter on the continent.

Douglas believed English courses were too flimsy, and lacking in imagination. Employing the creative course builder Pam Carruthers, he introduced beautifully built, imposing courses with fences including stone walls, sunken ditches, and a variety of water obstacles. His great innovation, in 1960, the imposing Derby Bank, remains a classic challenge in Hickstead's annual Jumping Derby Day. I wrote a history of Hickstead's first twelve years, in partnership with former BBC radio colleague Dick Tracey who later became Minister of Sport as a Conservative MP.

Life was never dull at Hickstead. Douglas, a barrister-turned-businessman, made his fortune with the family's caravan camps on the Sussex coast.

Then he persuaded others, notably Wills tobacco firm, to invest through sponsorship in his dream to create the best permanent showjumping venue in the country. Meteoric in temperament, generous to a fault, and much-married, Douglas's colourful life was a gift to Fleet Street.

The publicity he provoked was not always fragrant, but it widened public awareness of showjumping, and his beloved Hickstead. If you

Douglas Bunn, founder of the All England Jumping Course at Hickstead, a charismatic horseman and a good friend.

accepted an invitation to stay with Douglas and his increasingly extensive family you needed stamina. Dinner started very late, and would continue into the early hours, with plenty of fine wines consumed throughout. The conversation ranged far beyond the horse world.

Douglas seldom appeared from his bed before noon, but once he was up and about the tempo sharply increased.

In his box during his shows you would find interesting show business personalities, such as broadcaster Ned Sherrin and the Forces' Favourite singer Vera Lynn, as well as leading horsemen from home and abroad. As a very senior showbiz celebrity, Vera would sit for hours in the box, following the showjumping closely, then relishing lunch or tea in the box afterwards. Douglas ran a lavish hospitality suite at the back of his box, equipped with fine wines. There was no rushing meals here; there was a TV screen to allow the diners to watch the sport while eating.

The chat in the box was a considerable bonus, and there was always something new in the shows at Hickstead. Bunn created the first permanent working hunter course I had seen, and innovated a class for eventers who jumped in and out of the Hickstead main ring in an exciting blend of showjumping and horse trials. His new ideas, and the success of Hickstead, were not approved of in the early years by some elements in the postwar establishment of the British equestrian scene. However, peace was made eventually with such luminaries as Mike Ansell who had not at first enjoyed Douglas's outspoken independence.

One of Douglas's enduring projects was the sport of team 'chasing which he launched in 1974. The format, still working well, originally involved teams of four riders tackling a cross-country course against the clock. The winner was the team whose third rider had the best time.

Prestigious teams took part over the first daunting course at Hickstead: members of the House of Lords and House of Commons, and teams representing racing, eventing, showjumping and the services. It was such a thrilling spectacle, with exciting falls occurring frequently, that the BBC televised the early events live. The acerbic trainer Ryan Price rode the awesome course wearing only jodhpurs and a cloth cap. After crossing the finishing line he was naively asked by a TV reporter if he had been 'frightened'.

'Frightened? You must be fu***** joking!' replied Ryan live on television.

I was rash enough to take part in the first one, riding my impetuous mount Foxford. I filled a vacant position in a team of Masters of Foxhounds, led by Ian Farquhar, then Master of the Bicester and Warden Hill. We all wore traditional hunting dress, which meant that I had no more head protection than a top hat.

Foxford took me over the big timber and hedges with his usual boldness, but slipped up and fell over a comparatively easy fence, dumping me in the mud. Minus the top hat, I remounted and Foxford surged over the rest of the course confidently. We finished in sixth place.

There was a tussle over the future of the Royal International Horse Show which had to move from its original home at London's White City to an indoor setting at Wembley and then the National Exhibition Centre, Birmingham. The great summer show, whose title belongs to the

Mud-caked and hatless I rashly re-mounted Foxford to complete Douglas Bunn's first Hickstead Team 'Chase.

British Horse Society, would clearly be at its best outdoors, and there was competition from the Royal Agricultural Society who could offer their arena complex at Stoneleigh in Warwickshire.

In 1992 the BHS decided in favour of Hickstead, and as BHS Chairman I was more than pleased later to sign a contract confirming the future of the show at Douglas Bunn's Sussex site. He did the show proud from the start, and it continues to flourish at Hickstead, in contrast with the Stoneleigh site where the Royal Show has expired.

Douglas had spectacular fall-outs with people, but always made it up later. I was among hundreds attending his funeral when he died in 2009 aged 81. He was the least conventional public figure in the horse shows world, with a vision far beyond that of most of his contemporaries. We paid sincere tribute to someone who made a huge contribution to equestrianism in the 20th century – and generated a tremendous amount of fun.

DUBLIN AND BEYOND

I enjoyed Hickstead and all the many other shows I attended over my years at *Horse & Hound*. My favourite was Dublin Horse Show which still flourishes with a style rather lost elsewhere. On the opening day the judges and stewards appear in morning dress, and there are wonderful parades of horses throughout the show. There is a tremendous social programme of summer Hunt Balls and other shenanigans in the evenings: one year I found myself dancing Viennese waltzes late into the night with a lady from Vogue magazine.

Best of all are the wonderful hunter classes and breed classes showing off Ireland's superb young stock. The main ring offers the most superb equestrian spectacles I have seen.

Virtually every animal on the extensive showground at Ballsbridge is for sale. The show catalogue guides you to each horse's temporary box where you can inspect the animal closely. Wearing a flannel suit I climbed aboard a strawberry roan hunter cob and gave it a pop over some poles in one of the outer rings. The animal was not one of my best purchases, proving unsuitable for Leicestershire, but I sold it on as a show cob.

One of the joys of *Horse & Hound* was that I could sometimes visit major overseas contests, acting as visiting Editor and reporter. The first I attended was in Poland where I took part in a showjumping class for journalists, tackling a Grand Prix level course which had been much lowered, but was still daunting for a rider whose jumping experience was almost entirely in the hunting field. We rode local Polish horses, and much depended on your draw; I did not form anything like a winning partnership with my mount, and the class was deservedly won by a Dutch equestrian journalist.

When we visited a Polish horse-breeding stud I foolishly volunteered to ride one of their young horses, and to the joy of the other hacks on the trip the Editor of *Horse & Hound* was swiftly thrown over the animal's head.

Knowing something of their desperately oppressed modern history, by the Germans and the Russians, I thoroughly admired the Poles who were still under the Russian heel in the 1970s when I rode there. We observed the Polish crowd queueing patiently for hours for ice creams. They sat in almost total silence at the ringsides while teams from Russia and East Germany were jumping.

Taking part in shows on the spur of the moment was never wise. I was summarily bucked off by a mule in the ring of the World Circus on Clapham Common.

At Bertram Mills' Circus at Olympia, to amuse my children, I volunteered to ride bareback round the ring. I managed to stand up and maintain my position on the broad back of the cantering horse, and was beginning to think it was easy when the clowns pulled the suspending rope attached to my waist, and I soared round the ring well above the horse, scattering ball point pens and my wallet into the front row. Afterwards I had a hard job convincing the children my fall was not my fault.

EVENTING ROUND THE WORLD

It occurred to me that the best way of maximising the value of overseas trips was to take our readers with us. The response was almost overwhelming when I launched the first *Horse & Hound* Readers' Trip to the 1976 Montreal Olympics. David Johnson, a travel agent based at Hove, Sussex, managed the trip superbly, chartering a jumbo jet which he filled easily with eager enthusiasts, mainly eventing fans, but also showjumping and dressage supporters.

The readers' trip provided free travel for myself and a photographer, and added to *Horse & Hound's* profits. David, suave and polite, proved the ideal tour organiser for our readers. He became a great friend of mine, and I am forever grateful for his imaginative series of tours which delighted readers, and myself and my staff, over some 20 years.

The Montreal Games disappointingly produced not a single medal for the British equestrian teams, but this did not blunt the appetite for more *Horse & Hound* tours, even when healthy competition was launched by the excellent British Eventing Support Group. At Bromont, Montreal we saw Princess Anne re-mount after her horse Goodwill fell heavily in the cross-country phase. The Queen and Prince Philip were present, and were rushed to the fence in a car, but by then their intrepid daughter was on her way again.

Anne gallantly re-mounted to finish the course, although remembered nothing of it because she was concussed, and retired after this phase. Her British team-mates Hugh Thomas and Lucinda Prior-Palmer (now Green) were unable to complete the event due to injuries to their horses in the cross-country. Only Richard Meade completed the event for Britain, coming fourth, just outside the medals.

I admired him immensely since his gold medal achieved at the Mexico games in 1968, and further team and individual golds won at Munich in 1972. Richard had the sublime ability to raise the level of performance of every horse he rode. I rated him the best competition horseman I had seen, exhibiting an ice cool nerve in all circumstances, aided by a wonderful seat and hands.

Of all the competition sports, I always found eventing the most attractive, since I first visited Badminton Horse Trials in 1969, when it was won by Richard Walker on Pasha. How different was the great event in those days. I met members of my Hunt, the Portman, stewarding an open water fence far out on the course, near Luckington Lane.

Lucinda Green riding George to win Badminton Horse Trials in 1977.

Richard Meade schooling Laurieston before the Munich Olympic Games; one of the horsemen I admired the most.

The Portman's Master, Sir Peter Farquhar, was patrolling a stretch of the course, equipped with a whistle to warn of an approaching event horse. Spectators were sparse, and there was ample room for the Portman group to set up a sort of camp, brewing tea on a primus stove.

When a horse jumped the water we cheered right under its nose; when it fell in the water we hooted with laughter. It must have been quite off-putting for the riders.

'Fancy not being able to jump that!' said Sir Peter disapprovingly as another competitor had a splash.

The fences, designed by the course director Col. Frank Weldon, were large, imposing and inviting to a bold horse and rider. I believe this was in line with the original concept of the 'military', the continental horse competition which became eventing. Badminton's huge success and growth each spring brought national TV coverage to the sport. Course builders after Weldon began to produce clusters of combination fences which suited the TV producers, and the growing crowds who sat in small grandstands next to each cluster, especially those at the water complexes at Badminton and at Burghley, the course at Stamford, Lincs, which became the main autumn attraction.

Having enjoyed the sport so much from the 1970s I am inevitably one of the old brigade which deplores the modern tendency to build fences which are increasingly technical, and most of all I regret the FEI's decision to abandon the roads and tracks phase of the test, which allowed horses to be thoroughly exercised before they tackled the cross-country phase. Today we see the emphasis heavily on top marks in the dressage phase, too often unduly influencing the result.

The growth of the trade-stands area at Badminton into a mammoth commercial village has been copied at Burghley, at Blenheim, and elsewhere. Big profits are made from these enterprises, benefitting the estates which run them, and helping to pay for increasingly lavish course layouts with prepared going.

Because one horse can engage in few major events in one year, eventing cannot produce the flow of prize money available to the leading specialist showjumpers who can compete their horses frequently. The band of top-class riders calling themselves professionals, who dominate the leading positions in major horse trials, are outnumbered by many others who are immensely keen riders who put a great deal of enthusiasm into the sport, but cannot support themselves on prize money. They rely on the generosity of owners, plus working immensely hard as teachers and dealers, all too often having to sell the exceptional horse they have produced because they badly need the sale price.

'You are ruining my daughter's career', an eventing mother told me on the phone at *Horse & Hound*. She was complaining bitterly that we had failed to mention her daughter's sponsor in an event where the girl had finished within the top ten.

Douglas Bunn on his showjumper Beethoven.

I gently responded that as far as I could see, even with individual sponsorships which come and go suddenly, eventing remained a largely amateur sport, not a career, and was all the better for it. But those who entered it, as a long-term career should realise this, because they would find themselves working long and hard just to keep themselves in the sport.

Even though the risk element in eventing has been emphasised by some tragic fatalities and heavy injuries, there is no shortage of candidates for the great sport. Organisers still search for new forms of fencing which 'give' when a horse strikes them, but retain a cross-country solidity.

It says much for the enthusiasm and grit of each new generation of riders. Even if I am not so happy with the major changes in its format, I continue to admire the sport and those who compete.

For many years Marilyn and I were annual guests of David, the 11th Duke of Beaufort and his wife Miranda, at the great horse trials in front of the handsome Palladian house in Badminton Park. David is a wonderful host, and has done his utmost to retain the best elements of the sport at Badminton where he was himself a competitor in his youth.

The ritual of the opening night cocktail party, the veterinary inspections, and the event itself, culminating in the Sunday afternoon showjumping, still continue to delight enthusiasts – and long may they do so.

The growth of the sport in the 1970s, and its increasing international appeal, was a great asset to *Horse & Hound* early in my editorship.

We took hundreds of readers to the first World Eventing Championships held in 1978 at the newly-opened Lexington Horse Park in Kentucky. I had already attended a preview seminar at Lexington the previous year, but I was impressed by the lavish organisation of the great event. US leading rider Bruce Davidson retained his individual title, but the hosts had to swallow their disappointment when their neighbours, the Canadians, unexpectedly captured the team event.

Despite missing out on gold medals, the visiting Brits had a tremendous trip. The US showed British horsemen imaginative ways of linking competition with the cultural and historic appeal of the horse in ways we have still failed to explore. As well as wonderful competition facilities, Lexington Horse Park offers visitors a marvellous Museum of the Horse, and many other entertainments, plus visits to the fabulous racehorse studs where breeding stock luxuriate on the famous 'blue grass of Kentucky'. If only we had a national horse museum of the Lexington calibre in Britain.

For me the Lexington experience opened a new window on one of the most exciting and interesting explorations of my life as a horseman: the North American hunting field, and the remarkable men and women who hunt foxes and coyotes with some of the finest hounds in the world. *(See Chapter 13 – Hunting USA)*

In 1986 David Johnson organised our most ambitious readers' trip ever: to the World Championship Three Day Event held at Gawler in South Australia. It was a triumph in every way: the British won the team and individual gold medals, and the *Horse & Hound* readers had a great trip, with a stop-over in Singapore on the way out, and Bali on the return, having stayed in Adelaide during the event.

Lord Patrick Beresford as chef d'equipe had done a great job in ensuring the British horses were still in top competition form after the long flight to Australia. Ginny Leng won individual gold on Priceless, and with her in the team were Lorna Clarke, Ian Stark, and Clarissa Strachan. Anne-Marie Taylor was a creditable fifth as an individual rider.

Lying on a Bali beach afterwards I reflected that *Horse & Hound* should be covering international horsemanship more widely. The popularity of the horse worldwide was far stronger than I had understood. We had gained additional overseas subscriptions in North America and in Australia through flying the flag for the magazine at major events there.

I resolved to put forward a proposal for an international luxury edition of *Horse & Hound* which would be found in airport lounges worldwide and aimed at the major equestrian nations overseas.

I made my pitch to IPC management on my return, but although they listened patiently they were not willing to make the investment.

'Do what you are best at – keep leading the UK equestrian market – and do it even better,' was the verdict from the publishers.

Perhaps they were right, but we will never know...

CHAPTER TWELVE

WHAT TO WEAR, AND OTHER DILEMMAS

Controversy was no stranger to *Horse & Hound* under the firm guidance of Arthur Portman, its Editor for 50 years from 1890, and son of its founder Wyndham Berkeley Portman. Arthur's views on everything ranging from his disapproval of 'Fenians', to, amazingly, the Salvation Army, thundered forth in his weekly leader column until his death in an air-raid on September 17th, 1940.

I aimed to ensure that *Horse & Hound* would continue its first Editor's example of expressing firm opinions on the main issues in the horse world, although of course with a far more liberal stance than Arthur Portman's. There were plenty of issues from which to choose.

No subject proved more contentious than the simple question of what to wear when riding a horse. I upset more than a few older friends in the hunting world by summing up the issue as: 'Sanity or Vanity?'

Chinstraps? Most of the old guard of the hunting world were horrified. They were aghast when, in the 1980s, I abandoned the top hat to appear out hunting wearing such an abomination. Some were angry; others were bewildered; only a few were willing to consider such a huge step towards what was scornfully deemed to be the 'Nanny state'.

For many years I had worn traditional hunting clothes, top hat, red or black coat, white breeches, top boots and spurs, simply because it was expected. As a hunting correspondent I often wore a black cutaway

The Hon. Arthur Portman, Editor of Horse & Hound from 1890-1940. The magazine was founded by his father, the Hon. Wyndham Portman in 1884.

coat made-to-measure made by an Irish tailor in Co. Limerick whose prices were far less than London.

Arguably, the decision to stick to 'traditional' hunting dress in the late 20th century did the sport no favours by encouraging its enemies to blackguard it as a symbol of elitism in the class war. Far more important, the improved safety headgear used in other risk sports was dramatically more effective than a top hat or a hunting cap with a rigid peak, made of calico dipped in shellac. Its manufacture had not changed much for a couple of centuries at least.

The top hat either risked coming off or crumpling if you fell on to a hard surface. If you landed on your face the rigid peak on cap could snap your head back sharply, and break your neck, perhaps killing you, or consigning you to a life of wheelchair – bound paraplegia. Hard bowler hats are safer, but there is a risk of them coming off in a fall unless they fit uncomfortably tightly.

No matter what you wore, broken backs and necks were seen to be the traditional, inevitable toll of riding horses, especially if you wished to travel at speed over fences. Like most of my contemporaries in the hunting field I knew something of the risks, but felt myself to be virtually immortal.

I believed the worst would not happen to me, and anyway looking smart in traditional hunting dress was a morale booster. These illusions, prevailing throughout the hunting world, received a severe dent in November 1982 when Col. Andrew Hartigan, holding the prominent post of 'Silver Stick' (Commander of the Household Cavalry), was fatally injured hunting with the Grafton. His top hat came off and his head struck the road in a fall. He never regained consciousness and died a week later.

The British Army responded by ordering that all serving officers and men should wear modern headgear with chinstraps when hunting. Capt Ronnie Wallace, Chairman of the Masters of Foxhounds Association was a stickler for traditional hunting dress, but the MFHA cautiously advised Masters they should not object if their followers wished to wear safe headgear in future.

Professional hunt staff should be offered the option of wearing it. It was hoped this would offset insurance problems if hunt staff received head injuries while forced to wear traditional headgear. One Master in the Shires who set an excellent example by adopting a modern insulated cap with a chinstrap was Joe Cowen. When he visited Exmoor, Ronnie Wallace introduced him thus: 'And I believe that lurking under that dreadful hat is the Master of the Fernie.'

My traditional attire for many years as the hunting correspondent Foxford.

The MFHA decision was hardly a welcoming embrace for safer headgear, and the long-term result was motley in the hunting field, with all kinds of headgear appearing. In Leicestershire, led by the Quorn, Masters conceded that men could wear modern caps, but 'to avoid confusion' they had to be grey-coloured to differentiate them from the black caps worn by Masters. The argument that we could only recognise a Field Master because he was wearing a black cap was flimsy, but not contested.

The traditionalists scornfully dubbed the grey caps 'mouldy bowlers'. I was one of the first wearing these, and I was made well aware of the whiff of betrayal of 'traditional hunting values' floating around my head. There were mutterings, but no criticism, to my face. The traditional hat makers responded by producing a top hat which sat on top of a thin skull cap fitting tightly over the head. It must have been dreadfully uncomfortable for the few who wore it; from the back it protruded over the ears like the headgear of a Victorian stage villain.

A powerful ally in the move towards commonsense was Prince Charles. He soon exchanged his traditional velvet hunting cap for a modern version with a chinstrap in the hunting field. The Prince explained to his foxhunting friends: 'I wear a safety helmet with a chinstrap when I play polo. Why should I abandon safer headgear in the hunting field?' There was, of course, no rational answer, and the Prince's example did a lot to further the cause. The most powerful influence towards safety was the decision of the Pony Club to make modern headgear compulsory for all members.

This followed the first seminar of the newly formed Medical Equestrian Association at the Royal Society of Medicine's headquarters in November 1985. For me, it shattered any delusions about the real issues of head and back injuries.

In cooperation with the British Horse Society safety department, to whom much credit was due, a distinguished team of doctors spelled out clearly that head injuries could be reduced by as much as 60 percent through wearing a modern insulated cap, with a chinstrap. After attending the seminar, I grasped the nettle and launched in *Horse & Hound* a consistent policy in favour of safer headgear.

Going down the start of the Melton Hunt Club Ride, as number 34, I rode in a top hat and hunt coat. The more sensible competitors wore crash hats and back protectors.

At the seminar I was especially impressed by the Jockey Club's chief medical officer Dr Michael Allen who showed how seriously they were taking the safety issue. They were already ahead by insisting that jockeys wore crash hats, and later back protectors were to be enforced.

We reported future seminars by the Medical Equestrian Association, and supported moves to train paramedics working at horse trials and other horse sports.

The traditionalists' opposition that I experienced occasionally was more than compensated for by parents of riding children who praised the new headgear for protecting them from serious injury. Britain's countryside was increasingly full of hard surfaces, such as concreted farm drives, and slippery roads accounted for many falls.

Today you will still see many Masters of Foxhounds and huntsmen still wearing black caps, some insulated, but mostly traditional.

A few male followers still wear top hats, but there are many more examples of modern headgear worn by men and women. The issue of dress is vastly over-shadowed by the issue of whether hunting can regain full legal freedom again in Britain.

The riding sports all have firm rules about headgear, although dressage people have been agonising only recently about their adoption of modern headgear. It is interesting that side-saddle riding over fences is receiving a surge of new adherents, and some appear in the hunting field in top hats and bowlers. Traditionalism fights back, and I do not deny that adults should make their own decisions about what they put on their heads in a non-competitive sport. The strongest advocates for safer wear come from relatives who have suffered the trauma of seeing loved ones afflicted by life-long paralysis after a riding fall, however seemingly innocuous.

Paintings and photographs of the traditional hunting field are lent glamour and formality by top hats and old-style peaked caps, but they do not compensate for the traditional toll of broken necks and backs which we now have the means to lessen, although still far from eradicating.

After a Medical Equestrian Seminar in 1985 I advocated modern headgear, and adopted it myself. Here I am riding in a team 'chase in Yorkshire.

A QUESTION OF BREEDING

Another area where modernisation was firmly resisted in the postwar years was the breeding of horses intended for showjumping, dressage and eventing.

Was Britain right to place so much emphasis on the show ring when across the Channel the Europeans were concentrating on breeding 'Sport Horses' for athletic competition? The Germans and Dutch created a strong, lucrative market for their new-style Warmbloods.

Most continental breeders received worthwhile subsidies, either from the state, or from horserace betting. Ours receive neither, and they have been more heavily taxed in Britain, since the horse is not rated as an agricultural animal, because it is not raised for food. In fact horse-flesh is consumed in Britain in dog meat. In vain we tried to tell the Treasury that horse breeding was a form of agriculture, employing staff and keeping land down to grass, therefore environmentally useful.

The fatal flaw in our betting system allowing private bookmakers rather than a tote monopoly, has disadvantaged all areas of horse breeding in Britain through lack of subsidy from the huge betting profits made possible by horse breeders. The French and other tote monopolists gave funding for all types of equine breeding from their betting system.

Anyone breeding riding horses in Britain is all too likely to be in the category of 'fools breed horses for wise men to ride'. The financial rewards for such breeding can be small, or non-existent, except for high class sport horse and thoroughbred breeders, but they have borne an unfair tax burden compared to their overseas competitors.

It was heresy to express such views in the 1970s, but could it be that the traditional policies of Britain's main non-thoroughbred horse breeding body, the Hunter's Improvement and National Light Horse Breeding Society, were already out of date? The H.I.S, founded in 1885, was the guardian of the hunter type of horse, used by the military in two world wars as well in the hunting field and riding sports.

The H.I.S. made available good sound thoroughbred stallions to horse breeders, cutting the cost of a covering fee through a premium, or subsidy. The stallions were checked by vets and selected at an annual stallion show. The premiums were funded by the Tote and the Levy

Board, but by the late 1990s these subsidies were withdrawn due to racing's own problems which I have described.

Many good animals were produced under this system, but the major weakness in British horse breeding was the absence of any official grading system checking the soundness or quality of the mares presented to these stallions. Too many people were inclined to use, for breeding, mares that had broken down in their work, thus transferring to the next generation the mare's faults in conformation or constitution.

Already the Germans, French, Belgians and Dutch, were producing competition horses fetching huge sums internationally. They were producing their so-called Warmblood horses from their native breeds, such as Hanoverians and Holsteins, crossed with thoroughbreds, often using top British TB lines. Most importantly they were rigorously testing and grading mares as well as stallions.

I attended a leading German horse fair where continental breeders showed examples of their stock, but British breeding was only represented by the famous yellow display caravan of the H.I.S., manned by a Shires hunting character, the affable moustachioed Major-General Sir Evelyn Fanshawe and his assistant Mrs Betty Townsend.

Prince Charles set an example in the hunting field, wearing a chinstrap because he favoured "sanity before vanity".

'Competition horses?' said Sir Evelyn when I questioned him about H.I.S breeding policies. 'We already have the best competition horse in the world – the thoroughbred. And that's all we need!'

Sir Evelyn devoted his latter years to the H.I.S. literally to the end of his life: he died on a ferry whilst in cross-Channel transit with the H.I.S. caravan back from an overseas show.

The thoroughbred is, of course, the essential breed for racing, and thoroughbreds can compete successfully in other horse sports, especially eventing. But although our senior horsemen were sceptical, increasingly the continental Warmblood was chosen, even by British showjumpers and dressage riders, because its obedient, calm temperament enabled a high standard of accuracy in performance.

It was not until 1998 that the horse breeding situation in Britain was transformed when the H.I.S. was re-invented as a new body, Sport Horse Breeding of Great Britain, seeking to promote a British horse suitable for modern competition work.

PAINFUL SUBJECT

I made sure the controversy over breeding was fairly reflected in *Horse & Hound*. Other burning issues were the status of riders in the Olympic Games, and the use of phenylbutazone (bute) as a painkiller in competition horses. Prince Philip was an admirably pro-active President of the FEI, modernising the rules of many horse sports, and launching the new sport of competition carriage driving as an FEI event, in which he was an enthusiastic participant.

However, there was much angst in Britain over the FEI's decision to make a firm distinction between professional and amateur riders at Olympic levels. The British Federation, perhaps because of the royal connection, led the way in obeying this new international edict to the letter.

It meant that most of Britain's leading showjumpers were no longer eligible to ride in the Olympics because they were encouraged by the British Equestrian Federation, on behalf of the FEI, to declare their activities as dealers, riding for payment, or running professional yards.

Major-Gen. Sir Evelyn Fanshawe (seen left with Lord Kimball) favoured traditional breeding policies as President of the Hunters' Improvement and National Light Horse Breeding Society.

Alas, by 1975 over 40 of Britain's leading showjumpers had taken out professional licences under FEI rules, but virtually no other European equestrian nation's showjumping riders had done the same. So much for European unity! The continentals claimed they would be heavily penalised by European taxation laws if they became acknowledged professionals. There was much grumbling in British showjumping circles about Prince Philip's 'German cousins letting him down,' but other continentals were no better on this issue.

None of Britain's so-called professional leading show jumpers could be in our team at 1976 Montreal Olympic Games which I reported for *Horse & Hound*.

Without the likes of Harvey Smith, David Broome and others, we were well below strength, and finished only seventh in the team showjumping contest, while Germany's Alwin Schockemohle won the individual gold medal; Britain's best performance was achieved by Debbie Johnsey in fourth place. The winning French showjumping team included one rider who admitted to me at a press conference that he ran a riding school at home.

'How professional is that?' I questioned in my despatch to *Horse & Hound*.

It was not until after the 1988 Olympics that the International Olympic Committee (IOC) made all professional athletes eligible for the Olympics. The day of the 'shamateur' rider was over, and the gate to the Olympics was re-opened for all British showjumpers to qualify and compete again.

The increasing need to buy showjumping horses bred on the continent at huge prices, and the lock-out of 'professionals' in the Olympics were both setbacks to our sport at international levels. Since Harry Llewellyn on Foxhunter and his team mates triumphed in Helsinki in 1952, we were not to see Britain win Olympic team showjumping gold medals until the 2012 London Olympics.

The over-use of bute in horses as a powerful painkiller became a major issue in the 1970s when there was criticism of its use in horses taking part in sports. It was widely used in the sport of showjumping where horses tend to compete until a considerable age, sometimes over 20. Hopping over poles, however high, involves nowhere near the stress placed on a horse galloping and jumping at speed in chasing or horse trials. However, the elderly showjumping horse's joints can become creaky, and the animal benefits from a strong painkiller in the form of bute which can reduce inflammation.

The use of the drug lengthens the working life of the horse, but raises obvious welfare issues: just how long do you put off earned retirement for an old codger who has served you faithfully for many a year? Isn't it all the more likely, if you use painkillers, that the end of his showjumping life will be the immediate use of a bullet?

In eventing the indiscriminate use of bute is even harder to defend since it enables horses that are technically lame to continue in work in the most physically demanding of horse sports. Unfortunately one of the side-effects of the drug, if used far too frequently in large doses, was believed to be some degeneration of the animal's bone quality. There were some suspicious cases of high-profile horses collapsing with sudden, and unexplained fractures whilst in work, or even just exercising.

The Jockey Club commendably took the view that, as the guardian of the thoroughbred horse, it could not allow bute to be used on any registered TB horse in racing; an excellent decision which I supported and advocated in all other horse sports. Using bute not only made a lame horse able to compete, a form of cheating, but it allowed lame horses to be used for breeding, conferring their ills on the next generation. This was particularly true of navicular, the arthritic condition in the foot, which seems to be hereditary in some cases.

Prince Philip had firm views on the use of bute. 'It's perfectly alright to give a horse some bute to ease his pain. It's no more than me using an aspirin to offset my arthritis,' he said to me.

With the Prince at the helm, the F.E.I. adopted a policy of allowing partial use of bute in competition horses, but it proved to be an impractical policy. Testing for partial amounts of bute was expensive and difficult, made all the worse through different horses absorbing the drug at different levels.

Eventually the F.E.I. sensibly adopted the same attitude as racing, banning the use of bute entirely. In the racing world there is an exception in some USA States which not only permit bute being used in horses racing, but also Lasix, the drug which prevents a horse bleeding in its windpipe whilst racing. If a horse is being given these drugs it is signified in the racecard. Again, the tendency to carry forward these weaknesses to future generations is aided by the use of drugs among young mares and future breeding stallions.

In Britain the bute issue became so heated that I was called upon to debate it in no less a venue than the Oxford University Forum. The argument in favour of using bute was led by my friend Dorian Williams who shared a similar view to that of Prince Philip. As always, Dorian was affable and generous in debate, and the discussion never became

Prince Philip, as President of the International Equestrian Federation, made the sport of combined driving an official F.E.I. sport, taking part himself with skill and determination.

acrimonious – although my passionate opposition to bute must have had some effect, since the motion in favour of the drug was lost.

Prince Philip's attitude to *Horse & Hound's* stance on the drugs issue was not so affable.

'And you got it wrong again!' he charged me, when he came across me standing at the end of a presentation line at the South of England Show. He then proceeded to engage in a heated discussion on the bute issue, to which I responded with equal fervour.

'Good heavens!' said a lady dignitary next to me in the line, after the Prince passed on. 'Fancy arguing with Prince Philip! They'll be taking you off to the Tower of London!'

I replied that the Prince earned my utmost respect for expressing his informed views. He was an enthusiast discussing a subject on which he felt strongly. I knew that next time we met there would be no rancour. He was not one to hold a grudge.

I invited Prince Philip to write on the subject to *Horse & Hound* which he did, and we published his missive in the Letters column as if it was perfectly normal to receive such correspondence from the husband of the monarch – a privilege accorded no other publication, to the best of my knowledge.

I freely confess, as I did in public debate, that on the bute issue I believed in a different policy for non-competition horses. I used bute in a few cases on my older hunters, enabling them to continue in the hunting field a little longer than would have been possible otherwise. There was no pressure to win a competition; the old horse was simply made to feel more comfortable, but I never found it to be a long-term solution for serious foot conditions.

HAIL MOSCOW?

I was ticked off by a great many leading personalities in the horse world on the issue of Britain's participation in the 1980 Olympic Games, but interestingly not by Prince Philip who kept silent on this political subject. Mrs Thatcher, as Prime Minister, had predictably given a stern warning to British athletes not to take part in the Games because Russia was at the time invading Afghanistan. President Jimmy Carter led the

USA boycott of these Games, supported by 65 countries. To Margaret Thatcher's annoyance, British athletes went to Moscow, and won medals.

In *Horse & Hound* I urged British equestrianism to go to Moscow too, believing the Olympics should not be used by politicians to make protests. If we were to study the current liberal credentials of other nations before allowing them into the Games then there would always be large gaps in participation, and ultimately the Games would be wrecked. I even argued that it would be good for British young riders to meet Eastern European youth in a neutral sporting context.

Such liberal sentiments shocked sections of the British horse world, including some of the establishment at Stoneleigh which still contained a stalwart ex-military element. We published a highly critical letter of my views on the subject, from Lady Doreen Prior-Palmer, mother of the great eventing rider Lucinda, later Lucinda Green.

British equestrianism, then the most conservative of our national sports, decided not to go to Moscow, thereby causing some of our riders to lose their best chance of winning medals. About 80 nations did compete in Moscow, but predictably Russia led a boycott of the 1984 Olympics in Los Angeles.

General 'Monkey' Blacker, later President of the British Equestrian Federation, commented in his memoirs: 'The boycott resulted in the worst of all worlds. It was largely ineffective, spoilt the Moscow Olympics, had no discernible political effect on the Russians, made the West look rather silly, and was, in hindsight, an error.'

Although the modern Olympics have escaped the pro-am controversies of the 20th century, they will always be subject to international stresses and strains, and great vigilance is required by the IOC and national sporting bodies to ensure they are not endangered in future by attempts at gesture politics. The world did not boycott Hitler's 1936 Berlin Olympics, and the occasion provided a valuable warning of his abominable racism when he displayed it towards coloured athletes.

PUTTING SOMETHING BACK

An opportunity to put something back into the horse world which I had long enjoyed, occurred when I accepted the chairmanship of the British

Horse Society, soon after I retired in 1998 from IPC Magazines as a Board Member, and Editor-in-Chief of *Horse & Hound*, *Country Life*, *The Field* and *The Shooting Times*.

Dorian Williams and Mike Ansell had always impressed upon me the importance of the BHS, a registered charity, as the fulcrum of the British equestrian scene, with the Queen as its patron. It was a multi-faceted organisation, comprising two disciplines, eventing and dressage, and important service groups, including training, safety, welfare, bridleways access, and horse and pony breeding.

The BHS was affiliated to the Riding Clubs movement and it was the parent of the Pony Club. Showjumping had always stubbornly remained independent of the BHS, being administered by the British Showjumping Association.

Just before retirement from *Horse & Hound* I had been approached to 'do something about the BHS' by Lord (Sam) Vestey, who was Master of the Horse in the Royal Household. Somewhat rashly I agreed to join the BHS Board, and accepted the chairmanship of the Welfare Department before going on to become Chairman from 1998. I knew it would be a challenge, but it proved a far greater task than I had envisaged.

The Society was in trouble: eventing, dressage and the Pony Club had cut adrift to form wholly independent bodies in 1998. They had prospered during the postwar years as groups within the BHS, benefitting from a sharing of financial resources, and enabling members to join each group for modest increases in the basic subscription. As each sport became more popular small bands of activists sought 'independence' claiming they would get better administration and facilities on their own.

Meanwhile the British Equestrian Federation was assuming a much higher profile as the overall authority of equestrian sports, mainly because it was receiving far larger grant income from lottery funding.

The structure was complicated, and I met very few riders and horse-keepers who bothered to understand its ramifications. Increasingly, they tended to see the world entirely from their own specialist corner, which had been a major factor in the break-up of the BHS.

It had not been a tidy divorce. British Eventing, the new Horse Trials body, was aggrieved that an eventing fund remained within the

BHS. Its financial situation became perilous when the 2001 foot and mouth epidemic caused the cancellation of most of its fixtures, along with a great many other equestrian activities.

Although we felt the break-away from the Society should never have occurred, my colleagues on the BHS Board and I felt we should do all we could to assist the sport of eventing, and we gave significant grant support to British Eventing during the foot and mouth crisis. As a registered charity the BHS could not transfer its funds elsewhere, although it could make charitable grants.

Although many of us regretted the break-up at the time, horse trials and dressage have flourished as individual bodies. The raft of medals won by British horse sports at the London Olympics set the seal on their success.

Our task at the turn of the century was to ensure that the BHS did not collapse in the aftermath of the break-up. There was a strong movement among the British Riding Clubs to follow the break away from the BHS. After prolonged meetings and negotiations we persuaded them to stay, much to the benefit of both bodies.

The BHS itself was operating on an annual deficit; its staffing and expenses needed pruning; its merchandising department required re-organising; and it had an IT system which was not working effectively. Sadly we had to sanction the dismantling of the indoor arena, lecture rooms and library that had been established at the National Equestrian Centre, the dream of Dorian Williams and his colleagues as the postwar focus of UK horsemanship. The wooden building was in a dire state of dilapidation, and the Society did not have the funding to repair or rebuild it.

I was particularly downcast by this inevitable decision, remembering the vibrant enthusiasm of Dorian Williams and his colleagues for their dream project for education and training British riders. Nowadays equestrian students get their training at agricultural colleges which have established highly popular regional equestrian departments.

At BHS headquarters we embarked on a painful but necessary staff redundancy programme, effectively carried out by an energetic new chief executive, Hywel Davies, formerly of the Royal Highland Show. For six months before Hywel arrived I operated jointly as chairman and voluntary chief executive, a full time voluntary job.

Among many other radical changes, we had to complete a project to move the Society's headquarters from its leasehold wooden hut premises on the Royal Showground at Stoneleigh, Warwickshire, to former military hospital brick-built premises on a freehold site at Stoneleigh Deerpark nearby.

There was a deeply conservative element in the British equestrian scene who needed constant explanations and reassurance about the changes we were forced to make. While making financial cuts, we also achieved some innovations, including a new equestrian insurance scheme for members, the creation of a BHS Welfare Centre caring for abandoned horses and ponies, and a national hunter trials competition. I became heavily involved in setting up a new body, the British Horse Industry Confederation, to talk to government about equestrian issues.

The idea was suggested by Lord (Bernard) Donoghue while he was a Parliamentary Under Secretary at the old Ministry of Agriculture. My first contribution in getting the body underway was to achieve the cooperation of the Jockey Club through its chief executive, Tristram Ricketts. Bernard served as consultant on a body which is still a useful conduit to the government of the day, via DEFRA (Department of the Environment, Food and Rural Affairs).

Whether we liked it or not we were facing the registration of horses in the UK because of the requirements of the European Union. At the BHS we were strongly in favour of registration, partly to improve breeding standards by reducing the amount of random breeding of poor quality horses and ponies in Britain. It would also aid welfare standards by tending to retain ownership of horses and ponies in the hands of those prepared to take the responsibility of registration. The modern tendency for serious animal diseases to cross frontiers easily is another threat to our stock of equines, and registration is a help in controlling such outbreaks.

Princess Anne accepted the Presidency of the BHS while I was chairman, and I was grateful for her staunch support in the painful changes we had to make to keep the Society on the road to a new future.

It was the custom for the President to chair the BHS annual meeting in London. The Princess filled the role effectively during a meeting which proved anything but a polite formality, full of tough questioning from the floor. She took a genuine interest in what was happening inside the Society, and I gave her regular briefing sessions.

The Society's role as the horseman's friend has been well and truly vindicated. In an increasingly urbanised Britain the rider and the horse need a voice, and often a defender, on the basic issues of safety, education, welfare and access to somewhere to ride.

Nowadays the Society has a membership approaching 80,000, with over 30,000 members in affiliated riding clubs. It has replaced the headquarters we moved into with a brand new office building, now shared by the British Equestrian Federation, a coming-together I much welcome.

My successors at the BHS have done a marvellous job in establishing the Society firmly in the 21st century as the must-have support group for horsemen and women who want to maintain proper standards in riding and keeping their horses.

Sadly, the showground site at Stoneleigh has seen the closure of the Royal Show itself, an unthinkable loss during most of the 20th century when it was a major highlight of the equestrian calendar.

We had to make a decision at the BHS for a permanent new home for the Royal International Horse Show, the title of which belonged to the Society. The great Show had to leave London sometime after the old White City showground was closed. It was never the best solution to hold it indoors at the National Exhibition Centre at Birmingham.

We chose to accept the offer of Douglas Bunn to take the show under his wing at Hickstead. He ran the show with great enthusiasm, adding new classes, and respecting its traditions. Since Douglas passed on, his children and other members of his family continue to run the Royal International successfully at their famous Sussex venue.

We suffered disappointments, but the first Board of the depleted BHS succeeded in putting the Society on the road to recovery.

CHAPTER THIRTEEN

HUNTING USA

A modern Jorrocks would thoroughly approve of the American hunting world. Jorrocks in Surtees' 'Handley Cross' and in 'Jaunts and Jollities' warmed to the true hunting man who put the sport achieved with hounds well above the mere ride.

He would find plenty of foxhunters of that sort in North America. It was by chance that I experienced some of the most fascinating foxhunting of my life, while I was attending the 1978 world eventing championships in Kentucky.

I was introduced to one of the greatest hunting characters it has been my pleasure to meet, Ben Hardaway III, Master of the Midland, the pack based near Columbus, Georgia, which he founded in 1950. Much has been written about Ben, but he is one of those people larger than any description you could commit to print.

'Come and see my hounds,' said Ben in our first conversation at Lexington.

'I'd love to. I'll try to fix a visit down to Georgia,' I replied.

'No, come right now,' said Ben in his easy Southern accent. 'You can fly down for a few days when this show's over.'

'Which flight should I take?' I asked.

'My flight,' said Ben with a grin.

He ushered Jim Meads and myself onto his private jet aircraft which zoomed from Lexington, Kentucky to Columbus, Georgia in quick time. At Columbus airport, a car was waiting by the runway. Ben took the wheel and headed straight for the perimeter fence round the airfield.

Ben Hardaway, charismatic Master and huntsman of his own Midland pack in Georgia and Alabama.

'Got my own personalised exit,' said Ben. He pressed a button on the dashboard and a section of the fence obligingly swished back to allow us through.

If this all sounds like a man showing off, well perhaps it was, but Ben has a disarming capacity for laughing at himself, as well as the rest of the world. I suspect he could have made a comfortable living as a stand-up comedian if he had been born in a different cradle.

Heir to a major US construction company, Ben has been able to spend money lavishly on his favourite sport. In doing so he has generously provided many years of sheer delight to others who followed his hounds, and soon became his friends and disciples. He charged only ten dollars a year subscription to Midland Hunt members, but joked: 'And they get ten dollars worth of say!'

Despite the private aircraft, and the inherited fortune, there is nothing over-blown about Ben Hardaway's reputation as a hunting man. Like all true hunting men he is a keen naturalist who has deeply studied his quarry, mainly red and grey foxes and coyotes, and the highly challenging environment in which they are to be found. In his case it is a mix of wooded country around his homestead in Georgia, and a contrasting country of rolling grassland and scrub in the neighbouring state of Alabama, where he hunts from a secondary kennel at Fitzpatrick.

Through innovation, and experimentation, Ben has created one of the great working packs of the world, using hound lines from Ireland, France and America's Penn-Marydel breed. For years he wrestled with the problem of preventing his hounds from rioting on the lines of the

American white-tailed deer which have a very strong scent, and are abundant in his hunting country.

He told Jim and me the story which has become a legend among hound-breeding foxhunters both sides of the Atlantic: 'I put a rioting hound in a ten-gallon metal drum with a deerskin. Every time he sniffed at the deerskin I gave him a jolt with an electric prodder.

'Did he stop chasing deer? No he didn't. But he won't go anywhere near a ten-gallon drum!'

I wore an incongruous bowler and shirtsleeves to follow the Midland hounds in Alabama, riding a superb chestnut hunter from the Hardaway stable. Jim Meads donned knee-high leather boots, said to protect him from rattlesnake bites, all too possible a risk, as he followed and photographed Ben's hounds on foot. As usual Jim coped with the heat, and the snake threat, to produce excellent pictures accompanying my report published in *Horse & Hound* under the heading: 'Hunting the fox – in rattlesnake country.'

I soon realised I was hunting with one of the great amateur huntsmen of the time. There was no fuss nor flourish, just a close understanding of his hounds' needs in finding a fox, then maintaining the line until the end of the hunt.

Ben Hardaway's hounds hunted superbly in soaring temperatures.

I enjoyed following the Midland hounds in hunts across their Alabama country.

I saw a strong red fox get up in a grove of woods before flying across the grass at top pace, with the pack screaming on the line, having left covert together in great style. We had started at dawn, but by early morning the temperature had risen to over 80 degrees Fahrenheit, and dust was kicking up on the tracks between the grassland and crops. So much for our English venery which preaches that a good scent usually depends on damp ground and cold air.

Hounds engaged in a smart hunt across country, in which we jumped a plethora of timber fences, and galloped over the dry turf. Despite the shirt-sleeves I was streaming with sweat by the time the hunt had ended. There were flies and mosquitoes on the hack back to the Fitzpatrick kennels, but Ben cooled us off with a case of champagne straight off the ice.

I noticed with amusement that Ben Hardaway's first whipper-in, a black man named Jefferson (Tot) Goodwin, quietly rode away before the morning's sport ended. Tot had a hunting pack of his own to feed and exercise, Ben told me. The easy relationship between the landowning MFH and his black staff in the hunting field and at his home was a contrast with Alabama's segregationist reputation.

I saw more of this amity when Ben took Jim Meads and myself coon hunting at night in the woods near his Alabama kennels. Coon hounds were supposed to pick up the scent of the coon on the ground of the forest, and would then hunt the line to the particular tree which the quarry had climbed.

There were half a dozen coon hounds at the meet: slim, long-legged creatures with dome shaped heads, and floppy ears. They were owned by black farm workers who greeted us with laconic friendliness. We all sat down to eat hot stew and drink corn whisky, while the 'dawgs' hunted about in the woods. There were said to be plenty of poisonous snakes about, so we gratefully received boots and leggings as 'hunt dress'.

I was impressed by the voice of 'Ole Blue' a large blue-ticked dog who had a wonderful howl which echoed through the woods, raising the hairs on your neck.

While we waited Ben told me about his youth when he would sit in cornfields at night with older countrymen whilst their hounds hunted foxes in the dark around them. When these hounds picked up a line they would hunt it as a pack, and the waiting owners would pick out the cry of their own hounds, judging which one had hit the line first, and stayed in the hunt.

Wearing snake boots I joined in Ben Hardaway's night-time hunt for tree-roosting coons.

"Ole Blue", the coon hound with a wonderful howl.

This tradition of 'trencher-fed' hunting often derived from Irish immigrants who brought hounds to the US. We should not forget that the USA's 18th century founder, George Washington, was a keen foxhunter in Virginia, but he followed his hounds mounted in the style of the English gentry.

The next phase in the hunt, when the quarry was 'treed' by the hounds, was to shine torches up into the branches of the tree the coon had chosen for its escape. Theoretically the light would glint in the eyes of the coon looking down, and the hunters would then shoot him down. I have to report this phase was a total failure during my coon hunt, and I was not particularly sorry.

Ben enlivened proceedings by telling, in a Southern accent broadened for the occasion, the story of a coon hunter who once appeared at the meet with a monkey. The owner strapped a gun belt and a brace of revolvers round the monkey's middle. After a coon dog had bayed at the foot of a tree, the monkey shinned up it, but eventually climbed down having been unable to find a coon.

The monkey then advanced on the baying dog and shot it between the eyes.

When the dog's owner protested loudly, the monkey owner replied: 'Ah'm sorry about that, but if there's one thing this heah monkey hates more than a coon, it's a lying coon dog!'

During later US hunting tours I made happy return visits to Ben Hardaway's Midland Hunt, but none more memorable than to report his special foxhunting field trial in which I was one of the judges. It was far removed from anything I could have seen in the English hunting field (although the idea was later tried here briefly, and not pursued).

Foxhounds selected from a number of packs gathered at Ben Hardaway's Alabama kennels, and were hunted jointly in the early morning as one giant pack of about 70 couple; ostensibly under the control of one huntsman and a posse of whippers-in. To my surprise each hound had a large number painted in black on both flanks to enable identification by the judges.

I was one of several mounted judges following the pack, with the task of observing which hounds acquitted themselves best: finding the fox, maintaining the line, and if possible being among those in at the kill. We were also to note any hound which rioted on deer, earning disqualification immediately.

Brian Fanshawe, by then retired Master and huntsman of the Cottesmore, attended as a non-riding judge, travelling in a truck with Ben Hardaway who kept bellowing instructions and advice on his closed circuit mike. Whether it was possible for the huntsman to carry out any of these instructions, I doubt.

I waited patiently on horseback outside a covert soon after dawn on the first morning, when suddenly what appeared to be a large dog trotted out of the covert, approached me and stood nonchalantly for a while under my horse's neck, apparently listening to the sounds in covert. It dawned on me at last that this grey creature with pricked ears and intelligent eyes was a coyote, a legitimate quarry of the chase in America.

I stood in my stirrups and holloaed. The coyote looked up at me, almost in amusement, and trotted sedately away into the woods. I was to take part in several coyote hunts with hounds later. They were totally different to a foxhunt which can involve much local hunting, and casting back. The coyote takes off like a train, running hard virtually in a straight line, or a huge loop. He has a neat trick of crossing the line of another coyote in a far off covert, rather like a relay runner handing over the baton. The fresh coyote then takes off with tremendous zest, leading the tiring pack on a fruitless chase.

Coyotes are therefore hard to catch with hounds, but I saw a couple killed simply because they ran into high wire fencing which they were unable to jump. The death of one coyote by a pack of hounds is like a car-crash: immediately fatal for the coyote. The quarry dies in its own environment where it is itself a hunter.

This is far more humane than attempting to kill the coyote by shooting where the wounding rates are remarkably high due to the animal's tough constitution and elusiveness. During repeated visits to Hunts on the US East Coast I was told that coyotes from the West Coast states were gradually driving grey and red foxes out of their habitats, and were taking over as rapacious raiders of farm stock.

After each day's field trial hunting, my fellow mounted judges and I were interrogated on what we had seen of hounds working. My reports were probably incoherent; it was very difficult to assess which individual hounds were performing best. I declined to support a report that a hound from one pack had been seen hunting a deer.

Despite inter-pack competitiveness, the whole affair was conducted in a cheerful, celebratory atmosphere. Some of the Masters and huntsmen had driven many hundreds of miles to the field trial, and they were treated to Southern hospitality and music in a tent after hunting every day. It was tremendous fun, capturing something of the old frontier style of American living, and I felt privileged indeed to take part. I forget who won the prizes, and it really didn't matter.

One of my fellow judges was a keen lady foxhunter with a witty tongue, Daphne Wood who with her husband, Marty, had set up their own pack of foxhounds, the Live Oak, in the Panhandle area of North Florida. Marty, as chairman of the American Masters of Foxhounds Association invited me to speak at their annual gathering in New York in 1991.

It was a piercingly cold January, but plenty of warmth was generated by US and Canadian foxhunters as they lunched, dined and danced – the latter at a magnificent ball where it was mandatory for the ladies to wear silver and men to don scarlet hunt coats. Amid the convivial fun, the North American Masters held exceedingly well-organised and worthwhile seminars on hound breeding, hunt politics, and other matters. They run an excellent on-line website which is way ahead of hunting sites I have seen elsewhere, including the UK.

American and Canadian Masters were most interested in the growing political pressures on British hunting generated by the animal rights movement, and wanted to be fully informed. Once again I was impressed by the strong links forged between North American foxhunters and those in the UK. Some of the leading US Masters I met later flew to London to join the great marches protesting against Labour's ban on the hound sports.

The Americans can teach us something about the way to organise the sport in the modern world: US and Canadian Hunts are run on club lines, with the Hunt Kennels used as a social centre, rather like a golf club. Some make big savings through keeping followers' horses at livery at the Hunt Kennels, the profits enabling them to keep the Hunt Staff's horses free. Our system, in which most subscribers seldom have a chance to go to the Hunt Kennels and stable their horses elsewhere, is not so well suited to forming a closely knit membership unit. I hated to hear some British Masters refer to the subscribers as 'the customers'.

After the programme in New York, my wife Marilyn and I, with Jim Meads, continued an American hunting tour, kindly arranged by Russell Clark, Master of the Myopia hounds in Massachusetts, who we had met when he made hunting visits to the Quorn.

Russell meant well, but it was a tough schedule. We drove from New York down to the Green Spring Valley Hunt in Maryland, home of the daunting timber race, the Maryland Hunt Cup. Joint Master Frank Bonsal mounted me on a superb timber jumper, which was just as well, because some of the fences we faced during an excellent day's hunting needed to be tackled by an experienced horse.

We were splendidly entertained by senior Joint Master 'Duck' Martin and his family, and then drove down to America's classic foxhunting state, Virginia, having a day with the Elkridge-Harford on the way.

In Virginia I much enjoyed hunts with the famous Orange County pack, hunted by the veteran Melvin Poe. Their hounds really do have orange tinted patches. The Piedmont, hunted with skill by Joint Master Randy Waterman, have a grass and stone-walls country reminiscent of our Cotswolds, and I much appreciate the day on a grand horse loaned by the senior Joint Master Mrs Randolph.

The hunting dice rolled in my favour in a visit to the Middleburg Hunt where I arrived very late due to a mix-up over horses. The huntsman, Albert Poe, brother of Melvin, was just blowing hounds on to the line of a fox when I caught up. They soared away on a very good hunt indeed; the ride was great fun as we tackled a variety of timber, and the hound work was impressive, with hounds accounting for their fox.

In 2004, the American Masters of Foxhounds Association asked me to speak again at their January seminar, held in a snow-decked

New York. We were spoilt by staying in the Plaza Hotel, overlooking Central Park.

I was kept busy, speaking at a working lunch, a splendid dinner, and a presentation session when I backed my talk on UK hunting with a video of the Cottesmore running well across the Rutland terrain. The Americans could not have been more hospitable and appreciative. The supportive relationship between American foxhunters and those in Britain and Eire is indeed a bright strand in the sporting world.

After the 2004 New York programme I flew down to the Live Oak country with Marty and Daphne Wood. Their white-fronted mansion in its own parkland reminded me of a set from *Gone With the Wind*. Hunting takes place in and around thousands of acres of coniferous forests, much

Marty Wood III, Master and huntsman of his Live Oak pack in north Florida.

of it owned by the Masters. Alligators and snakes can be found all too easily in the Panhandle's tropical clime, and like many packs the Live Oak hounds hunt bobcat as well as fox or coyote.

When we weren't hunting, the Woods took me on highly enjoyable quail shooting parties, riding on mules, and shooting over the heads of dogs who put up the game. Success in this sport depends on more shooting skills than I possess, but it does not result in big bags even for the best shots. I much preferred it to the big pheasant and partridge shoots of the UK where hundreds of birds are put up only to be shot down.

Over several decades I hunted with more than a score of North American packs from Ontario down to Alabama. They mixed efficiency with informal fun, and a warm welcome to visitors. In those areas deficient of hedges, banks or strong timber, the riding challenge is far less than crossing a stiffly fenced English or Irish country. This helps to concentrate minds on the hound work.

Occasionally I found some testing country : for example, there was a day with the Eglinton and Caledon Hunt in Canada when I was thrilled by a coyote hunt in a snowstorm in which we were jumping almost blind over big timber 'line fences', boundaries between large enclosures.

It was part of a six day Festival of Hunting, visiting and hunting with a different pack each day, and addressing their Hunt Club dinners in the evenings. The first half of their season would soon be stopped by their fierce northern winter: I recall listening to the howling of timber wolves on snow-clad hills while I lay in bed in a Canadian timber farmhouse.

The Canadian programme of daily ''untin' and talkin'', as Jorrocks put it, was a physical challenge, which I thoroughly enjoyed, until the very last day with the Toronto and North York pack when I managed to pitch head-first over a small timber fence my horse refused. It was a riding error: I should have put my legs on harder.

After my mild concussion was quickly checked at a local hospital – how different from the waiting in A-and-E at home – I went to the Toronto and North York Ball that night, dancing until the early hours.

As a result of my Canadian trip I was invited back to judge hunter classes at the 1994 Royal Canadian Winter Fair, one of the greatest

Marty Wood and his wife Daphne, his Live Oak Joint Master – in celebration with photographer Jim Meads.

shows in the world. I entered the lavish show ring as a passenger perched high on the top deck of a four-in-hand coach – and only just ducked my head in time as we passed under a metal strut, missing decapitation by a fraction of an inch.

In the ring, a team of Trakehner horses bolted out of control, crashing their coach into ours, rocking it perilously. Another coach driver coolly averted more disaster by steering his team into the side of the runaway coach stop it. One horse fell amid a splintering of coach and poles, but grooms leapt to the horses' heads when they stopped. Amazingly no-one was injured – and the band played on. It was quite an entrance.

The rest of the show went without a hitch. If I was not the most illustrious hunting correspondent in the annals of sporting history, I was certainly one of the luckiest.

Chapter Fourteen

ADVENTURES IN IRELAND

The railway engine driver seemed very angry. He had stopped his engine, and was standing on the track waving his arms as the County Limerick hounds ran across the lines.

'No he's not angry. He's just waving to say he's seen the fox cross the line,' said the Master confidently.

Lord Daresbury was right. His hunting country was deeply rural, and people knew the priorities when his Limerick pack were hunting a fox.

An even more remarkable sign of hunting's place in rural Ireland occurred when the Limerick pack jumped a stone wall into the playing field of a village school. I was amazed when the huntsman followed, and then the Master gave us a lead over it too.

Children were at play as we surged across one end of their recreation area. They waved their arms and cheered enthusiastically as the Hunt went by.

Even in the most rural areas of England in the 'seventies I could not imagine these incidents occurring without causing adverse press comment.

Hunting with hounds in 2015 remains legal in the Irish Republic, and in Northern Ireland, which is the only area in the United Kingdom to reject hunting ban legislation. This is due to the much closer relationship between town and country throughout Ireland. People in Irish urban areas have not been overwhelmed by the animal rights propaganda which has been so successful in Britain.

Having reported Ulster's 'Troubles' in the 1970s for BBC television, I am under no illusion that the Emerald Isle is entirely about jolly rural pastimes. The hunting field does, however, bring out some of Ireland's best qualities: humour, good fellowship and warm friendliness to visitors.

I enjoyed immensely all my hunting trips to Ireland, some of the most memorable incidents taking place before or after the day's sport. For example I attended a Co. Limerick Hunt Ball in the company of Audrey King, a senior English lady of the Hunt who braved the big Limerick banks mounted side-saddle.

Hunting with Lord (Toby) Daresbury, senior Master of the Co. Limerick pack of Old English bred hounds.

Audrey, one of a coterie of English hunting ladies who had emigrated to Ireland to hunt with Toby Daresbury, had been a noted beauty, and still had considerable style and poise. It was a pleasure to dance sedate waltzes with her. We were on the floor when I was aware of the sound of breaking glass 'off-stage', and a few raucous shouts. My companion did not turn a hair.

'It's just the boys having a little fun in the bar,' Audrey reassured me. Soon several men staggered on to the floor, scattering broken bottles over quite an area. The dancers continued to scrunch across the fragments with no sign of concern.

I recognised one of the revellers when he emerged from the bar: Mr P.P. Hogan, one of the great hunting characters of Limerick, a superb horseman who had given me a tremendous lead over fearsome banks that very afternoon.

Now he had a glass in hand, and was smiling happily. Then he turned round, and I saw that his scarlet tailcoat had been ripped from collar down to the bottom hem, and now hung in two limp wings.

'Must have been in a bit of argument perhaps,' murmured my dance partner, giving the impression nothing untoward had occurred.

Lord (Toby) Daresbury, Master of the Limerick for 30 years, and huntsman for many of them, had a sense humour entirely suited to hunting in rural Ireland.

'What do you do with your old hunting clothes?' I heard a young lady ask Toby at a meet.

'I fold them up, put them by my bed, and then I put them on again next morning,' he replied gravely.

Toby was utterly devoted to the Old English type of Foxhound, having latterly followed his father into the Mastership of the Belvoir in the 1930s, giving a tremendous lead across the Vale as Field Master. I asked him how the mounted field knew he was the Master as he wore a cutaway coat and top-hat instead of a skirted coat with a cap.

Mrs Bunny McCalmont, wife of Major Victor McCalmont, Master and huntsman of the Kilkenny.

'If they didn't know who I was they shouldn't be out hunting with me,' he replied.

After the war he transformed the Limerick hounds into a Belvoir-dominated Old English pack, hunting them himself, and proving they were just as effective over a big bank and ditch country as they were soaring over the old turf of Leicestershire. Toby was inclined to refer to 'modern Foxhounds' as 'barking dogs.'

I used to accompany him to the Irish Hound Show where visiting young English judges of the Ronnie Wallace 'modern Foxhound' school would usually dismiss first from the ring the Old English Limerick hounds.

'I'm so glad they didn't make one of my hounds champion – as I should have had to shoot it,' said Toby mildly as we drove away from the show at Clonmel. He continued to support the show whatever the judges did, and occasionally his hounds won the two-couple class as an example of an entirely level pack of a distinctive type.

He had lost his third wife, the former Lady Helena Hilton-Green, in a hunting fall with the Limerick in 1972. Known as 'Boodley', she was the former wife of 'Chetty' Hilton-Green, famed Master and amateur huntsman of the Cottesmore. I recall her as a warm and vibrant personality, and a great horsewoman. Toby's first wife, the former Joan Sherriffe, died in 1926 from injuries received in a fall while hunting with the Quorn, only seven months after their marriage. Two years later he married Joyce Laycock who bore him a son, the Hon. Edward Greenall, but she predeceased her husband in 1958.

Since Boodley's demise, Toby's household was run by his companion-housekeeper, the diminutive Meriel 'Merry' Atkinson, a doctor's daughter from the Belvoir country. She was skilled at rearing hound puppies and foals. Once after a fall, she had clambered on to a stone wall, and shouted 'Pony, pony!' Her homebred horse stopped, wheeled round and galloped back to the wall where she calmly re-mounted.

I saw the entire Limerick pack running hard after a fox across the park at Alta Villa. Just at that moment Merry appeared and called 'Puppy, puppy!' to some whelps she was feeding. At least four couple of the hunting hounds veered away from the pack, and ran up to her, somewhat to the irritation of the Toby's professional huntsman, Hugh Robards.

I was aghast during another Limerick hunt when hounds crossed the deep and swift-flowing River Deel. Robards and P.P. Hogan never hesitated, but leapt their horses down off the bank; the horses were almost completely submerged, but then rose and began to swim the river, emerging at a cattle watering place on the far side.

It seemed far too cold a day for water sports such as this, and although the Field Master also took to the river, I set off along the bank for half a mile until mercifully I found a bridge. Looking round I noted that three-quarters of the mounted field had followed me.

I managed to hunt with most of the Irish packs during more than 30 years of visits. The glorious old turf, and miles of jumpable walls in the Galway Blazers country was a special delight. I was once mounted on a superb five-year-old, supplied by the famous dealer Willie Leahy. Barbara Rich, the Leicestershire dealer, had asked me to ride the horse and report back as she had a client for it.

After a wonderful day on what proved to be a superb hunter, I was hacking back to Leahy's horsebox when a visiting Englishman complained about the dreadful falls he had suffered from his hireling.

'I was going to ride a much better horse – but I hear they gave it to some bloody hunting correspondent.' he said bitterly.

With the Co. Limerick I learned to jump Irish walls and banks mounted on my host's superb hunters.

*Lady Daresbury,
known as "Boodley",
and like her husband
a former Leicestershire
hunting personality.*

Willy Leahy was renowned so far and wide, that there was a card in a telephone booth in New York's Central Park, advising his telephone number to anyone who wished to hunt with the Galway Blazers.

In the Tipperary country I experienced one of the best days of my life, following a pack which screamed across a very wet country all day, hunted with great verve by their red-headed English Master Michael Higgens who you could easily have mistaken for an Irishman, so well did he fit into the landscape.

No Irish hunting tour could be complete without visiting the iconic Scarteen, the Black and Tans, so-named after the distinctive pack of Kerry Beagles hunted by the Ryan family for over 300 years.

Head of the family and Master of the pack, Thady Ryan, courteous and silver tongued, was among the most popular personalities in Ireland, and was at the height of his reputation when I hunted with him. His natural charm, and his relaxed but effective way of hunting hounds, earned him legions of supporters, especially visiting Americans, some of whom stayed as guests in the Ryan home.

I recall Thady's wife going from one horse to the next at a meet, taking off sandwich boxes which first-time American visitors had strapped to their saddles.

'You won't be needing them; you won't have the time to eat,' she laughed.

She was right: a run across the Scarteen banks behind the Kerry Beagles was a hectic experience in which normal time and space no longer existed.

At the end of one such run, during a dig in the hunting field, I recall Thady bothering to dismount to show an American how to blow the hunting horn, although the huntsman had to resume the saddle quickly when his hounds characteristically used their own initiative to run fast to a holloa indicating another fox was seen in a distant field.

The independence and sensitivity of Kerry Beagles requires special handling, which may explain why you will not see them elsewhere in mounted Foxhound packs. Thady's son, Chris, once brought the Scarteen hounds to hunt with the Cottesmore in Leicestershire. The Kerry Beagles clearly hated the number of horses thundering across the grass behind them, and during a stop for second-horses some of the pack took refuge under the Hunt lorry.

In the afternoon the mounted field thinned, and at last the Scarteen put down their noses and ran a stirring hunt, with their distinctive cry. They preferred horses to be the other side of an Irish stream or bog during a hunt.

In the Meath country I was thrilled by a wonderful hunt which included crossing part of Fairyhouse Racecourse. We jumped some of the white-painted timber enclosing the paddocks, and left the racecourse to encounter formidable water-filled ditches. Reading a biography of the sporting Empress of Austria I noted that she and her companion, Bay

The great Irish hunting personality Thady Ryan, Master and huntsman of the Black and Tans, crossing a bank neatly at speed.

Middleton, had similarly ridden across the same racecourse in the late 19th century. It seemed more evidence that foxes tend to run similar lines of country for generations.

With the Kilkenny I followed hounds across 'Murder Mile', a sequence of huge stone walls which rolled alarmingly as your horse tried to bank off them. Fortunately I was mounted on a superb hunter, by the same sire as the chaser Captain Christy, provided by the Kilkenny's legendary Master and huntsman Victor McCalmont who was a leading bloodstock breeder.

His wife, the English-born Bunny McCalmont, used to organise a marvellous picnic hamper which followed us during the hunting day, and to which she and her guests repaired at frequent opportunities. Bunny, a well-upholstered lady with a warm sense of humour, answered the door when I first visited the Kilkenny.

'You're the Editor of *Horse & Hound*?' she asked. 'Goodness. I thought he was a little old man with a white beard.'

When I visited her in company with the sporting artist John King he received a shock at dinner. The butler ceremoniously lifted a silver cover off John's plate to reveal a jock strap. For the first and last time, I saw John blush.

'They sent it on from your last port of call at Toby Daresbury's,' said Bunny. From then on she referred to him as 'Jockey King'.

Falling off in Ireland usually meant getting extremely wet in a bog or a water-filled drain as they call a wide ditch. I had my share of this experience, including ejection from the saddle when a three-year-old I was riding stepped into a drain as if it was not there, and plunged into the drink. Unfortunately we scrambled out on different sides, and I had to wade through the water again to try to catch my errant mount, but he was soon trotting purposefully after the fast-retreating mounted field. I had a long, squelching trudge across bogland back to a lane where the hirer stood holding my horse, enquiring with a grin: 'Got yer bum wet did yer?'

I had been told at the meet the horse was a four-year-old, but as it was before Christmas he was still technically only three. There was more than a hint as to his inexperience when the hirer asked me to give him my whip and my spurs before we moved off.

'Would you like my Hunt buttons as well?' I shouted back as the young horse put in a buck when hounds moved off.

After the fall, the young horse never put a foot wrong for the rest of the day. Knowing my horse's youth, I was apprehensive when, on the top of a very steep bank, a piece of barbed wire sprang up in front of him. He paused, and delicately lifted one front leg, then the other, over the wire, and then launched himself off the far side of the bank with great care to land well beyond a ditch. I was told that in Ireland foals out at grass learn such skills at their mare's side, and on top of that bank, as I saw my future distinctly threatened, I was fervently grateful my mount had benefitted from early natural training.

In general the pace of hunting in Ireland is slower than the English Shires, and for that reason I believe it is possible to survive falls which would be more horrendous at a strong gallop on firmer going.

Occasional mishaps never dissuaded me from returning to hunt in Ireland every season for nearly 30 years. There is a carefree attitude to the Chase in Ireland which appeals, and I adore Irish-bred hunters who find a 'fifth leg' in dealing with the most hair-raising obstacles. The problem was that too many Irish dealers and hirers were inclined to over-use their horses as three and four-year-olds, often causing joint problem and lameness in later life.

I am told that during its recent economic boom, some of Ireland's hunting countries were squeezed when notable areas of rural Ireland became built-up, and far more barbed wire was used in increasingly intensive stock farming in some areas.

But governments north and south of the Irish Border firmly have refused attempts to ban hunting with hounds. The rural community has a significant voice, and Irish packs of hounds are still hunting the abundant fox population in traditional manner.

If by some miracle of rejuvenation I was able to resume hunting I would head for the Emerald Isle as quickly as possible to taste again joys of the Chase untrammelled by the political bigotry and ignorance which has afflicted hunting hounds in the English countryside.

CHAPTER FIFTEEN

COME TO THE BALL

Blearily looking out of my hotel window at dawn on a Friday morning in March I detected the cause of the noise that was waking me up.

A gentleman in a scarlet hunt evening coat was lying on his back in a bus-shelter in London's Park Lane blowing a hunting horn. He was a left-over reveller from our annual eccentricity at Grosvenor House, the *Horse & Hound* Ball.

I inherited this phenomenon, a sort of tribal rite set to dance music, from Walter Case, without realising the full extent of the commitment.

By the time I arrived as Editor our metropolitan hunt ball had been regularly targeted by Britain's small, vociferous animal rights movement. Groups of them were held back by police and temporary railings on the pavement of Park Lane as guests arrived at Grosvenor House.

The anti-hunters shouted insults, whistled and occasionally threw unpleasant small missiles. Their worst effort was pouring paint stripper on a yellow Rolls Royce delivering people at the hotel, only to find the occupants of the car were not going to the Ball.

One year the lights mysteriously went out in the ballroom, but the band played on, and dancers were only too happy to smooch around in the dark. Another year the automatic sprinklers were activated over the dance floor, but dancing continued, with the revellers blithely ignoring the downpour as they would in the hunting field.

These were rare hitches inside the ballroom, and I deeply suspected anti-hunting factions for both these disruptions, but it was never proven.

Horse & Hound Ball guests were never deterred by the noisy reception on the street. Princess Anne, although barely out of her teens, marched firmly past an especially raucous reception from the antis when she arrived as a guest of honour.

When I apologised to her as I met her in the reception area, she said briskly: 'No problem. Just a lot of nonsense.'

She could have opted for a discreet entrance through the back doors of the hotel, but never did so. The Princess's sangfroid was tested again when I escorted her down the stairs into the Great Room: suddenly a woman dashed up to us in a threatening manner, exclaiming to me: 'There's somebody in my seat. You're in charge here! What are you going to do about it?' She was hastily escorted away by security staff, and the Princess did not even blink, although I had to cope with an attack of the giggles.

The great event had started not as a hunting icon, but as a fund-raising dance for good causes in the horse world.

Just after the war our irrepressible hunting correspondent Bay de Courcy-Parry, who wrote as 'Dalesman', urged the revival of 'Horseman's Dances' to raise money and have fun amid postwar austerity.

The first was held soon after *Horse & Hound* had lost several issues due to 'the fuel emergency.' Despite the economic gloom, a committee of horsemen with *Horse & Hound's* backing, held a 'Horseman's Dance' in 1947 at Grosvenor House in Park Lane, in aid of the National Horse Association's Horse and Pony Benefit Fund.

It was a huge success, packed with young men and women yearning for glamour and fun amid postwar austerity. The flavour of the dance became that of a Hunt Ball, with much of the support coming from packs in the Home Counties.

The following year, despite a snowstorm and petrol rationing, the Ball moved to the Park Lane Hotel and adopted the magazine's title, immediately becoming one of the most popular fixtures of the London winter season. Only a small note in the editorial pages was necessary to ensure an attendance of over 1,200 diners and dancers, revelling in the gusto of the largest Hunt Ball in Britain.

With most men wearing scarlet, blue or green Hunt coats, some of ancient vintage fitting all too tightly, accompanied by ladies in refurbished ball gowns, the occasion had a reassuring message that it was still possible to have a good time in a fast changing world where the Socialists were already threatening to ban foxhunting.

The 1949 *Horse & Hound* Ball at the Park Lane Hotel earned a totemic place in hunting history, and established it as a defiant pro-hunting symbol in the metropolis. That same afternoon MPs voted in the Commons to defeat a Private Member's anti-hunting bill. Farmers from the West Midlands rode their horses through central London, blowing hunting horns, to protest against abolition.

Defeat of the bill was a cause for huge celebration among the *Horse & Hound* diners and dancers, and they gave a tremendous welcome to the mounted protestors when they arrived at the Ball. 'Master', 10th Duke of Beaufort, gave a rousing speech in celebration of the Commons victory, and welcoming the protestors. Thereafter he never missed attending the Ball for well over 30 years. The mounted protestors formed a permanent group of hunt activists in the West Midlands under the name of 'The Piccadilly Hunt Club' whose lively annual dinner I was summoned to address several times.

Walter and Violet Case maintained the *Horse & Hound* Ball as a major London event until his retirement at the end of 1973. It was organised with great efficiency by Dorothy Finch, an unflappable lady in IPC Magazines' events office. After Dorothy's retirement we took on the organisation temporarily in my office and then handed it to public relations consultant Bridget Jennings.

The Ball returned to Grosvenor House in 1951, and remained there for 43 years; the hotel staff were excellent, serving over 1,200 dinners with remarkable speed, and then coping with a long night of jollifications.

It was an occasion when our readers' expectations dictated the course of events, a prime example of promoting a magazine's title. In those days we did not use focus groups to find out what our readers wanted.

The sense of excitement was palpable in the darkened Great Room of Grosvenor House as the guests assembled at tables marked by twinkling silver lights.

There was a well-established ritual which everyone thoroughly enjoyed. First there was series of champagne receptions, the largest held behind a curtain for the Editor's guests, up to a hundred strong.

Dorian Williams brought warmth to the role of Master of Ceremonies for many years, succeeded after his death in 1985 by his TV colleague Raymond Brooks-Ward, and then Michael Tucker, nowadays the leading equestrian commentator. Like foxhunting itself, the *Horse & Hound* Ball was used by left wing animal rights groups as a symbol of the upper crust in Britain's perpetual class-war. The truth was, like Royal Ascot, it gave hard-working people a chance to dress like peacocks as a change from drab every-day garb. The

Marilyn and I, about to host the annual event which "had a well established ritual".

unaffected energy and exuberance of the horse world at play belied the stereotypes of a languid upper class.

The very small aristocratic element at the Ball was accentuated by the intermittent attendance of royalty, and the faithful support of the Duke of Beaufort, but they were far outnumbered by the very wide cross-section of people who nowadays enjoy riding horses in pursuit of hounds: mainly businessmen, professional people and farmers.

Perhaps because most of them were physically fit, with considerable stamina, they surged on to the dance floor after dinner to dance with tremendous energy, and were never ready to go home after the last waltz at one a.m., which we later extended for another couple of hours.

Princess Anne continued to be a guest at the Ball after her marriage to Capt. Mark Phillips. She sat next to me at dinner, chatting seriously about horse issues. At first she found it hard to relax amid the press of people, but she began to unwind as she met friends in the eventing world among the throng, and ventured on to the dance floor occasionally.

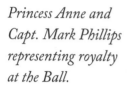

Princess Anne and
Capt. Mark Phillips
representing royalty
at the Ball.

Mark Phillips's capacity for chilling out was all too evident the first time he came as Anne's husband: he fell fast asleep at the dinner table, leaving Anne to do the talking. He had been exercising horses early that morning we were told, and he took Anne home soon after midnight.

Ironically, Mark was to become one of the most popular communicators with *Horse & Hound* readers through writing an insider's column on horse trials which the magazine still carries today.

The most relaxed royal guests at the Ball, and clearly enjoying themselves, were Prince and Princess Michael of Kent who both hunted regularly with the Duke of Beaufort's. I also saw them out hunting on a brave visit to the Belvoir one Saturday. They both had falls, but remounted cheerfully, and continued to battle through the throng jumping exuberantly over the Vale of Belvoir.

Princess Michael was ready to start the dancing with me as soon as dinner was finished. Tall and shapely, she was a good dancer, and readily accepted invitations on to the dance floor from numerous gentlemen who suddenly appeared at the Editor's table.

I noted that the Princess seemed to be attended by a photographer we had not commissioned – and sure enough, a full set of pictures of her dancing at the *Horse & Hound* Ball appeared in *Hello!* magazine.

After an hour of dancing, the next stage of the ritual was the annual horn blowing competition, divided into classes for professional hunt staff and amateur huntsmen who were often Masters of Hounds. Ronnie Wallace had won the contest at the 1947 Ball, and thereafter attended as a judge with a colleague, and the Editor as referee.

When I first took on this task I was surprised by the seriousness of the judging, and the keenness of the competitors. However, the younger element were dying to get back on to the dance floor.

Sydney Lipton and his orchestra, long experienced in the West End and at Hunt Balls, provided the dance music for many years. I liked his traditional repertoire of numbers, and best of all they were not too loud, so that one could hear oneself speak at the dinner-tables. As the years rolled by I sympathised increasingly with elderly guests, such as Anne, Duchess of Westminster who responded cheerfully to my invitation to dance, with: 'No thanks darling. M' feet have given out.'

Sometimes we unwisely accepted the urgings of Douglas Bunn to 'go on somewhere' after the Ball. Usually he took us to Annabel's in Mayfair which despite its popularity I found fairly unexciting compared with nightclubs I had visited in the East as a reporter. I returned to the Grosvenor House in the early hours worn out, and then rose after a couple of hours' sleep to dash to the office to select the pictures of ball-goers for publication in next week's issue.

Raymond Brooks-Ward, attending with his wife Denise, succeeded Dorian as MC.

I was cautious about innovation at our Ball, but I introduced one wildly popular new feature which I had seen at a provincial hunt ball: just after dinner one of the top military bands would arrive on the dance floor, and give a stirring display of counter-marching. When this culminated in *Rule Britannia* and *Land of Hope and Glory* the assembly was entranced, standing up to wave tiny union jacks which we provided. I noted wryly that these little plastic flags bore the words 'Made in China'.

The best one-off interlude was a cabaret act generously provided free by one of my favourite

Walter Case escorting the royal couple.

comedians, Jimmy Edwards, then a Joint Master of the Old Surrey and Burstow. The be-whiskered Jim played various brass instruments with droll variations, much to the pleasure of the older generation, although the young were impatiently waiting to get back on to the dance floor.

As musical tastes became ever more pop-orientated we introduced a disco in the balcony area, and on the dance floor Sydney Lipton gave way to the Johnny Howard band, far more vocal and strident, and wildly popular with the young. Sadly, all conversation for the rest of us was stifled after dinner.

The editorial and advertising staffs had their own table at the Ball, and our publishers kindly stayed at their own table, realising that the Editor was not actually having a night off.

The greatest *Horse & Hound* Ball marked the magazine's centenary year, 1984. Francis King, still our publisher, produced some money to fund the largest guest list ever. Normally the Ball was entirely self-supporting, and always made a significant profit donated to an equestrian/hunting good cause. It generated enormous goodwill and promotion for the magazine as well, but despite this I could see warning signs that its days in London were waning. We gave a centenary dinner for the magazine in addition, with Princess Anne as the main speaker, and eloquent contributions from Dorian Williams and others. I was touched by the real affection for the magazine expressed in letters of goodwill from far and wide.

In the 1990s we had to devote increasing editorial space to promote the Ball; it was becoming far more expensive to run; and the magazine industry was under greater pressure to maximise profits in the teeth of tougher competition and rising costs. Younger publishers at meetings I attended sometimes asked 'What is the ball for?' I attempted explanations of *Horse & Hound's* 'mystique', and received the answer: 'You mean brand values?'

In 1995 when I was Editor-in-Chief, I approved the brave attempt of my successor, Arnold Garvey, to save the Ball by moving it to the middle of England – in the Birmingham Metropole Hotel at the National Exhibition Centre.

It was a sell-out, very well supported by the Midland Hunts, but the growing animal rights movement did not miss out on an increasingly strident demonstration outside the hotel as guests arrived. As usual the

Dorian Williams was Master of Ceremonies and Ronnie Wallace judged the hornblowing contest.

diners ignored the protestors, and the Birmingham hotel staff were magnificently supportive.

But after several years at the NEC Arnold Garvey moved the Ball back to London, returning to its roots at the Park Lane Hotel. It was an enjoyable evening, but the input in effort and money from the magazine required to run such an event was growing, and reluctantly the unique event was allowed to die before Arnold's seven year tenure as Editor ended. The last one I attended was dominated by a fund raising auction; it seemed the imperatives of economics had overtaken a fun evening.

Hunt Balls all over England were by then holding hunting horn competitions, and the importance of these social events in funding each Hunt were becoming more important. Going up to London for a night out was increasingly expensive.

So the *Horse & Hound* Ball survived for more than 50 years, but like so many traditional events it was overtaken by 'progress'.

No doubt the anti-hunting movement notched up its demise as a victory, but it was never intentionally a flag-waving exercise for hunting – just people harmlessly having a good time.

Princess Michael descending the stairs into the ballroom; our glamorous guest-of-honour at the Ball.

Chapter Sixteen

THE TURF

It would have been impossible to become an effective Editor of *Horse &
Hound* in the 1970s without knowledge and affection for the world of the
Turf.

Racing was just as much a main staple of the magazine's format as
hunting, ensuring the title's place at the top end of the market. We were
read by Jockey Club members as much as by the ladies and gentlemen of
the Masters of Foxhounds Association, by horsemen and women of all
varieties, and by the staff in tack rooms of stable yards serving all areas
of the horse world.

My affection for British racing has long been tempered with
irritation at the unfair way it is funded. Reading back-numbers of *Horse
& Hound* I came across the frequent fulminations of our founding Editor
and proprietor, Arthur Portman, against private bookmaking firms
operating off-course. He pointed out forcefully that racing made betting
possible and should therefore see a fair proportion of the profits returned
to the sport. Portman's arguments are still basically valid today: the
fundamental flaw in British racing remains that the flow of the profits
the sport generates goes out of the racing industry and into the betting
industry, much of it based offshore. Other major racing nations operate
Tote monopolies and return far higher percentages of the profit on the
turnover to racing. This makes possible far higher prize money, more
investment in racecourse facilities for race-goers, and financial support
for thoroughbred horse breeding, including grants towards TB-cross-
breeding too, thereby benefitting the horse industry as a whole.

I have seen Tote monopolies in operation in the U.S., in France, Hong Kong, New Zealand and Australia. Their racing industries received up to ten percent returns on total betting turnover, whereas for many years British racing received less than one percent. The creation of the Betting Levy Board to skim off a profits tax from bookmakers each year, with a limited Tote operation up against fierce competition from the privately-owned bookies, has not worked well for the sport. On-course bookmakers contribute to the traditional atmosphere of British racing. They could have been allowed to continue operating on-course, whilst ensuring that the hugely lucrative off-course betting is run under the pari-mutuel systems such as the French operate, resulting in far higher average prize money in their racing.

British racing is still under-funded because the goose that lays the golden eggs is starved of a fair percentage of the massive profits it generates for privately owned bookmaking firms. In March 2015 the Chief Executive of the British Horseracing Association stated gloomily: 'We are still in the situation whereby the vast majority of bets placed by punters outside of betting shops are making no contribution to the finance of the sport. This is unsustainable, and there is recognition that this needs to change.'

I nodded approvingly when the leading Irish trainer Willie Mullins said prize money at the 2015 Cheltenham National Hunt Festival should be doubled.

I continued Portman's policy in supporting a Tote monopoly in *Horse & Hound's* front page column 'Town and Country', which I wrote throughout my editorship. It was a compliment to the magazine's influence that a leading bookmaker sent a letter of protest – but significantly chose to address it to the proprietors of the magazine.

The bookmaker's letter received an admirable reply from IPC's board affirming the right of an editor to express opinions freely. I made sure the bookmakers' case was published in the magazine, but I noted with amusement thereafter that I was no longer invited to promotional lunches and dinners held by London's leading bookmakers.

The government has since sold Britain's Tote to a firm of bookmakers, and there is absolutely no prospect of an off-course Tote monopoly in this country financing the sport. I do not in any way criticise the bookmakers or the way they conduct their business in the UK, but it is worth pointing out that the system adopted in this country could have been so much better.

I was aware of the fun element of racing from an early age. Although I have never been addicted to betting the turf played a large part in my life from childhood. My mother's job towards the end of the war, and thereafter, was to work in the Exchange Telegraph 'blower's office', an essential service to the bookmaking community long before information could be relayed on-line.

Mother was one of a small group of women sitting in a Bournemouth office wearing telephone head-sets, receiving the betting prices from representatives at the racecourses in action that day, then relaying them to the bookmakers' offices in the region who paid for the service. When I visited the office as a school boy I was fascinated by the noise and the tension as the girls shouted the odds, and wondered how mother withstood the stress. Sadly, after some years the 'blower' sessions brought on heavy migraines and mother reluctantly gave up, losing a job she enjoyed and much-needed additional income.

Our wartime Christmas was sometimes improved by the arrival of a present to my mother, such as a turkey, from bookmakers. Since my mother was now so involved in daily racing, at home we followed the sport more closely. We crowded round our ancient valve radio to hear hectic commentaries on the Grand National and other major races, delivered in the plummy tones of Raymond Glendenning.

After I joined the *London Evening News* reporting staff in 1957, at the tender age of 23, my interest in horses soon became known to the News Editor, Sam Jackett. I did not explain that I actually knew very little about current horse-racing, and with some trepidation set off at Sam's behest to cover some of the biggest racing fixtures of the day.

The racing editions of the *Evening News*, the *Star*, and the *Evening Standard*, were published in mid-morning, and were valuable sellers to London's millions of punters. The racing editions were succeeded by up to half a dozen more editions during each day, produced at hectic pace against intense competition between the three evening newspapers. We staff reporters chasing news stories were expected to phone in our copy ahead of the news agencies as well. Although I had spent a year on a good provincial evening paper, in the Chichester office of the *Portsmouth Evening News*, at first I found keeping up with the hectic Fleet Street regime extremely testing. Fortunately I had verbatim shorthand, and enough stamina to pound the streets of London endlessly. Much of the work was crime and court reporting which I enjoyed, but I missed the green fields of Dorset and Hampshire, and the possibility of riding horses ever again seemed remote.

I owe a great deal to Sam Jackett and his senior colleagues, whose tough exteriors filled the cliché of cloaking hearts of gold. They instilled in me the discipline of composing reports at great speed, often dictating without notes inside street telephone boxes besieged by irritated Londoners seeking to gain entry. On a really big court story the copy would be sub-edited, and actually printed in the current edition, before I had finished dictating the whole story to one of the team of the copy-takers in the news room, wearing head-phones to type at furious speed all day – one carbon copy to the news editor, the original to the sub-editors.

My orders from Sam Jackett were to spice up the sober coverage of the racing staff with colourful news stories and previews. The *News* specialist racing team, led by the veteran pundit Tom Webster, were civil, but barely tolerated my intrusion on their territory, and never invited me into the official racing scribes' press box. I did not care: I tended to cover the stories the race reporters avoided, such as the young Queen and her house-party riding on the course at Ascot before the day's racing.

Much to my surprise, and through sheer luck rather than expertise, I pulled off a coup when attending an Epsom Derby early morning exercise gallops the day before the classic race on the famous Downs in 1960. Even as an amateur horseman, I recognised that a horse staggering when suddenly pulled up from a canter by its jockey, was likely to have broken down. I ran breathlessly from Tattenham Corner nearly to the finish where the animal was now lying down, and an Epsom vet, George Forbes, arrived swiftly to confirm that the horse had broken its near fore fetlock, and had to be put down. The horse lay on the course only a few

Lester Pigott and St Paddy on the way to the winner's enclosure after the 1960 Derby, led by trainer Noel Murless.

lengths before the Epsom finishing post, a point I made fully in my report.

I was ever grateful to the urbane Peter O'Sullevan and Clive Graham of the *Daily Express*, who courteously told me the animal's name, Exchange Student, a stable companion of the Irish hot favourite Die Hard. The two pundits were completely unconcerned that I was from the rival Rothermere group. Their cooperation was anything but typical of Lord Beaverbrook's editorial news staff. I phoned through a speedy story to capture the *News's* first edition front page lead, scooping the other evening papers and agencies. A certain amount of equine knowledge proved useful in lending a fraction of authority to my hasty report, and they welcomed it warmly in the newsroom. The great bonus was that the *Star* and *Standard* missed the eyewitness story, and never caught up in later editions with my report.

My gateway to the turf was wide open that year: I had been sent to cover the first Flat race of the season, the 1960 Lincolnshire

Handicap, then held on Lincoln's own delightful course. It was exciting to watch cinema newsreel teams film the race on huge cameras with tripods mounted on their cars roaring alongside the Lincolnshire course. At the end of the race they drove off the course to a nearby airfield to rush the film by small aircraft to London for editing and processing to appear in London cinemas that very night. I phoned hasty copy after snatched interviews with the winning connections, but I cannot pretend my story was of startling originality.

A far bigger challenge awaited: I drove from Lincoln over the Pennines in my first staff car, a tiny Austin A30 saloon, to Aintree where the former Gaiety girl, Mrs Mirabelle Topham, was in charge of the crumbling shambles of her late husband's race course. She was fighting for the survival of a Grand National meeting desperately in need of investment, although it made millions for the world's bookmakers.

The delightful if formidable Mrs Topham chatted away amiably to the young man from the *Evening News*, although I doubt that later she liked my report of bushes growing out of the bricks on the grandstand, and sagging racetrack rails in need of repair and painting.

Neville Crump's ex-hunter from the Scottish Borders, Merryman II, won the 1960 National, ridden by Gerry Scott. It was the first to be televised, watched by a ten million audience, and the last National before the great perpendicular fences were sloped back, not at that time for 'safety' reasons, but mainly to bring more top-class chasers back to Aintree, in which it partly succeeded.

Television was increasing public interest in racing, and my role as a news reporter on course seemed established at the big fixtures.

Sometimes I worked on major racing occasions in partnership with my first wife, Mary Watson, a New Zealander who I met when she was an *Evening News* feature writer.

Mary covered social scenes at Royal Ascot meetings while I prowled about in search of news stories. Wearing with some discomfort a hired top hat and tails, I found Royal Ascot a bore. Unfortunately the Queen's daily arrival on the course in a royal carriage came into the category of a news story, and I made a terrible muddle in reporting the colour of the Queen's outfit, gladly handing over this vital task to my wife.

At the 1960 Derby my services as a news reporter were far more important than usual. It proved to be such a sensational day that the London evening papers re-made their front pages for a new Derby splash story in every edition, each one more sensational.

In late morning Winston Churchill's horse Vienna was suddenly withdrawn after being pricked in the foot by a blacksmith; a railway signal man fainted in the heat, and the royal train was held up, bringing the Queen to the course later than usual.

The race itself was dramatic because the favourite Angers broke a bone, and had to be put down. The winner by three lengths was St Paddy ridden by Lester Piggott.

I was among the crowd of reporters quizzing Piggott after the race.

'When did you think you were going to win, Lester?' they asked.

In his dry voice, he croaked laconically: 'Last night.'

'Were you worried about the horses in front of you coming round Tattenham Corner?' was another question.

'Well I wasn't worried about the 'orses behind me, was I?' came another brief rejoinder from the enigmatic jockey who had just won his third Derby.

Worn out at the end of a long, hot, and very tiring day, I confessed on the phone to the copy-taker in the office that I had not had time to put on a bet.

'Don't worry,' he said. 'You picked St Paddy in the Press Club sweepstake; you've won hundreds!'

In fact I had won about £250, a huge sum in 1960, and we used the cash to help finance a voyage of which I had been apprehensive, but had agreed to make almost as part of the marriage vows: to visit New Zealand to meet my wife's family.

I worked for a nearly a year on the *Auckland Herald*, and enjoyed many aspects of my allotted role as the 'Maori Affairs Reporter', given to me, so it was said, because I brought a 'fresh mind' to the subject. This entailed long car drives to far-flung Maori settlements in the Taupo area of New Zealand's North Island. Maori affairs were initially interesting, but somewhat palled as a future way of life, and I did not see myself getting immersed heavily for the rest of my life in New Zealand's news scene which, in the 1960s, seemed to be jogging along even more slowly than it was in my *New Milton Advertiser* training days in the New Forest.

This is a short-sighted and unfair summing up of New Zealand's splendid way of life, but I admit that in my twenties I was impatient and impetuous. We returned, after six weeks of sea travel, to London where miraculously I attained another Fleet Street reporting job despite the calamity of the Star newspaper having closed down, causing a glut of refugee reporters to the other two evening papers.

Fortunately, within a fortnight, I was on the staff of Beaverbrook's *Evening Standard*, appointed by Ronnie Hyde, the most awesome News Editor in Fleet Street. Tall, immaculately-suited, with grey wings of hair, and a drawling accent, Ronnie was famous for ruling his team of reporters with an iron hand. When one reporter had phoned in his story he was switched to the news editor to exclaim brightly: 'OK Ronnie, I'm on my way in.'

Hyde's reply, after reading the copy, was famously: 'On the contrary dear boy, you're on your way out.'

For reasons I still ponder, Hyde liked me, and appointed me deputy news editor after a three years' stint as reporter. We formed a friendship which survived my departure into the world of TV reporting, and magazine editorship. I was touched to find he had requested I should deliver the address at his funeral in St. Bride's, Fleet Street.

Ronnie loved racing and most other sports. He soon began sending me to major racing occasions as well as leading news stories.

Sent to Epsom for the *Standard* in 1962, I was utterly amazed to be involved in a second Epsom Derby drama, far greater than that of 1960. Twenty-six runners in the '62 Derby were galloping down to Tattenham Corner when seven horses fell in a dreadful melée, one of them fatally breaking a leg. I was standing at ground level at the rails by the finishing post as riderless horses galloped behind the leaders in a scene more reminiscent of the Grand National. It was said to be the most dramatic Derby since the Suffragette Emily Davison fatally threw herself in front of the King's horse in 1913.

The disaster enabled Larkspur, a 22-1 outsider, to romp home to produce trainer Vincent O'Brien's first Derby triumph.

Amid vast confusion and noise I extracted quotes from shocked trainers of fallen horses, and crumpled jockeys. Thanks to Hyde's organisation I was able to use an exclusive land-line in the paddock by the Finish to phone my story for a major re-plate on the last edition, earning a joint by-line alongside the *Standard's* racing correspondent Peter Scott. The intro to our front page splash was:

'The 1962 Derby ended in a fantastic mixture of triumph and tragedy this afternoon. The Irish colt Larkspur romped home a 22-1 winner after a pile up in which seven horses fell. Six of the jockeys were taken to hospital and three of them were detained. A woman spectator and a boy were also taken to hospital. One of the horses involved, King Canute II, broke a leg and was destroyed.'

The rank outsider, Larkspur, on his way to win the dramatic 1962 Derby in which seven horses fell.

I was ahead with the story because the racing correspondents were held up leaving their press box high in the stands by excited crowds surging down the stairs. While I was phoning my copy, I could see the racing press shouting and waving their arms in a scrimmage on the steps down to the paddock.

Next morning Hyde made a rare error in forgetting to send anyone to Epsom Hospital where three Derby jockeys were lying injured.

He sent me late, and I missed a hospital press conference, only to wander without permission into a ward where I found jockey Tommy Gosling sitting up in bed, being visited by his pretty fiancée. He chatted away about the disastrous race, and it made a nice exclusive for the Standard, magisterially acknowledged by Mr Hyde.

I reported Gosling as declaring: 'It was the roughest I can remember in the nine Derbies in which I have ridden.'

In 1964 I made a major career move, abandoning my secure post as Hyde's deputy to which I had been promoted, and any possibility of succeeding him. I was desperately frustrated by my indoor role on the *Standard's* news desk, and I wanted to enter the rapidly-growing world of television news.

My by-line on the Evening Standard front page reporting the Derby "of triumph and tragedy".

My aim was to become a TV and radio reporter, covering stories internationally, but first I badly needed basic experience of this new medium. I accepted a post as News Editor of Southern TV, based at Southampton.

For the first time since I had attended as a schoolboy, I thoroughly enjoyed a visit to the Portman Hunt's point-to-point, held in a beautiful downs setting by the ancient Britons' earthworks at Badbury Rings.

I have relished point-to-pointing ever since, and would swap any a major racing occasion for an afternoon with hunting people watching genuinely amateur riders riding over fences purely for fun.

Later at *Horse & Hound* I explored the hunter 'chase scene: amateur riders competing under Rules on racecourses.

My introduction was the annual springtime weekend meeting at Stratford-on-Avon where the Final Champion Hunter Chase was run for the *Horse & Hound Cup*. Founded in 1958 this was the second oldest sponsorship in British racing, the first being the Whitbread Gold Cup.

It was a highly enjoyable racing treat for myself and most of the editorial staff, and for some of our IPC management. We were given a warm welcome by the Rowe family and their colleagues on the Stratford board.

Racing on the Saturday was preceded by a lunch in a marquee where I was impressed to see such heroes as the great 'chase jockey Fred Winter, now a trainer, in company with other leading National Hunt figures. It was a reminder of the family atmosphere of the winter sport, with owners, trainers and riders coming from similar rural backgrounds.

They were celebrating the final day of the 'chase season, which closed until the autumn. 'Chasing was a smaller sport when it was seasonal, but it has to be admitted that it still only comes alive as a major attraction in the winter months; the needs of the betting industry had a great deal to do with today's prolongation of lesser races through the summer months, despite harder going and smaller spectator crowds.

Attending far-flung courses to present trophies for races sponsored by *Horse & Hound* enabled me to explore delightful areas of Britain I should otherwise not have known. It was one of the best ways of making new contacts valuable to the magazine.

*My **Evening Standard** interview with jockey Tommy Gosling after the 1962 Derby disaster.*

Walter Case, my predecessor, had embarked on a sponsorship of a race at Newton Abbot where the Clerk of the Course was Claude Whitley, long-time Master and amateur huntsman of the South Devon Hunt.

Claude, and his wife Susan, became firm friends, and I returned to the South Devon country to report hunting with Claude's hounds on the beautiful moorlands above Newton Abbot.

I was also out on a spring day when Ronnie Wallace brought the Heythrop hounds to hunt the South Devon country. Ronnie dismounted ponderously to walk with his hounds while they drew a large area of sun-drenched gorse.

'Fancy getting off his horse to draw! He'll never find there; I drew it blank myself last week,' said Claude, looking down from his horse high on a hill among the heather. Suddenly there was a whimper, then a crash of hound music, and the Heythrop hounds were away on the line of a strong dog fox – giving us a five-mile point across Dartmoor until caught above ground. I was riding a borrowed ex-point-to-pointer, and had a superlative ride which included jumping some Dartmoor stone walls.

'Wallace was a bit lucky wasn't he?' said Claude over a hearty Devon hunting tea in his farmhouse. It was six o'clock and through the window I could see Ronnie in the distance on his second horse, pounding across the moors on his evening hunt.

I extended our race sponsorships to hunter 'chases at Plumpton in Sussex, where the chairman was an interesting sporting character, Isidore Kerman. He was a London solicitor with a flair for property investment in top-class restaurants such as Scott's, and other enjoyable ventures which included a stake in Wimbledon Greyhound Racing track where I was his guest.

I had met Isidore out hunting with the Old Surrey and Burstow, and I was soon among the many who appreciated him as a man of great style and acumen whose advice and company was always worthwhile.

We took on new race sponsorships at Wetherby in Yorkshire, and at Kelso which enabled me to explore the Scottish Borders, following up with visits to the Scottish packs hunting this beautiful area.

Racecourses were delighted to accept sponsorships for quite modest sums from *Horse & Hound* because they appreciated the extra publicity they received in the magazine.

Credit Call, ridden by Joey Newton (left), on the way to winning the Horse & Hound Final Champion Hunters Chase Cup at Stratford-on-Avon in 1975.

Presenting a Horse & Hound Cup at Plumpton to winning 'chase owner Bill Shand Kydd, with Isidore Kerman looking on.

Racing remains a fundamental part of the British way of life, which still stutters into life on major sporting occasions. Wouldn't it be wonderful if, at long last, racing found a way of persuading politicians that changes are still urgently needed to the betting laws to ensure it is properly funded?

CHAPTER SEVENTEEN

HORSEY FAMILY NUMBER ONE

'I'm taking the short route. Hold on!' shouted the carriage driver. I was sitting next to him as he swung his team of four horses downhill diagonally, heading for the limpid surface of Virginia Water in Windsor Great Park.

The four–in–hand driver, known as a 'whip', fished a hunting horn out of his breast pocket and blew it as we hurtled down the hill. From then on, I remember events as if it was a slow motion car crash.

How ironic, it occurred to me, to die as a travelling referee in the 1975 International Driving Grand Prix in Windsor Great Park, when I could have done it so much more easily reporting the Vietnam War.

Two things happened: a leading wheel of the coach hit a huge boulder; and when they got to the edge of the lake, the team of horses ran back up the hill, tipping the wagonette on its side, and dragging it behind them.

I was underneath when the vehicle hit the ground. The driver kept firm hold on the reins and leapt over me, running up the hill and hauling his team to a halt at the top. I recall every detail because a picture of the spectacular capsize won a 'Sports Picture of the Year Award'.

My next memory as I lay on the ground getting my wind back was of a lady in a white riding mackintosh and a headscarf looking down at me, and asking in a cut-glass accent: 'Are you alright?'

215

I was about to expostulate that things weren't too good, when I recognised the lady as the coach's owner, Her Majesty the Queen. The driver was Lt.Col. Sir John Miller, Crown Equerry in charge of the Royal Mews at Buckingham Palace, and he was driving the Queen's team of greys and a bay to a wagonette. He had been in the lead after the dressage.

'Oh, I'm fine, Ma'am,' I said. 'Perfectly alright, thank you.'

It seemed the best thing to say when the sovereign enquires about a calamity in her vehicle. What I might have said to anyone else was something more pungent.

While I got to my feet I became aware that the drama was about to change into a farce. The navigator John Marson and a groom at the back of the carriage were spilled off the back of the wagonette but were unhurt.

I reported in *Horse & Hound*: 'The nearside large rear wheel was smashed. By some miracle, which I was not exactly praying for, a woodcutter soon materialised with a saw, and quickly provided two birch branches.

'With hideous enthusiasm, volunteers lashed the branches to the axles, leaving the wagonette listing at 45 degrees. The horses were harnessed again, and Sir John – carnation button hole still intact – completed Section C.'

Sir John resumed his driving set, not at all ruffled, and I numbly regained my position next to him. We set off down the hill, this time at a walk, with the carriage leaning precariously on the skid-stick on my side.

This time the horses braved the lake water, and waded through it remarkably calmly. I had started the trip with a clipboard and a stopwatch, but both had disappeared. Now I clung to the edge of the carriage, as it threatened me with immersion in Virginia Water.

We emerged on the other side of the lake, and lurched on for some yards, until Sir John said brightly: 'Ah, this is the cantering section.'

To my further consternation, he encouraged his team forward with his driving whip. There was a nasty grinding sound as the skid stick disintegrated. We came to a shuddering halt, and my side of the carriage hit the ground again. This time I fell off to land on my feet.

Disaster: I was the travelling referee when the Queen's team of horses, driven by Lt.Col. Sir John Miller, bolted back from the edge of Virginia Water, capsizing their carriage and smashing a wheel.

The grooms began to unhitch the four horses from the carriage, and I was asked to lead one of them. Just as we were walking away, a large dark green Range Rover halted. The lady at the wheel, wearing a headscarf, was not amused.

'That's quite enough, John,' said the Queen. 'Take my horses home immediately!'

Back at the Members' tent at Royal Windsor Horse Show, to which the driving marathon belonged, I received a written invitation to dinner that evening at Windsor Castle. It proved to be a large-scale party where the Queen who personally expressed sympathy and apologies 'for what happened to my team' received us.

I was seated on a table with Princess Margaret, and a couple of military attaches. I seemed to spend a lot of dinner re-lighting the Princess's cigarette, held in a long holder. The conversation was light and

I clung on as the Crown Equerry tried to finish the International Driving Grand Prix in Windsor Great Park, but the Queen ordered him to stop.

frothy, and did not include mention of driving carriage horses.

Sir John Miller was one of the most remarkable horsemen I ever encountered: as Crown Equerry to the Queen for 26 years (1961-87) he was in charge of all the horses used in royal ceremonial events, and he assisted the Queen in breeding horses and ponies of all kinds.

Of slim build, with a clipped military moustache, John Miller, was not an imposing figure, but he had a steely core which you learned to respect. As a Welsh Guards officer he was awarded an MC in the Normandy campaign; as a horseman I saw him ride and drive in the most perilous circumstances without the slightest sign of nerves.

At our first meeting he invited me for a drive through central London on one of the carriages from the Royal Mews at Buckingham Palace where he occupied a house near the stables.

'Steam gives way to sail' he barked as he swung the vehicle round Hyde Park corner among a heavy welter of buses and cars, forcing some to stop or change course. I was not surprised to learn that he had previously survived a carriage capsizing with him when the horses bolted amid Oxford Street's traffic.

On horseback in the hunting field he was equally impervious to risk, often taking his own line over a stiff country, sometimes to the fury of a Master of Foxhounds.

'There he goes again!' said Fred Barker, Field Master of the Quorn, as John Miller emerged over a hedge in certain fields which Barker had not wished to take the mounted followers. If Miller did transgress on land 'forbidden' to the Hunt he would go to see the farmer that evening after hunting to apologise and explain, perhaps inviting the farmer's family to an outing at the Royal Mews.

Some thought Miller overly pompous. The Queen valued him as a knowledgeable horseman, but was rumoured to have said: 'John sometimes thinks he is more royal than we are.'

His obituary in the *Daily Telegraph* said he was 'rather less genial to those who social position was unclear to him'. I discovered John Miller had a mischievous sense of humour underneath his serious mien, and he possessed the shining virtue of genuinely liking and understanding horses of all kinds, actively working for their welfare. He became one of the friends in the horse world I valued most.

Horse & Hound was received as essential reading in the most horsey family in the land. The Queen's interest in horses began during her childhood, riding ponies at Royal Lodge in Windsor Great Park where she spent much of the war. Princesses Elizabeth and Margaret rode in the wartime show which was to become the magnificent Royal Windsor Horse Show we know today.

It was an unmissable part of my calendar at *Horse & Hound*, and I soon became friends with Geoffrey Cross, chairman of the show. Moustachioed and military of bearing, Geoffrey was a son of a Windsor forage merchant, and had done well running a stud farm in Ireland for a wealthy owner.

He had a disarming speech impediment which caused him to refer to the Queen as 'Vee monarch'. In latter life he formed a romantic partnership with Ethel Hyde-White, estranged wife of the elegantly amusing film actor Wilfrid Hyde-White; Geoffrey spent much of the year with Ethel, sitting by the pool in a Palm Springs, Florida, condominium.

The royal connections meant the show had military and ceremonial trappings far beyond most other horse events, including displays by the Household Cavalry and the King's Troop Royal Horse Artillery – plus such traditional Army contests as tent-pegging.

Geoffrey was adamant on maintaining 'vee highest standards', and one area he was particularly keen on keeping at top-level was the most lavish hospitality tent I saw at any show. Breakfast, lunch, tea and dinner were served magnificently, and when his guests returned to the tent somewhat chilled after a May evening session, there would be multiple glasses of brandy awaiting them. He was an amusing and thoughtful host.

Sir John Miller, intrepid horseman, hunting with the Quorn in his senior years.

Geoffrey latterly spent much of his day in the tent, but would hurry outside to the royal box, announcing: 'Get to the box. Vee monarch is coming!'

Cross was a joint founder of Royal Windsor Show when it began as a Wings for Victory show in 1942 during the war. The other founder was Count Robert Orssich, a former Hungarian cavalry officer, and the premier show horse producer of his day.

In the postwar years Geoffrey formed the Royal Windsor Show Society, and raised the fixture to new heights, partly through obtaining high-class sponsorships from London's West End. Its fixture in early May was inclined to be visited by remarkably cold and wet days, especially calling for arduous support in the evening sessions, but the show never lacked plenty of spectators. Geoffrey said there was no question of changing the show's date because it fitted in with the Queen's summer calendar of royal events.

From her father, King George VI, the Queen inherited a deep interest in thoroughbred breeding and racing, and as an adult she has widened her interests into breeding horses and ponies of all kinds: from polo ponies to competition horses, even to the breeding of drum horses used by the Household Cavalry. In 1984 the Queen sent *Horse & Hound* 'warm congratulations' on our centenary. When she visited the offices

Showing the royal visitor our historic back-numbers.

of IPC at King's Reach Tower, on February 16th 1978, it was taken for granted *Horse & Hound* would be her first call, and we were proud when her visit to our patch over-ran the timetable considerably. We arranged a series of photographic displays of leading horses, and the Queen studied them closely, often asking the true horseman's question: 'And who is that horse by?' Too often I had to gesture despairingly for help from my staff, and they did not know either.

When the Queen looked at a picture of Prince Philip in a spectacular driving spill, I pointed out the magazine had never published a picture of anyone falling off a horse until 1968.

'Now you seem to do nothing else but that,' the Queen laughed.

Told that the *Horse & Hound* circulation at that time had risen to a record 75,000, the Queen said: 'It's quite astonishing that so many

Royal pleasure unlimited: the Queen presents the Grand Military Gold Cup to her mother, Queen Elizabeth, after her horse Special Cargo had won the annual race then sponsored by Horse & Hound.

are interested in the sport.' She added that after the visit she would read the magazine with even greater interest.

When I took over as Editor I discovered that a special copy of *Horse & Hound* was delivered every week to Buckingham Palace on a Thursday night, prior to its public sale on Friday morning. It was collected by a horse-drawn carriage which picked up documents at various central London offices for the royal household, organised by Sir John Miller at the Royal Mews. This had not been advised to the front desk

The Queen Mother at Horse & Hound's offices, receiving flowers from Caroline Standing, later my secretary.

staff when we moved from Holborn to new offices on the South Bank at King's Reach Tower in the later 1970s.

I picked up a telephone call from the front desk one Thursday evening, to hear a rich Cockney accent enquiring: 'There's a geezer down 'ere wot's arrived in a 'orse and cart to pick up a copy of 'orse an 'ound for Buckingham Place. Is that right, or is he 'avin' us on?'

I explained hastily that it was perfectly correct.

Sadly the practice ceased soon afterwards when a Scotland Yard special branch officer called at my office to advise me they had picked up a tip that an extremist group was planning to intercept the carriage as an anti-hunting protest. To my annoyance the carriage delivery had been reported in the gossip column of Titbits, another magazine published in the group. Thereafter *Horse & Hound* went to the Palace in a car.

There was hardly an area of the magazine in which Equestrian Family Number One was not involved: the Queen's intense interest in racing and bloodstock, shared by the Queen Mother; Prince Philip's polo and carriage driving; Princess Anne's eventing and race riding; and Prince Charles's polo, hunting, race riding and team chasing. Most other members of the royal family were taught to ride when young as a matter of course, a tradition ever since kings rode with their armies into battle.

Prince Philip, having served since 1964, was succeeded in 1986 by Princess Anne as President of the International Equestrian Federation (FEI) to continue the royal involvement in equestrian politics. Zara Phillips' immense successes as European and World eventing champion have continued the royal equestrian story into the current generation of royal riders.

I was invited into the royal box to meet the Queen at the first Royal Windsor Horse Show I attended in 1973, and thereafter I met Her Majesty and some other members of the royal family frequently in the course of an equestrian year. For nearly 20 years this included having lunch with Queen Elizabeth the Queen Mother at Sandown Park before the annual running of the *Horse & Hound* Grand Military Gold Cup. I did not realise the extent of royal involvement in this venerable amateur steeplechase for military riders, founded in 1841, when we accepted an invitation to sponsor it in the 1980s.

It was quite a modest investment – prize money was only a few thousand pounds – but it proved to be a marvellous promotion for the magazine: the race was often televised because of its royal connections, and featured heavily in the racing press.

I had not anticipated that the race always took place on the first Friday in March, the day after the *Horse & Hound* Ball, which meant I had very little sleep before driving swiftly to Sandown attend the Queen Mother's reception in the royal box which started at 12 noon prompt. Frequently the Queen was present as well, and was host at the adjoining lunch table.

At lunch I was relieved to find the conversation was anything but confined to racing. It was fascinating to hear the Queen Mother talk about the first and second world wars as if they were yesterday. She was especially happy when I mentioned foxhunting in Leicestershire, recalling the 1930s when she and her late husband rented a house at Naseby in Northamptonshire where the future King George VI hunted with the Pytchley and other Leicestershire packs.

The Queen Mother retained a connection with Shires foxhunting through loaning several of her retired steeplechasers to the Quorn Hunt where they were ridden with great dash across country by huntsman

Michael Farrin. I suspect Sir John Miller was more than a little involved in arranging this, since he was a keen Quorn follower.

Public interest in the Grand Military grew rapidly when the Queen Mother's horse Special Cargo won the race three years running, 1984-5-6, ridden by Gerald Oxley. After each running the Queen Mother would exclaim to her group of racing friends in the royal box: '*Wasn't* that a good race!'

Later one season I was invited to a small party at Clarence House where we watched a film re-run of Special Cargo's triumphs, and one could not blame our royal hostess for exclaiming: '*Wasn't* that a good race!' I was told the Queen Mother's recording of the race was nearly worn out from frequent use.

My wife Marilyn and I noted with some amusement that for some of the Queen Mother's elderly friends, the afternoon at Sandown became something of an ordeal for them in which they did their best to keep up with her energy. Wearing her usual off-the-face brimmed hat, a matching coat and carrying a large handbag, she would ignore the lift and trot down flights of stairs to make her way to the paddock to see the Grand Military runners parading.

After the race she would make her way blithely down to the unsaddling enclosure to present the cup, her step quickening even more when, with a beaming smile she was the winning owner receiving the great gold trophy from her equally delighted daughter, the Queen.

As the Queen Mother entered her nineties we could see little let-up in her gusto during an afternoon's racing. Towards the end of the afternoon her royal box guests, who included such elderly racing luminaries as the sporting brewer Col. Bill Whitbread and his wife, and Lord and Lady Grimthorpe from Yorkshire, would discreetly retire to the royal box toilets where the gentlemen would hastily shave, and the ladies would endeavour to change rapidly into their evening wear.

The programme was scarcely begun: after racing the Queen Mother was whisked back by car to Royal Lodge in Windsor Great Park, with police escorts. The rest of us tackled the huge rush-hour traffic on the M25 to get from Sandown round to Royal Lodge. When we arrived we joined a lengthy queue in the garden to the front door, of Army officers and their wives, and other friends.

The indefatigable royal hostess, changed and refreshed, greeted each of us at her door, and we entered a large reception room where a cocktail party for well over 100 military people and their wives ensued for the next couple of hours at least. Some of the elderly subsided into seats at the side, and I felt like joining them, but it was necessary for most of us to keep on our feet, and keep our wits about us, for the Queen herself frequently attended this post-race party, sometimes accompanied by other royals, including Princess Margaret and occasionally Prince Charles who was at the time increasingly keen on National Hunt racing.

The Queen Mother would sit talking to her trainer Fulke Walwyn, but showed absolutely no strain to be on her feet again to say farewell individually to each of her guests. As I exited on one occasion I bent down to stroke one of the Corgi dogs at her feet, and nearly got my hand bitten off.

The Queen Mother, accompanied by her Private Secretary Sir Martin Gilliat, left, was fascinated by our racing pictures.

'Oh dear, have you upset him?' asked the Queen Mother. I muttered an apology and vowed never to go near another royal Corgi. Queen Elizabeth never failed to thank me personally for the sponsorship, soon followed by a hand-written letter of thanks; a level of politeness unmatched in any other of our sponsorships.

Often Marilyn and I would retire from the Royal Lodge party to a local hotel for some badly-needed sleep. Sometimes however, I was mad enough to drive straight from the royal party up to our cottage in Rutland because next morning I would hunt with the Belvoir on an exciting Saturday fixture in the Vale. I am deeply in debt to my wife for tolerating such sporting zeal.

Although I firmly believe our constitutional monarchy best suits Great Britain as head of state, I was not an especially intense royalist before taking over at *Horse & Hound*. I reported for the Evening Standard Prince Charles's first day at Gordonstoun School, and had written-up the Queen's presence at race-meetings, but I was never a regular royal correspondent.

I found myself increasingly admiring the way in which all the royals put something back into the horse sports they enjoyed so much, contributing hugely to everyone else's pleasure. Proximity to the royal family increased my admiration for them.

It was clear they found all things pertaining to horses an escape and relaxation from their eternal schedules of formal engagements. On a Sunday afternoon at Smith's Lawn, Windsor Great Park, I would observe the Duke of Edinburgh drive the Queen from the Royal Mews at Windsor Castle, clearly because he was enjoying it. On several occasions when *Horse & Hound* sponsored a match I was invited to join them for tea in the small royal pavilion on the polo ground. The Queen poured tea from a silver pot, and handed round cucumber sandwiches.

I began to relax more than usual in royal company until HM said brightly: 'What was wrong with that picture on the front page of *Horse & Hound* last week?'

I choked on my sandwich. In our last issue we had published a full-page colour picture of the Queen riding side-saddle at the head of the Guards after Trooping the Colour. Our printers had made a technical error in reversing the picture from left to right, and we had to stop the run to correct the picture, but some had been distributed, including the one to Buckingham Palace.

Although the picture at first glance seemed perfectly normal, the Queen's legs were on the off-side of her horse instead of the near-side, as normal in side-saddle riding.

When I explained this, and apologised profusely, the Queen smiled warmly and said: 'Well, I did wonder.....'

Not a single one of *Horse & Hound's* knowledgeable readers wrote or telephoned to point out the photographic error on our front page.

Despite my experience in John Miller's carriage driving debacle in Virginia Water I weakly agreed to referee in Royal Windsor Show's driving marathon the following year.

This time I was seated next to a grimly silent German driver who occasionally flicked me in the face with his whip. He seemed extremely efficient, and I was not at all worried when his team broke into a canter as it approached a small stream on the course. The carriage leapt off the bank into the water, bounced in the air and turned over on my side. I was completely immersed, losing my clipboard and stopwatch yet again, but surviving with only a few bruises.

'What happened, love?' asked Cynthia Haydon, England's greatest lady whip, when she officially invigilated the bedraggled Editor afterwards. After I explained the upset, and apologised for the loss of the equipment, Cynthia beamed: 'Don't you worry. He must have been a silly booger!'

Mainly because I did not want to lose a season's foxhunting through an injury caused by falling off a horse and cart, I ceased refereeing after the second crash, but my respect soared for those who excelled at top-class carriage driving, including Prince Philip. He had helped frame the rules for the sport, and took it up in 1971, using horses from the Royal Mews which he trained at Sandringham.

The drivers were genuine sportsmen from a wide range of jobs and businesses, many of them very down-to-earth, and I noted that Philip was genuinely popular among them. Like the Queen he has amazing physical endurance: in his nineties, as well as standing for hours at royal functions, he is still driving teams of ponies around Windsor Great Park.

As well as enjoying the driving, like his uncle Lord Mountbatten he exhibited an obsession with the minutest detail of his sport. In the driving world you need to be aware of an endless amount of harness and carriage design detail. Prince Philip translated his considerable knowledge of Competition Carriage Driving into a book of that title, published in 1982.

I cherished a moment when he was explaining something technical about a harness item called a swingle-bar to a rapt equestrian audience at Buckingham Palace Royal Mews. 'Any questions?' said the Prince. A voice from the back asked a question about an impending royal marriage. A Fleet Street tabloid reporter had enterprisingly gatecrashed the occasion to put the query.

'Who was that?' demanded a furious Duke of Edinburgh.

'This is not that sort of press conference. Get that man out of here immediately!'

Another royal author, similarly keen on technical details, suddenly appeared in my office unexpectedly one morning in 1976. The front desk asked if I could take a visit from Lord Mountbatten. And there he was in my office, the illustrious Naval person I had first observed as a child attending the annual horse show at his home at Romsey in Hampshire where my mother's family had lived.

I had followed his life ever-after with great interest, and was to be much saddened and angered by his assassination by the IRA in 1979.

Mountbatten took a seat, and thrust across the desk a copy of his classic book *An Introduction to Polo* by Marco. He had first published it in 1931, he explained. Now he thought it was necessary to re-publish the book in its sixth edition. Standards needed to be brushed-up among younger players, and he believed his book could play its part.

Would *Horse & Hound* be interested in reviewing the new edition, and publishing an excerpt? Would I not? Mountbatten, after a lifetime in the public eye, had a good grip on the timing and format needed to promote his book to best advantage, confirming his reputation as an arch-fixer.

He made brisk arrangements and departed. I would much like to have chatted to him about world affairs and history but by coincidence I sat next to him soon afterwards at an equestrian veterinary dinner where we were both to speak.

'I'm going to be a bit controversial,' said Mountbatten with a grin.

He did cause a certain *frisson* by spending much of his speech extolling the benefit of certain herbal remedies for horse ailments, and Faradism, electric pulses to cure bad backs, warning against too much use by vets of chemicals and surgery.

The vets were not enthusiastic about herbal cures for horses, but the Earl was a hard act to follow and my after after-dinner speech fell more than a little flat.

Prince Charles wrote the foreword for Mountbatten's book, having been given a copy to study 15 years earlier when he was learning to become a high-goal polo player.

His early years had not been marked by natural riding ability to the level shown by Princess Anne in her teens. Charles admitted he had 'rather got put off' jumping through riding an ill-behaved pony that stood on its hind legs. He did not enter the hunting field until the age of 27, on 28th February 1975 – and the news was broken by *Horse & Hound* in an exclusive report, written by Foxhunter Number One, 'Master' the 10th Duke of Beaufort. 'Master' phoned me in a state of some excitement, to tell me that the Prince of Wales had ridden with the Beaufort hounds, and they had enjoyed a tremendous day.

It was a special fixture because the ground had been very wet, and the Duke had stopped hunting temporarily; he was not planning to resume until March. Only a field of 30 were out, and Charles hunted in 'ratcatcher' dress, a tweed coat with bowler hat, brown breeches and polo boots.

Master's own report told of an exceptional day's sport, culminating in a run with a five-mile point which ended with hounds marking their fox to ground in a cave near Sherston. Charles rode Pinkers, a reliable cob loaned by Princess Anne's in-laws at the time, the Phillips family. He thoroughly enjoyed himself, and was thereafter one of the keenest of foxhunters. I published the report in full, and it was later picked up by Fleet Street, although the Prince's new enthusiasm was not given much weight at first – until the anti-hunting lobby began to issue protests.

Charles began to appear in the hunting field at a variety of Hunts without prior warning to the mounted field, now wearing a velvet cap, not a top hat, with a specially created blue 'Windsor Coat' with a scarlet collar and cuffs, and silver buttons bearing the Prince of Wales crest. To avoid attracting attention to his presence, the Prince did not attend the meet, but joined in soon after hounds moved off.

He launched on a tour of hunting countries throughout Britain, usually accompanied, and much encouraged, by Sir John Miller. My own hunting was now based in the Quorn country, where we became well used to visits by Charles, now rapidly improving as a rider across natural country, although taking a full share of spills as well as thrills.

As a hunting correspondent I became used to seeing the Prince visiting Hunts far beyond Leicestershire. He spoke at hunting dinners, and attended Peterborough Royal Foxhound Show.

The Prince of Wales, wearing his specially designed hunt coat, and modern headgear, hunting on his strawberry roan mare Reflection.

I recall him raising plenty of laughs at an MFHA centenary dinner when he remarked that he did not recognise many of the lady foxhunters at the dinner 'because they are wearing a lot less make-up than they do in the hunting field'.

I took good care not give any clues in *Horse & Hound* about forthcoming royal hunting visits, and published pictures well afterwards. It was noted with pleasure in hunting circles that the Prince's foxhunting was soon accepted as a matter of fact in the media, and was not used inordinately as part of the hunting controversy which in the 1970s and 1980s was still a long way from the levels of parliamentary interest which occurred at the turn of the century and led to anti-hunting legislation.

Charles was prepared to speak out in defence of the sport, citing the conservationist values of maintaining coverts, woodlands and hedges. He made a point of insisting on hunting being carried out according to the Master of Foxhounds Association's code of conduct, and he befriended professional hunt staff, inviting many to visit his home at Highgrove in Gloucestershire. Some, including Michael Farrin of the Quorn and Jim Webster of the Belvoir, were invited to Charles's wedding to Diana.

As well as meeting him in the hunting field, I often saw the Prince at informal hunt teas in farmhouses and cottages. He said he met more 'ordinary blokes' in the hunting field than anywhere else in the countryside. Finding horses that suited him was something of a problem at first. Prince Philip's description of a horse as 'the great leveller' proved all too true at times.

In Leicestershire we revelled in the story that Charles one day mentioned with disappointment to a well-known Yorkshire dealer, Trevor Banks, that a horse he had bought was not jumping well out hunting.

With a straight face, Banks replied: 'I'm afraid my horses don't jump very well until money's in the bank, sir.'

'Oh dear,' said Charles. 'Haven't we paid for it John? [Miller]. You'd better do something about this quickly.'

I was close by during a hectic Saturday afternoon with the Belvoir in their Vale country when members of the mounted field surged forward to jump a narrow set of rails. Charles tried several times to take his place to jump, but each time he was baulked by a queue-jumper.

Hounds were running on far ahead, and the Prince was missing the hunt. He trotted to the back of the queue once again and said with a rueful smile: 'Ah well. I can't do anything about it. I just wasn't brought up to barge.'

When Mrs Rosemary Partridge subsided to the ground during a day with the Quorn, Charles considerately dismounted, and said:

'Oh dear, Rosemary. Is there anything we can do?'

'Yes,' said Rosemary. 'Kiss me.'

Prince Charles's foxhunting years helped him to explore British country life at all levels. He visited many small packs in remote areas as well as riding in the more fashionable Shires. He knew what it was to be shouted at by a farmer who did not want anyone on his land, not even the Prince of Wales. He knew the disappointments of a poor day's sport when scent was non-existent, and the thrills of a brilliant day when hounds ran hard. The Prince was anxious not to attract still more attention to foxhunting as a controversial sport, and regretted that it was not helpful for the Quorn to be constantly referred to by Fleet Street as 'Prince Charles's favourite Hunt'.

Charles became even better known to the readers of *Horse & Hound* when he took up the hazardous sport of Team 'Chasing, joining 'The Ratcatchers' team formed by the top-class show rider and hunting man David Tatlow, based near Stow-in-the-Wold. Tatlow helped the Prince to improve his riding still further, and Charles was in the Ratcatchers' team when they achieved notable victories.

Although the royal involvement was helpful overall for horse sports, the involvement of Prince Charles and Princess Anne became accepted as the norm.

John Oaksey, our great racing correspondent, noted with satisfaction that the 'highly infectious bug of riding over fences at speed has bitten Prince Charles good and proper'.

This followed Charles's brief attempts to become an amateur race rider, which no doubt earned him further spills and thrills, but were ultimately clouded by misfortunes which he bore with fortitude. His own chaser Allibar tragically collapsed and died after being ridden at exercise, and his hasty replacement mount Good Prospect gave him much publicised falls in the *Horse & Hound* Grand Military Race at Sandown in 1981, and again at Cheltenham the following week.

Many who met Prince Charles through the hunting and equestrian world, appreciated his sense of humour, his courage and his honest attempts to make the best of his sport for himself and others.

I was among those who felt considerable sympathy when he experienced so much negative and one-sided press reporting and comment during and after his marriage break-up with Princess Diana.

The qualities he showed so strongly as a horseman and hunting man, surely played a great part in helping him to make such a success of so many of his charitable activities, to create a successful second marriage, and to play his public role effectively as our future King.

The horse's special value to a future monarch was perhaps best summed up by the Elizabethan dramatist Ben Jonson:

> *Princes learn no art truly, but the art of horsemanship,*
> *The reason is the brave beast is no flatterer.*
> *He will throw a Prince as soon as his groom.*

CHAPTER EIGHTEEN

THE BATTLE

After taking over the editorship of *Horse & Hound* it seemed to me I had little choice when required, but to use my own broadcasting and writing experience to aid the battle to defend hunting with hounds from banning legislation. It was of course entirely in line with the magazine's policy, but joining the battle on the wider front became inevitable for me.

My pro-hunting broadcasts earned me a sporadic supply of abusive mail from the more extreme anti-hunters, sometimes threatening or desiring my early demise. When I visited the Lake District as part of a BBC Radio 4 'Any Questions' team, there was a question on hunting.

My reply was cheered to the echo by the Lakeland hunting people who were well represented in the audience. During my regular appearances on 'Any Questions' in the 1970s there was a notable difference when the hunting subject came up during a programme in an urban setting, but prejudice against hunting was generally far from strong in those days.

After a slowish start, the hunting world's defence in maintaining sport in the face of saboteur action, where it occurred, began to improve remarkably. There were plenty of ex-military men, and ladies, among hunt followers, and they often displayed a useful skill in tactical defence.

The most effective tactic I saw was employed by huntsmen who simply picked up their hounds and took them far away into country difficult to reach from the roads. This was not always possible, but it was preferable to avoid a situation where huntsmen and their staff engaged in any sort of argument with the sabs.

Some Masters who hunted hounds as amateurs were the saboteurs' favourite targets. They liked nothing more than obtaining a highly irate Master in a red coat swinging his whip to keep the sabs away from his hounds. We learned to dismount, and take off our headgear, when interviewed by television reporters at meets. Image remained a potent factor in the hunting war.

The British Field Sports Society, formed in 1930, remained the hub of hunting's defence until 1998 when the Countryside Alliance was born. Ronnie Wallace made sure he was the BFSS vice-chairman as well as his major role as chairman of the Masters of Foxhounds Association.

He recruited me onto his 'public affairs' committee at the BFSS. It comprised a membership of people with media and political experience, including John McCrirrick, the TV racing pundit, and Charles Goodson-Wickes MP who was to become BFSS Chairman. McCrirrick was a useful contributor to policies designed to give hunting with hounds a better voice in showing the public that it was not an indefensibly cruel activity, but actually an effective form of wild-animal conservation.

From my twenties when I began to hunt more intensively, I had looked harder at the ethical and practical issues involved in hunting. I found ample evidence that totally justified the continuation of the sport in the interest of the quarry species – and the environment in which hunting took place. Hunting foxes with hounds is infinitely more humane than all other methods widely used in Britain, and foxhunting with hounds bestows major conservationist benefits for the fox and its environment.

Planting coverts for hunting was a major benefit to wildlife of all kinds. Much of our rural landscape owes its diversity and beauty to hunt coverts planted for many generations. When a fox is hunted by hounds it is killed immediately it is caught, or it escapes unscathed. There is no convincing evidence that the experience of being hunted causes permanent harm.

Before the Hunting Act 2004, the fox, the deer and the hare were culled by the Hunts as a conserved quarry. The packs operated under rules of conduct imposed by the hunting organisations, such as the MFHA and the Association of Masters of Harriers and Beagles. They all observed close seasons when hunting stopped while the quarry species were breeding. The intent was to control local populations of foxes, deer and hares to meet the wishes of the farming community, but certainly not to eliminate them.

I soon learned the extent of the alternative means of 'control' of these species in our countryside. It is possible virtually to eliminate foxes in a quite wide areas, by a draconian use of snaring, trapping, poisoning, and the use of guns in night-time 'lamping' exercises, whereby the fox is lured towards a light by simulated sounds of a fox-cub in distress.

This is especially effective in the breeding season, all too often resulting in a vixen killed above ground, leaving her litter of cubs to starve to death in an earth. Worst of all is the night-time baiting of foxes with terriers after they have been dug-out; an exercise only exceeded in cruelty by the rightly illegal activity of badger-baiting.

If you liked to see foxes in our countryside, then a properly-run foxhunting country was the place to see them before the Hunting Act 2004 became law in February 2005. Since the iniquitous Act, foxes are much harder to find in too many rural areas, and shooting has become far more intensive.

Anti-hunting bodies mistakenly advocated shooting as the 'humane' answer to fox control. There is ample evidence that foxes are extremely hard to kill with a gun with the first shot; the wounding rate has been set at about 40 percent, which can hardly be claimed as humane. The same is true of attempts to shoot hares and deer. After large-scale hare shoots there are more than a few hares left lying wounded to be picked up and dispatched later.

I became called on all too frequently by the BBC and other broadcasters to defend hunting in an increasing welter of debates on TV and radio. Some were stimulating and fun; some were a wearisome chore because the anti-hunting speaker often relied only on emotion instead of discussing the case for wild animal welfare.

I much enjoyed debating hunting on Radio 4 with the great Methodist preacher Donald Soper who I had listened to at Hyde Park Corner with great admiration in my youth. He thought hunting was a 'sin', but agreed amicably there was no discernible support for this in the Bible, and he admitted that many clergy had hunted.

Soper discussed the hunting issue in a measured intellectual manner which must have disappointed the producers who wanted plenty of heat as well as light. I felt privileged to have broadcast with him, and wished there were more opportunities to speak on the hunting issue on an ethical basis, rather than it becoming a 'yes you did, no I didn't' argument.

Regular opponents in media debates were the current directors of the League Against Cruel Sports. I must admit I quite enjoyed jousting with Richard Course, the most successful of the Directors of the LACS. He was a sort of 'cheeky chappie', exhibiting something of a sense of humour during a broadcast debate, and I grew to know his main ploys of argument very well. He would talk amiably after a broadcast, in contrast to some who slunk away silently.

Course's most effective feat was to persuade the Co-operative Wholesale Society to ban hunting on 50,000 acres of prime farmland which it owned throughout England. This resulted immediately in a few Hunts losing much-valued hunting territory, including the Fernie in Leicestershire and the VWH in Wiltshire.

The BFSS ran a protest meeting in Brighton to coincide with the Co-op Party's annual conference. The Co-op refused to receive a delegation from us, although one of their senior figures, a Mr Mani, appeared briefly at our meeting. He said he had never seen hunting, but it was against his beliefs to take life.

Mr Mani smiled politely, gave a little bow, and walked out before we could contest his view. Afterwards Ronnie Wallace and I sat on Brighton beach with our feet cooling in the water. We reflected wryly there were tougher times on the way, and our side needed to raise its game.

Richard Course's other line of attack was to encourage left leaning county councils to ban hunting on thousands of acres they owned. Their problem was that virtually all the tenant farmers on county council-owned land would not implement such a ban The staunch support of most farmers has been hunting's greatest asset against all attempts to banning the presence of hounds in our countryside before and after the Hunting Act.

The League's biggest victory would have been a proposed ban on 8,000 acres of council owned land in the cream of the Shires in Leicestershire where the Quorn would have been sorely afflicted. Brian Fanshawe had only recently come to Leicestershire to become Joint Master and huntsman of the Cottesmore, a role he filled with skill and enthusiasm.

He showed the same level of leadership in chairing a vigorous campaign against the Leicestershire County Council ban mooted by Labour councillors. I was among the small group organising the response on behalf of the Hunts.

After intensive lobbying of the County Councillors, we paraded every local pack of Foxhounds and beagles in a demonstration outside Leicestershire County Hall while councillors debated the subject. The hunting demonstrators bearing placards ranged from eminent Masters of Foxhounds to housewives and children; it gained huge national and local publicity.

No party had overall control of Leicestershire County Council, and although the attempt to ban hunting was defeated, we noted grimly it was only by one vote. Later in the 1990s the BFSS achieved a High Court judicial review which found that a hunting ban imposed by a local authority could not be legitimate whilst the sport was sanctioned in law. But Richard Course's local government campaign had earned the anti cause a great deal of time and space in the media.

It was all the more ironic that after Course retired from the LACS he contributed an article to *Horse & Hound* recanting his view that hunting with hounds should be abolished, admitting that the prosecution of the anti-hunt case would not advance fox welfare and could not be justified.

A later LACS chief executive, James Barrington, has taken a similar stance after leaving his post, and is director of the Middle Way Group which promotes a solution whereby hunting would be allowed in future under government licence. He is one of the most effective voices in support of hunting with hounds.

Millions of pounds of ratepayers' money in a number of councils was wasted on a fruitless exercise, but this was to be dwarfed by the taxpayers' cash about to be expended by Labour governments in Westminster on the hunting issue.

Hunting much improved its defence tactics. We made films explaining the conservation values of hunting; we taught Masters and others how to be interviewed; we appointed Hunt monitors to watch out for saboteur activity, and there were under-cover activities to learn more of the anti-hunters' plans for action. I found myself helping to script, and provide the voice for an excellent pro-hunting film produced by John Hawksworth who lived and hunted in the Cottesmore country.

He had excellent credentials in the media: he had produced and scripted many episodes of the hit series 'Upstairs Downstairs', and other popular TV programmes. We chose the Fernie as the Hunt who would gallop, jump, and show their hounds on TV, with excellent interviews coming from huntsman Bruce Durno, and a raft of local characters.

The film was shown on national TV in the BBC's 'Open Door' series for minorities to express their views, but it was only sanctioned after the anti-hunting brigade had been given the same time on air.

It was clear to us that a Labour victory in a General Election would vastly increase the pressure on hunting, and at last we were beginning to plan for the future more effectively.

The most left-wing element on Labour's backbench was using proposed anti-hunting legislation as a ridiculous revenge on the 'Tory toffs' in return for Mrs Thatcher's closure of coalmines, a surrealistic example of how foxhunting has been distorted as a class political emblem. 'Remember the miners!' shouted Labour's backbench when hunting was debated.

I ran several articles in *Horse & Hound* on the need for hunting to spend still more time and money on improving its image, and its public face. This was not well received by some in the upper ranks: Sir Stephen Hastings MP, the current BFSS chairman, phoned me to deliver an angry rocket for 'rocking the boat'.

I protested mildly that pro-Tory newspapers frequently gave constructive advice to the Conservative party on future strategy, and that's what we were doing with the BFSS. Hastings, a keen Leicestershire hunting man, cooled down quickly, and we continued to work together amicably. The truth was that one of the biggest successes of antis was the continuing drain on pro-hunting financial resources, causing continuous

On 19th February 2005 we held a march of over 700 mounted hunting people in Melton Mowbray, protesting against Labour's Hunting Act.

fund-raising. In *Horse & Hound* we supported fighting funds for hunting, and donated from the proceeds of the *Horse & Hound* Ball.

Sure enough Labour's landslide victory on May 1st 1997 precipitated the Foster Private Members' Bill later that year, seeking to ban hunting with hounds. With the aid of a fierce body of anti-hunting opinion on Labour's backbenchers – banning hunting was a lifelong tilt at the 'toffs' for some of them – the Bill was carried with a 260 majority.

After retiring from the *Horse & Hound* editorship I took an active role as Leicestershire Chairman of the Countryside Alliance, and later as Chairman of the Midlands Region. We organised trips for huge parties of Midlands hunting people to attend the great pro-hunting rally and marches in London and elsewhere.

We held a mass protest of the Shires Hunts near Melton Mowbray, in which an effigy of Tony Blair was burnt, an exercise born

of frustration. Over 700 mounted hunting people took part in a protest ride we organised through Melton Mowbray, historic 'capital' of foxhunting, ending in rousing speeches in the Market Place, led by our MP Alan Duncan.

Despite much difficulty in gaining permission from the police, Geoff Brooks, the staunch pro-hunting farmer who had cared for my horses, organised a protest ride supported by over 1,000 hunting people on horses and

My friend Geoff Brooks who organised the Melton Mowbray protest, and another in Leicester.

ponies through part of Leicester, but not the centre of the city owing to police objections. It was described as the largest equine incursion into Leicester since the Battle of Naseby in 1654.

That evening we saw BBC TV assiduously 'balance' their report by giving equal time to just a handful of anti-hunting spokesmen present, using the usual emotive terms of 'barbarism' rather than a reasoned case. Every time we captured the attention of the media with a major effort we simply provided an easy platform for our opponents. All our protests were to no avail because a party political game was in full swing in Westminster, with hunting as the football.

By now Blair's New Labour was piling on the pressure on hunting as a class symbol to be eradicated, ludicrously giving the subject so much government time that it was estimated over 120 hours of debate was expended in the Commons before the Hunting Act was achieved on 18th November, far exceeding the time given to debating the Gulf War. Overall some 1100 hours of parliamentary time had been devoted to the subject in recent years in private members bills and committee hearings.

Wholly inappropriate use of the Parliament Act finally over-ruled the objection of the House of Lords to the enactment of one of the silliest pieces of legislation ever to emerge from our Mother of Parliaments.

Its anomalies include legality under the Act to kill a rat or a rabbit with a dog, but not to hunt or kill with hounds a hare or a fox. Foxes can be flushed from covert by a couple of hounds to be shot, but only if the landowner wishes it to protect reared game, such as pheasants, rather than farm stock!

Having given many hundreds of hours of my time, over so many years, to the drawn-out battle to save hunting with hounds from such legislation, I felt drained, and saddened by the passing of the Hunting Act. I saw country people in tears at the last meets held in Leicestershire before the Act was enacted the following February. Jubilant interviews with some anti-hunters revealed only too clearly that their main ambition was to 'hunt the hunters'; we were indeed a divided society when it came to rural issues.

Hunting with hounds is a very difficult subject to defend in debate; it is so far removed from the life-style of the majority of modern urban Britons, that they have no conception of the case that foxes are better conserved through use of a pack of hounds, than the spurious case that shooting is a quick, and almost painless death, as seen in a fictional shoot-out on TV every night. We had failed to make this case to the House of Commons and most of the public, most of whom cared very little about the issue anyway.

The BFSS ran a superb rally in Hyde Park, and later the Countryside Alliance did a magnificent job in organising the two major

Countryside Marches through central London. Every effort was made to present country people as polite, law-abiding citizens, praised for picking up their litter after their London protests, and for not engaging in street punch-ups.

I was present when this facade cracked once, on Wednesday September 15th 2004 when the Commons debated the second reading of Labour's Hunting Act. Inside Parliament Otis Ferry, newly appointed Joint Master of the South Shropshire, and seven other young hunting men, created parliamentary history by invading the floor of the Commons to interrupt the debate, and cause a short suspension of the sitting.

I was among the 20,000 or so pro-hunting people packing Parliament Square outside the Commons. The normally 'polite' country people were actually beginning to protest in an aggressive way, despite the pleas of Countryside Alliance stewards who had vainly tried to steer a protest march away from Parliament. I still have doubts that they were right to do so.

Scuffles developed between police and protestors by barriers set up in front of the House of Commons. Police batons were used immediately, and I saw several young men on the ground with blood streaming from their heads. Ambulances were rushed to the scene; there were to be some unpleasant pictures of the clash in next morning's papers, and claims that the police had over-reacted.

It was clear from the words of Labour's Rural Affairs Minister Alun Michael, who had the dire task of shepherding the Hunting Act through Parliament, that the government feared far more strife on the streets than ever occurred. Vainly Mr Michael tried to delay the implementation of the ban for two more years to give Hunts time to wind down, and ensure 're-homing' of their hounds.

In fact, there were no more protests of any size in central London between the Second Reading Debate on September 15th, and the final passing of the Act on November 18th. There were pro-hunting protestors outside Parliament that day — but it was too late.

A Labour non-hunting friend of mine in politics said afterwards: 'Where were you all after the second reading? The hunters went right off-radar. There was to be no long-running country versus town war.

Vainly attempting a humorous protest against a hunting ban: girls with a banner saying "hunting is better than sex" in the Countryside Alliance's Liberty and Livelihood march through London on September 22, 2002.

This helped Tony Blair allow his backbenchers to have their wish for a hunting ban to be implemented straightaway – taking place only three months after the passing of the Act.'

And so it was. The hunting community is essentially law abiding and probably incapable of mounting the sort of violent anarchy that the anti-Poll Tax riots created in central London, thereby achieving their aim.

Perhaps I was wrong in believing that the Hunting Act was not inevitable, but I still have grave doubts over the decision not to accept a Middle Way solution for hunting in 1998, and again in 2002, whereby the government offered Hunts a future under licence run by an independent authority. It would have been much better than the current situation under the Hunting Act.

245

However, ten years on from 2005 when the Bill was enacted, I would never have believed that, despite the iniquitous legislation, all the Hunts in Great Britain have survived, and are still active. Only hare coursing ceased as an official sport.

It is a testament to the strength of rural communities that this is still the case. Most landowners and farmers continue to allow hounds onto their land to do whatever they can within the terms of the Act. Hunting with hounds is manifestly not the same, and there must be considerable doubt that it will ever return to the traditional, unfettered sport of the past.

Sadly, since 2004 the status of the fox has fallen in our countryside from favoured quarry to be culled and conserved, to vermin which must be utterly destroyed, especially in areas where new shoots demand their gamekeepers protect reared game from the slightest threat of predation by foxes.

Snaring and indiscriminate shooting of foxes is rife in many areas of the countryside, neither offering a more humane option than hunting with hounds whereby the fox was either killed outright or escaped completely unscathed. I have seen too many foxes wounded by shooting, or maimed through losing legs in snares, freeing themselves after hours of agony. Self-regulated hunting for foxes for sport was far less intense, with greater welfare benefits in the control of fox numbers according to the needs of local agriculture.

There are increasing rural 'black holes' in the countryside where hardly a fox is to be seen, although fox populations inside London and other main urban areas have soared. Many urban foxes live by dustbin scavenging; they suffer from mange and injuries received from vehicles on busy roads. Is this an ideal 'solution' to fox conservation?

After a life-time of hunting before the Hunting Act, and many years devoted to its political defence, there are grounds for being deeply depressed by the present situation which is far from static: the political battle over hunting is by no means over, and bands of saboteurs still raid some Hunts, claiming they are breaking the terms of the Act.

Anti-hunting MPs in the Commons want to amend the Act to make it impossible even to take a pack of hounds out into the countryside.

It is unlikely the status quo will last forever under a change of government. Jeremy Corbyn's brand of far Left Labour politics would seek to make the Hunting Act even more restrictive.

Currently 186 packs of Foxhounds are recognised by the MFHA; it is estimated that 45,000 people are Hunt members; the breeds of hunting hounds have survived; hound shows are flourishing; youth is still keen to follow hounds, on horse or on foot. I enjoy seeing them enjoy themselves when I follow the Leicestershire packs by car. It renews my faith in the resilience and optimism of most British people.

All is not lost: there is still plenty of reason to hope our countryside will be hearing the hunting horn for many years to come, certainly well beyond my lifetime.

I wish those who follow hounds today the traditional benison: 'Good Hunting!'

Breaking in Josephine's son, Henry: I am about to lunge him with Georgina on board soon after we backed him. He went on to be an advanced eventer.

Foxford carrying me brilliantly around the formidable Hickstead Ride course – before he fell!

CHAPTER NINETEEN

MY HORSES

Now in my eighties, and having been forced to leave the saddle by ill-health, I dream of horses frequently. I awake in the morning still haunted by memories of galloping effortlessly across old turf, of steadying my horse coming into a fence with a forbidding ditch in front, of soaring over, landing perfectly, then galloping on to more bliss on horseback. Sometimes I dream of falling off, but then I wake up unharmed.

Late in my riding life I attempted to breed the hunters I rode. It proved not to be a cost-saving exercise, and often I was reminded of the adage 'fools breed horses for wise men to buy'.

Yet there were many rewards, and moments of sheer joy, when a young home-bred horse proved he really could do the job for which I had bred him: following hounds across country with courage and skill.

Long before I edited *Horse & Hound* I stumbled into magazine writing and equestrian and hunting authorship, largely through necessity. In the early 1960s I needed extra income to pay for my addiction: foxhunting. Hunt subscriptions then seem tiny compared with today's, but measured against a young journalist's income they were a burden.

I had to ask the Old Surrey and Burstow Hunt Secretaries if they would allow me to pay the annual sub of £30 in two halves, and they kindly agreed. It was costing me up to £10 per week to keep my blue roan Irish hunter Ballyn Garry at livery.

Limerick horse dealer Michael Moran showing me Josephine, the wonderful hunter mare I bought in 1979.

If I had to pick one horse who has served me the best, it would be my Irish mare Josephine, a great mount in the hunting field, and a wonderful brood mare later, producing some excellent hunters.

At the hospitable table of Lord (Toby) Daresbury at Askeaton, Co. Limerick in August 1979, I mentioned I was looking for another horse, and someone suggested I call on Michael Moran who had several for sale at his farm nearby.

The buying process was extremely casual. Hatless and wearing a grey flannel suit I walked with Michael into a large field bordered with stone walls and patches of hedge, where about 30 horses grazed. He saddled up a five-year-old chestnut gelding which he said had hunted all last season.

After saddling up the chestnut, Michael handed me a piece of stick he had just pulled from a bush, and invited me to 'have a little ride'. There was to be no dealer's show by a smart lad in the saddle showing me the horse's paces. Michael gestured to the stone wall, and invited: 'Have a pop over that...'

It seemed a tall order for a horse out at grass, but I faced up to the wall, and the horse cleared it adequately, taking a strong hold.

Only because it seemed too easy to buy the first horse I had ridden, I asked him if he had anything else.

'There's a mare over there, might suit,' he said eventually. Saddle and bridle were transferred to a bright bay mare with a black mane and tail, a small white star on her forehead, a snip of white on her muzzle, and two white socks. She was a bonny mare, aged six. Michael said she had been out 'now and again' with the local Stonewall Harriers.

Although much the same height, 16.2½ hands, the mare seemed far more substantial. She had a splendid shoulder and neck, well sprung ribs and strong quarters. I felt instantly at home and relatively safe on her back.

Unlike the gelding, the mare did not pull hard going towards a jump. I realised with a pang I had not chosen the same place where I had jumped the other horse: there was an awkward undulation, almost a scoop in front, and heaven knew what lay beyond. She measured the wall carefully, then jumped it economically and cleanly, and jumped back into the field just as carefully.

When Mr Moran revealed in his farmhouse kitchen that he wanted 'thirteen hundred pounds for the gelding, and eleven hundred and fifty for the mare,' that clinched it; my fragile economics backed my sentiment. Her name was Josephine, said Michael, and she was worth the money as a brood mare alone.

We did not haggle. It was less than I could expect to pay for such a horse in England at that time. When I returned to Buckinghamshire, the lady who looked after my horses said: 'A mare? I thought you had more sense than that.'

Josephine carried me superbly with all the Shire packs, and up to a dozen other widely different countries. She proved adept at finding that 'fifth leg' at moments of peril. The mare showed no sign of mare-ish temperament when in season, and I recall her stopping only once in the hunting field: she saw her reflection in a water-filled ditch just in front of a Belvoir fence, and halted with her head down staring into the water, whereupon I hurtled over her head to be completely immersed.

I was attending a Quorn dance when the news broke that Josephine had given birth to a splendid colt foal. I wrote regularly about my attempt to breed from Josephine in *Horse & Hound*, by Geoff Brooks's stallion Flint Hill, and selected the name Foxhill Joseph from a host of suggestions submitted by the readers.

My first harsh lesson about breeding occurred when the foal was a yearling : suddenly it was losing weight and did not appear to move properly behind. A veterinary diagnosis was that we had bred a foal with the 'wobbler' syndrome, synsataxia, incoordination of movement through the spine.

There was much sympathy from the readers when I had the foal put down. Fortunately we had put the mare in foal again, this time to Geoff Brooks's stallion John O'Gaunt, a 16.3 hands dark bay horse by the TB stallion Hoarwithy out of an Irish Draught mare. John O'Gaunt was a successful showjumper as well as a hunter, and had a scopey, accurate jump.

This time Josephine produced a handsome bright bay colt, with three white socks and a white star and I named him Jonjo after the great steeplechase jockey Jonjo O'Neill, nowadays a leading trainer.

Altogether Josephine produced nine foals, losing her last one when she was aged 23, but then acting as foster mother to an orphaned thoroughbred foal through the National Foaling Bank scheme.

Josephine died aged 26 at the International League for the Protection of Horses sanctuary at Snetterton in Norfolk to which I made donations, and raised money. She lived a long and well-fulfilled life, and privately I shed tears when I heard she had passed away peacefully in her paddock. I had so many happy memories of Josephine and her varied offspring.

Josephine's first foal, Jonjo was one of the naughtiest young horses I ever encountered, always inquisitive and ready for a lark. I think I made a mistake in leaving him with his increasingly disenchanted mother far too long.

Since I was writing about Jonjo's progress I somewhat rashly decided to have Jonjo broken-in by the new wizard of the equestrian

Josephine carrying me safely over a hunter trial course.

scene, Monty Roberts, the American trainer who uses an extraordinary technique to accustom a young horse to the saddle, and to be mounted, in just one session, compared with the traditional breaking-in process which may take longer and sometimes relies on a lot of breaking-tackle being strapped onto the horse. Monty calls his technique 'starting' a horse, and always says that a great deal of schooling is still necessary later.

Having arranged Monty's first UK tour, I included the three-year-old Jonjo in the young horses to be 'started' during his exhibition at the National Equestrian Centre, at Stoneleigh. All went to plan: Jonjo duly responded to Monty's remarkable system of 'advance and retreat' communication, soon accepting a saddle and bridle for the first time, then standing without demur as Monty's assistant mounted him. We were all amazed and impressed when Monty achieved this with a string of different unbroken young horses inside a high wired round enclosure.

Marilyn and I took Jonjo home to Leicestershire, and with some trepidation followed the trainer's advice to ride him again the following day.

He still accepted the saddle and bridle, and stood meekly while Marilyn bravely mounted him while I hung on to the bridle, and led him round at a walk. I still feel qualms about my rashness in allowing my cherished young wife to take such a risk, but Marilyn has never been short of courage, and at the time it seemed safer for the heavier, stronger person to remain holding Jonjo's head.

The first of Josephine's nine foals.

Next day I mounted him, riding him to follow Marilyn giving a lead on another horse. Jonjo stopped at a bridge where he could hear water rushing underneath, and took a lot of persuading to cross it. Apart from that he gave no trouble. It was extraordinary; it all seemed to good to be true – and it was.

No blame to Monty Roberts, but I suspect that I did not devote quite enough time thereafter to the normal schooling process of a young horse, long reining, lunging and groundwork under saddle. Whatever the reason, and much of it was Jonjo's high level of intelligence which questioned everything, he proved to be a remarkably difficult ride in the hunting field when I began to take him out with hounds as a four and five-year-old. Although he would happily jump obstacles at home, in the hunting field he would refuse without warning a perfectly routine fence. He shied at imaginary obstacles, and exhibited a talent for bucking and rearing when least convenient.

I sent him to be schooled over fences with Stuart Campbell, one of the best trainers of young horses in the Shires, who reported back: 'He's going better now, but I reckon he's bone-headed. He just doesn't get it. It may be a long time before he does.'

Soon after that I was riding Jonjo with the Quorn from their opening Kirby Gate meet when hounds ran from their famous hill-top covert Gartree Hill. They surged away along the ridge from the covert towards Thorpe Satchville. Jonjo gave an extra strong pull, and cantered with ears pricked towards the first of an inviting line of cut-and-laid fences. He leapt it with purpose, landed neatly, and then treated every fence we encountered with equal confidence. I was absolutely elated, and sent warmest thanks to Stuart Campbell because his schooling had clicked in Jonjo's mind after all. As Monty Roberts preaches, training horses successfully is far more to do with encouraging cooperation than attempting to achieve it by brute force.

It would be good to recount that Jonjo thereafter was a totally reliable hunter. He was never quite that: although he was an exciting, bold ride, but he was somewhat unlucky in acquiring small injuries. He developed an ability to cast shoes, and to brush his hind fetlocks. He could be unpredictable, once during routine road exercise leaping a fence at the side of a lane, and carrying a girl groom far into the fields beyond.

After four seasons he contracted sarcoids, wart-like skin tumours on his neck. They responded to treatment, but took some time, and by now I had other young horses entering the hunting field. Marilyn made contact with a keen hunting couple in the Flint and Denbigh country, Ralph and Sue Collins, who were pleased to take Jonjo on permanent loan. They gave him a marvellous home.

Sue was assistant to an eminent veterinary surgeon, Derek Knottenbelt, and able to deal with any further evidence of sarcoids. Ralph says he enjoyed a great deal of excellent hunting on Jonjo and later I sent him another of Josephine's offspring, Jonjo's full brother Ranksborough. Thanks to the care of the Collinses, both horses are enjoying a happy retirement in their twenties.

Breeding and keeping horses to hunt absorbs an enormous amount of your time, and money, but it added a new dimension to my hunting. In my sixties and early seventies I was still riding young horses, getting enormous pleasure out of introducing them to the hunting field, even if it meant riding further back in the field while they were learning.

Using a Hunters' Improvement Society stallion Henricus we

produced a gangling foal, Henry, who grew to 17 hands. He was a slow developer who did not take rapidly to the cut-and-thrust of the Leicestershire hunting field. I sold him, since I was hard-up and had too many horses, to an event rider Peter Liffen who showed much patience and skill in producing the horse up to top level, including a win at the Blenheim trials.

Willoughby, a fiery chestnut colt, son of Josephine by John O'Gaunt, was not quite big enough for me, and we sold him as a show horse where he was successful, but he ended up as an excellent Leicestershire hunter for the Earl of Verulam, mainly in the Fernie country.

Josephine produced a further useful colt by Geoff Brooks's Warmblood stallion Armando, which I gave to Geoff, and was sold on as a leisure ride. Then came the splendid, upstanding hunter type, Ranksborough, sired by John O'Gaunt, and named after a famous Cottesmore covert. Headstrong, and unpredictable, he was not an easy ride in the hunting field at first, but he became a mount I appreciated enormously; athletic and agile, he never fell, and could manage any obstacle with ease – but he could put in a rare late stop at a fence he mistrusted.

He won the hunter championship at Rutland Show, and notched a Highly Commended rosette in a four-year-old hunter class at the Royal Show. Before the class began a Hackney horse driving class exited into the collecting ring, causing an astonished Ranksborough to fly-buck spectacularly, nearly unseating me.

Josephine's seventh foal, again by John O'Gaunt, was her first filly. We called her Ella's Gorse after a Quorn covert, but she was too light of frame to carry me in my sixties. She was particularly headstrong, and needed careful handling, but was broken in quite easily by Ruth Matthews who kept her for me in the Cottesmore country.

When we advertised Ella for sale as a three-year-old, I was surprised to get an enthusiastic response from the other side of the Atlantic. Peter Heydon, a publisher living in Michigan, wanted a filly as a present for his wife Rita who was very interested in breeding from a horse with performance potential. We sold Ella for £4,000, and she was shipped by air to the US where she settled down as a riding horse, and later as a brood mare.

*Ranksborough,
the best hunter
I bred from
Josephine.*

When I bought hunters, I could seldom afford to pay top market prices, so most of my steeds were 'characters'. The afore-mentioned Foxford was the only Irish horse I owned whose pedigree I could trace. In most cases, when asked about the sire, the dealer would say: 'And who would you like him to be by?'

Foxford was bred at Moorestown Stud by Capt. Charles Moore, former manager of the Queen's studs. The big raking gelding with prominent pin bones, was a son of Sadlers Wells out of a hunter mare who pulled a harrow between the turnips. Billy Oliver, who kept a livery yard at Wendover where I had other horses, warned me: 'He's not an old man's horse, mind.' This was an irresistible challenge, and for sheer excitement Foxford beat anything I owned.

He took a tremendous hold in the hunting field, and was reckless over fences, never refusing anything in front of him. As recounted earlier in 1975 he carried me safely over the Melton Hunt Club Ride, and that same year (see Chapter 11) I rode him in Douglas Bunn's first team 'chase over a big course at Hickstead.

On road exercise at home Foxford took great liberties: he once backed into a village shop window, causing huge cracks, and worst of all he jumped on to the bonnet of a small saloon car, demolishing the vehicle; fortunately my third party insurance paid up.

I had half a dozen memorable seasons on Foxford until at the age of 12 he became a 'wobbler' through a degenerated motor nerve, probably due to a fracture in his pelvis early in his life, revealed in a post mortem. Having heard the news in my office, I closed the office door, locked it and wept.

Among a highly varied collection of hunters I bought, as cheaply as possible, was Soloman, a stocky, powerful black horse with a Roman nose. I purchased him from Sir John Miller the Crown Equerry, after the hard-pulling horse had 'run away' with a lady rider to whom the Colonel had previously sold the horse. Much later, after Solomon gave some tremendous hunting in the Belvoir country, Sir John revealed: 'I am afraid he wasn't really sound.'

I replied: 'Well, thank you for telling me!' In fact, I had already paid for an operation on Solomon's dodgy splint bone, and had him Hobdayed. Although he had been a Household Cavalry mount, Solomon knew a lot more than mere ceremonial duties. Amazingly he would lower himself and soar over big hedges in the hunting field like a top-class chaser. He took a tremendous hold, and never refused in the hunting field, but I discovered that if you put him at an artificial schooling fence he was adept at dropping his shoulder and putting you on the ground immediately. I suspect he had suffered harsh training methods in his youth.

'Frank the Shank' was a desperately hard puller I bought for only a thousand pounds from a dealer who could not find a home for him. 'Becher the Creature' was an impetuous chestnut gelding who would 'miss out' the odd fence but somehow keep his feet. But he was a tremendous ride, adoring the non-stop formula of drag-hunting, and team 'chasing. On exercise he would suddenly veer off the road, once disappearing completely into a huge ditch, only to scrabble out like a large badger. In Geoff Brooks's yard we managed to lessen Becher's impetuous behaviour by cutting out corn from his diet; he over-reacted to protein, and hunted quite happily on regime of hay and bran.

In Ireland I haggled for some time with the excellent dealer Sean

O'Shaughnessy in attempting to buy Clonard, an upstanding dark-bay gelding who had won £100 in Foxhunter level showjumping. Then I remembered that the Irish punt was sinking fast against the English pound, and there was already a 12 percent reduction in the price we were discussing.

I was actually in the car leaving the yard when O'Shaughnessy tapped on the window.

'Have I bought him?' I asked.

'No, 'tis stolen him, you have,' said the dealer with a grin.

Soloman acquitting himself well over the walls of the High Peak country.

But he gave me some 'luck money' to seal the deal, and could not have been more helpful in shipping him to Leicestershire. Connell, as I re-named him, was one of the best hunters over a stiff country I ever rode. He had great natural jumping ability, and went well in only a plain snaffle. He would slow down and stop if I shouted 'whoa!' as he had been trained to do when being long-reined as a young horse. He later proved as adept in crossing the big fences in the Portman's vale country in Dorset, as he had been in the Shires. At home he was easy to handle, apart from jumping out of his field, and learning to open the latch in his loose box.

Sadly his career ended through failing sight, another reminder that you must cherish your horses while they are fit and well, always bearing in mind that cruel fate can take them away so quickly. Among my highly varied hunters bought economically, was Lucy, a grey mare who I later learned had bucked her previous owner over a hedge on the way to a meet.

I soon discovered for myself her readiness to buck extravagantly, but it was redeemed by her excellent jumping ability. She gave me some top-class hunting in the cream of Leicestershire, never falling, and purely by luck she never unseated me when bucking, although several grooms were thrown off and most of her exercise had to be led from another horse. I sold her as an excellent broodmare; one of her foals was good enough to appear in the Italian three-day-event team.

Red, an impetuous chestnut I bought from a friend, the Leicestershire dealer Vere Phillipps, was an exciting ride as a young horse, but settled down to become a great partner for my step-daughter, Georgina, who won several showjumping classes with him. He ended his days a favourite ride for schoolboys at The Elms preparatory school, near Ledbury.

The last horse I bought was the most extraordinary. Monty was a 16.3 hands coloured horse with brown and white streaks more reminiscent of an Appaloosa than a skewbald. His mare had been purchased as a hunter from a market. She was considered overweight but on November 11th, entirely the wrong time for foaling, she was found in her box with a coloured colt.

First named Armistice, he was re-named Monty, and hunted as a large cob with great zeal by the Belvoir hunting farmer and contractor Charlie Brown. I had seen him going well, and as he would not pass a vet as one hundred percent sound, I made a cheap offer for him which Charlie declined, but suddenly accepted a week later.

Monty, my last hunter, here ridden by my step-daughter Georgina Crowhurst.

Monty was past his best; his legs were knobbly with old injuries, but he was gallant and willing. I thought he would be a confidential mount in my late sixties and early seventies, and so he proved.

Monty was easily the best hack I ever had, patiently standing to open gates, and behaving impeccably on and off the roads. In the hunting field he could clear big fences if given plenty of time, preferring timber to large spreads. Although slowish, Monty could keep in a hunt if you did not rush him, and I much enjoyed my days on him. I was thrilled when he was placed second in a local working hunter class, simply by jumping the course clear in the best time.

He was an endearing horse in so many ways, and was much enjoyed as a hack by my step-daughter when he was in his early twenties. I was fortunate to find a wonderful retirement home for him with Cottesmore farmer and horsewoman, our friend Lesley Cripps, who hacked him with much pleasure, but now gives him a splendid complete retirement from work in his late twenties.

I owe all the horses and ponies I owned, bred and borrowed, so much for the best of my fun. My attempts to describe these joys are far short of the reality of the pleasure they gave, despite occasional shocks and disappointments. I shall always be immensely in debt to the horses, and those who looked after them for me.

I couldn't believe it: my home-bred Ranksborough had just been awarded the Ridden Hunter Championship at Rutland County Show after winning the heavyweight class as a four-year-old.

Chapter Twenty

DOWNS AND UPS

If foxhunting is 'the image of war, without its guilt, and only five and twenty percent of the danger', as Jorrocks averred, there is still bound to be some grief.

All forms of riding incur a risk once you put your foot in the stirrup. Indeed, disaster can occur when you are on your feet near a horse. I had a share of the grief, but I count myself sublimely fortunate, in avoiding horse-riding's minimal, but still dreadful, toll of paraplegia wreaked by broken backs, or grievous head injuries.

After surviving a round of bullets through my camera car in Cambodia, and other near misses reporting wars in Vietnam and the Middle East, I had the foolish notion when I gave up news reporting that my hazardous assignments were over.

When I walked away unscathed after my young horse somersaulted over a hedge in the Vale of Belvoir I should have fully understood the warning contained in Jorrocks's precept.

If you escape the worst you tend to re-mount, comforted by the illusion that it 'can't happen to me'.

I damaged myself more as a hunting correspondent than war reporting, but in over 60 years' riding I escaped lightly with only two trips to hospital. The first was in 1975 when I inadvisedly rode a borrowed horse in the second of Douglas Bunn's new Team Chases at Hickstead.

My horse fell early on the awesome course, and I was carted to hospital with a cracked pelvis, but only stayed in one night.

The second serious accident illustrated just how inconvenient, if not life-threatening, a riding injury can be. It occurred at a low point in my life in 1987 when my short second marriage had just broken up. To use an equestrian metaphor this was a sudden heavy fall at the time from which it is hard to regain your feet until you have recovered your breath. As Jorrocks said: 'A fall is a h'awful thing!'

The blow struck in October while I was cubhunting with the Belvoir on an excellent Irish hunter I had bought that summer from Leicestershire's famed hunting doctor and dealer, Tom Connors. He and his wife Jill were kind and generous friends who entertained me to many a hunting tea at their Muxlow home after a day with the Quorn.

My worst riding fall occurred when the sun was shining, the ground was all too firm, but there was a scent, and hounds ran with a joyous cry from Hose Thorns, the famous covert surrounded by grass and fly fences in the heart of the Vale of Belvoir.

It was all too tempting to abandon the usual cubhunting practice of standing around coverts. Robert Henson, Joint Master, led us in a smart canter in pursuit of hounds, and over the first fence, some innocuous rails.

My horse jumped it well, but on landing he skidded on a rut, and fell heavily on his side, crushing my left leg.

'Which hospital do you want to go to?' they asked me as I lay crippled on the ground.

'Take me to the Nottingham pay beds,' I said, remembering the advice of Ulrica Murray Smith, Master of the Quorn, if disaster struck.

This proved to be a historic myth when I arrived at the Queen's Medical Centre, Nottingham. There were, of course, no pay beds. The hospital porters would not even carry me into A and E because I had arrived not in an ambulance, but in a car driven by a kindly hunting friend, Sue Parr.

A small nurse eventually arrived with a flimsy wheel chair and, aided by Sue, gallantly pushed me into the emergency ward. My stoicism failed amid agony when they tried to pull off the boot from the crushed leg.

'Cut the thing off!' I shouted, disregarding the cost of replacement.

I shall always be grateful to Sue Parr for insisting that, as I had health insurance, I should nominate the best orthopaedic surgeon available.

The distinguished Nottingham surgeon John Webb is famous for repairing injured foxhunters in Leicestershire. He was on holiday, but his partner Christopher Colton turned up, and plated my fractured tibia and fibula in two lengthy operations within a week.

While I was on the trolley on the way to the second op, woozy from a pre-med, a Belvoir hunting friend, Tony Fenwick, appeared, and thrust a sheaf of papers onto the sheets.

'It's a report of our team 'chase. Hope you can get it in next week,' he said.

I croaked that I was not in the best position to help, but normal service would resume as soon as possible.

A week later the union-minded porters refused to carry me out of the hospital to an ambulance because it was from a private hospital in London. So once again I was trundled awkwardly in a wheelchair by a small nurse.

I thought I had arrived in heaven when they asked me if I would like a gin and tonic at the Devonshire Street hospital in the West End. My bedside became a convivial party as a host of friends arrived, including Douglas Bunn with a bottle of champagne. I was much cheered again when Peter Davis, then chief executive of our parent company Reed International, arrived with solicitations and another bottle of bubbly. Sir Peter and his wife Sue have been our good friends ever since.

Nothing could go wrong now, I assured myself, after enduring yet another operation, a skin graft. I was lying in bed, looking forward to leaving the hospital next day when I heard the BBC TV weather forecaster Michael Fish somewhat flippantly deny an unofficial report from a woman caller that a hurricane was heading for Britain. The dramatic sequel to that report, The Great Storm of 1987, is now part of British history.

It was like a return to a war zone that night, as I lay in my hospital bed while the violent cyclone hit London, having rampaged along the

South Coast. The wives of an Arab potentate in the next room screamed and wailed. The lights went out as power failed, and I could hear the crash of glass from shop windows several blocks away.

I was jinxed again. All hope of leaving hospital seemed impossible, but I was amazed when a driver arrived to whisk me away and made nothing of threading round fallen trees in Regents Park to find a way past North London's street chaos. I recuperated in a Bedfordshire cottage for several weeks, commuting to the office on crutches after an absence of only a fortnight.

The sensible, rational course of action at the age of 52 might have been to give up riding to hounds, but I resumed hunting, with the Oakley, in January. It was not what the doctor ordered, but one of the fundamental tenets of a horseman is that after a fall you should re-mount as quickly as possible if you wish to keep your nerve. The same applies in all of life's ups and downs, but it was sheer luck that I did not pay a higher price from my worst hunting fall.

After two more operations in the following summer to remove the plating from my leg, in October 1988 I entered a happy and settled period of my life when I had the immense good fortune to marry Marilyn Crowhurst.

Since we married, nearly 30 years ago, we have gained from sharing our interests in horses, and much else. Marilyn is immensely supportive, enabling me to enjoy my retirement in Rutland where there is still hunting with the Cottesmore in one of the best surviving hunting countries in the Shires.

It was after one of the home-bred horses, Ranksborough, dropped me on to a tarmac road, causing spectacular bruising, that I finally decided the time had come, aged 73, to give up riding for the second time.

I had temporarily abandoned the saddle several years earlier, after a short spell of ill health, but I soon resumed for a few more seasons' hunting. I made that decision after I went to a meet where a man I did not know was riding Ranksborough as a 'spare horse'.

'Look, he's recognised your voice,' said the rider who had been loaned my precious horse for the day.

Sure enough, Ranksborough's ears were pricked, and he was

looking at me with great interest. I rubbed his ears, which he always liked, and he nuzzled me. Normally I try not to be sentimental about each horse – loving them all deeply is another matter – but on this occasion I choked a bit.

A few days later I asked if I could have my horse back, and soon I was riding him in the hunting field again. As well as hunting I had long enjoyed hacking out in Rutland, often with my step-daughter Georgina, a consummate rider, and a keen member of the Cottesmore Pony Club, now a lawyer.

Mostly it was sheer bliss to be in the saddle again, but increasing pain, and something worse, was afflicting me, and I knew I would have to make the hard decision to give up before long.

Soon after leaving the saddle for the last time, after being dumped on the road, I had another battle to face: prostate cancer. Marilyn insisted that I sought advice just in time, and it was her care which helped save my life through a period of treatment which was more traumatic than I had foreseen.

In retirement we embarked on the unthinkable task of learning to play bridge, and after the rigors of instruction at Stamford Bridge Club it has provided hours of fun, if not great expertise on my part. The best way to keep fit after abandoning riding has been provided by our Border Collie who demands daily walks.

My recovery from cancer reinforced my appreciation of each daily pleasure of life, never taking anything for granted. I realised how fortunate I was compared with grievously afflicted younger patients I met in the Royal Leicester Infirmary's marvellous oncology department.

Nowadays I gain great pleasure from the riding achievements of my three grand-daughters in New Zealand, Brianna, Katrina and Lara, encouraged by their parents, my daughter Maxine and her husband Hamish. I am also fortunate to have a talented grandson and grand-daughter, Caleb and Tabitha, the children of my son Marcus and his wife Annie who also live in New Zealand. Marcus and Maxine have both carved admirable careers in television production.

Riding confers many benefits, not least the habit of re-mounting after you fall off, when facing life's obstacles. Hunting brought me many rewards, not least through forming partnerships with so many horses in a demanding, but non-competitive, sport. The goodwill and friendships formed in the hunting field can last for a life-time. I shall always be grateful to the farmers and landowners over whose land I was privileged to ride. Their support has been the key factor in the preservation of hunting in the British Isles.

I would urge parents to follow Winston Churchill's advice in encouraging children to ride, but ensure they are taught properly, enroll them in the Pony Club – and see they respect their mounts as friends to be cherished, rather than exploited solely as a means to rosettes and glory.

My story is that of a keen, if only moderate, horseman. I was fortunate to discover you do not need to travel abroad to seek adventure and fun. It is readily available in our own wonderfully diverse countryside. I hope enough of rural Britain will be preserved for many future generations to enjoy riding over grass and fences in pursuit of the sweet cry of hounds.

At this stage of my life, my sporting journalistic career is best summed up in the poem, 'The Good Grey Mare' by George Whyte-Melville, from which the title of the magazine was derived:

> *I have lived my life – and it is nearly done –*
> *I have played the game all round;*
> *But I freely admit that the best of my fun*
> *I owe it to horse and hound.*

INDEX

Italics denote photo references

My youngest grand-daughter Lara with Danny after a win in a New Zealand Pony Club event.

A Short History of Foxhunting
Alastair Jackson & Michael Clayton £14.99

Right Royal
John Masefield £20

Hoof-beats through my Heart
David Edelsten £7.99

The Racingman's Bedside Book
Compiled by Julian Bedford £18.95

The Byerley Turk
The True Story of the First Thoroughbred
Jeremy James £8.99

Saddletramp
Riding from Ottoman Hills to Offa's Dyke
Jeremy James £16.99

Vagabond
A horseback adventure from Bulgaria to Berlin
Jeremy James £16.99

The Yellow Earl
Douglas Sutherland £20

My Animals and Other Family
A Rural Childhood 1937-1956
Phyllida Barstow £16.99